This is such a fascinating book with a powerful message: All young people need to feel that they matter. A must-read for anyone interested in the mental health and well-being of children and adolescents.

—**Rory O'Connor, PhD,** Professor of Health Psychology, University of Glasgow, Glasgow, Scotland, UK, and author of *When It Is Darkest: Why People Die by Suicide and What We Can Do to Prevent It*

From the first page, Dr. Flett draws readers into a fundamental understanding of the need for children and adolescents to feel that they matter. He explores what mattering is, why it is important, and the potential consequences to youth from feeling that they don't matter, including addiction, aggression, depression, and suicide. A leader in the field of mattering research, Dr. Flett works to ensure that people of all ages feel that they are important to and valued by others.

—**Robin Kowalski, PhD,** Professor of Psychology, Clemson University, Clemson, SC, United States

In an engaging style, Dr. Flett makes a clear case for why "mattering matters" to the healthy development of children and adolescents. This groundbreaking resource provides a comprehensive summary of the theory and research on mattering, and is a must-read for clinicians, researchers, educators, and trainees who are interested in supporting resilience and flourishing among our next generation.

—**Randi E. McCabe, PhD,** Professor, Department of Psychiatry and Behavioural Neurosciences, McMaster University, Hamilton, ON, Canada; Fellow of the Canadian Psychological Association; and coauthor of *Cognitive-Behavioral Therapy in Groups*

If you've ever wondered what truly makes children and adolescents feel seen, valued, and connected, this book is for you. It introduces the powerful idea of "mattering"— a concept that many don't realize is central to everything from mental health to motivation and social development. With clear insights and real-world examples, the book helps parents, educators, and anyone who cares about young people understand how deeply mattering impacts their lives and well-being.

—**Virgil Zeigler-Hill, PhD,** Distinguished Professor of Psychology, Oakland University, Oakland, MI, United States

Gordon Flett's work offers a comprehensive assessment of early life experiences of mattering to others. This book will benefit clinicians, academic researchers, and parents. I highly recommend it.

—**John Taylor, PhD,** Professor and Director of the Center for Demography and Population Health, Florida State University, Tallahassee, FL, United States

Dr. Gord Flett has taken up the scholarship of mattering, and its implications for children and youth, in an energetic and compelling manner. *Mattering as a Core Need in Children and Adolescents: Theoretical, Clinical, and Research Perspectives* is a critical addition to the necessary discussion of how to prevent maltreatment, emotional abuse, and neglect, as well as violence to self and others. This book should be required reading for public health officials who seek to build multisystemic resilience, promote mental health, and reward good citizenry. In short, this evidence-based presentation attests to the finding that people who feel they matter, *do* things that matter. Now, more than ever, we need this book to guide us towards a reinvigoration of positive relationality.

—**Christine Wekerle, PhD,** Associate Professor, Pediatrics and Psychiatry & Behavioural Neurosciences, McMaster University, Hamilton, ON, Canada

MATTERING AS A CORE NEED

in Children and Adolescents

Gordon L. Flett

MATTERING AS A CORE NEED

in Children and Adolescents

Theoretical, Clinical, and Research Perspectives

AMERICAN PSYCHOLOGICAL ASSOCIATION

Published by
American Psychological Association
750 First Street, NE
Washington, DC 20002
https://www.apa.org

Order Department
https://www.apa.org/pubs/books
order@apa.org

Typeset in Charter and Interstate by Circle Graphics, Inc., Reisterstown, MD

Printer: Sheridan Books, Chelsea, MI
Cover Designer: Anthony Paular Design, Newbury Park, CA

Library of Congress Cataloging-in-Publication Data

Names: Flett, Gordon L., author. | American Psychological Association.
Title: Mattering as a core need in children and adolescents : theoretical, clinical, and research perspectives / by Gordon L. Flett.
Description: Washington, DC : American Psychological Association, [2025] | Includes bibliographical references and index.
Identifiers: LCCN 2024032468 (print) | LCCN 2024032469 (ebook) | ISBN 9781433842788 (paperback) | ISBN 9781433842795 (ebook)
Subjects: LCSH: Adolescent psychology. | Child psychology. | Developmental psychology.
Classification: LCC BF724 .F53 2025 (print) | LCC BF724 (ebook) | DDC 155.4--dc23/eng/20241125
LC record available at https://lccn.loc.gov/2024032468
LC ebook record available at https://lccn.loc.gov/2024032469

https://doi.org/10.1037/0000449-000

Printed in the United States of America

10 9 8 7 6 5 4 3 2 1

To my wife, Kathleen; our daughters, Hayley and Alison;
sons-in-law, Mark and Jeremy;
and granddaughters, Mae and Leora

Contents

MATTERING AS A CORE NEED

in Children and Adolescents

INTRODUCTION

Ten-year-old Mary lives with her mother, father, and older brother at an army base. Space has been made available at this base for people with limited financial resources, which certainly applies to Mary's family. At one point previously, they had lived in a modified garage. To Mary, today seems like a school day just like every other school day. Mary gets dressed, has her breakfast, and heads off to school.

Her day is uneventful until school is over and Mary heads home. She gets back to the army base and goes to where they live, but something is very wrong. Her mother, father, and brother are gone! All their stuff is also gone! What has happened? Imagine the distress of 10-year-old Mary and what she had to be thinking. There was no sign or clue where her family had gone. Were they abducted? Did she go to the wrong residence? Is it a bad dream? Kids sometimes run away from home, but when do parents run away from home?

Mary is close with her parents and brother. She knows she matters to them, and they matter to her, so they certainly didn't simply decide to up and leave without her. She knows they must be somewhere, and she must now focus on finding out where they are. It is upsetting for Mary, but only a bit

https://doi.org/10.1037/0000449-001
Mattering as a Core Need in Children and Adolescents: Theoretical, Clinical, and Research Perspectives, by G. L. Flett

because she knows in her heart they will either find her or she will track them down. Her bond with her family and the connection she carries with her is a source of some comfort.

But what if Mary didn't matter to her parents or wasn't sure she mattered to them? The thought might cross her mind when she found everyone and everything gone that she had been abandoned. Perhaps they made a tough financial decision and picked her older brother Billy over her because Billy is now old enough to work and help with the family finances. Or maybe she has become an earlier version of Kevin McCallister from the *Home Alone* movies—maybe they just forgot her! If she had become consumed with fears and worries about not mattering, this new situation might confirm what she anticipated all along. Now, she feels like she is being held hostage by emotions. Mary tells herself that she must calm down and find her family, but she can't because her feelings of not mattering add to her sense of feeling alone. She is preoccupied and distracted by feeling so isolated.

What happened to Mary's family? Military personnel visited the family right after Mary left for school and told her parents that the family had to be relocated, and it had to happen right away. There was no warning and no time to get a message to Mary. They planned to have her brother Billy meet Mary and direct her to where they now lived, but he had been briefly delayed.

I have heard versions of this story many times. Mary was my mother. I sometimes heard this story and other stories from my grandmother because I grew up in a home in Ontario with our extended family living with us (i.e., my maternal grandmother, grandfather, and aunt). My aunt was a later arrival to the Andrus family, and her presence was like having a slightly older sister. I witnessed for many years how much family members meant to each other, so it was easy for me to envision the 10-year-old Mary and her penchant for just keeping calm and carrying on. My mother used to tell me that when she found everyone and everything gone, she didn't know what to think at first, but she knew beyond a shadow of a doubt that they would come back and find her.

This book is about the feeling of knowing you matter to significant others versus feeling like you do not matter. The real-life scenario introduced earlier illustrates how the feeling of mattering can be a vital resource for children in understanding their worlds; however, the feeling of not mattering can be a barrier that can make upsetting situations even more upsetting. Children who have a feeling of mattering to others carry a connection and sense of attachment that comforts them even when they are alone. However, children who do not have a feeling of mattering to others can feel even more alone and disconnected.

This book is about mattering research and theory in children and adolescents; however, the story of 10-year-old Mary reminds us that it is really about the life experiences of individual children and adolescents everywhere. The working premise is that the need to matter is universal and applies to everyone. When this need is satisfied, mattering is a psychological factor that has the potential to lift up all children. The approach taken here is that every child and adolescent would benefit from the feeling of mattering to others because every child and adolescent needs to feel a sense of importance and significance to others.

The central premise of this book is in keeping with initial claims about the importance of mattering when the concept was first introduced. Rosenberg and McCullough (1981) described the mattering construct in detail and showed, using data from four samples of adolescents, that "the adolescent high on parental mattering lives a richer, fuller, more satisfying life" (Rosenberg, 1985, p. 219).

This book essentially begins where my previous book on the psychology of mattering left off (see Flett, 2018a). The first book ended with a call for "the need to matter" to be formally enshrined as a sacred right of children and adolescents around the world. It noted that the United Nations Convention on the Rights of the Child (1989) culminated in globally agreed on rights of children, including the right to care and protection and the requirement to always prioritize the best interests of the child. The one right missing from the list is the child's right to matter and have a feeling of mattering to the people in their life and their community. It was stated,

> We have an obligation to provide each child with the positive sense of self and the psychological feeling of security that comes from knowing that she or he matters to the people in her or his life. This right fits nicely with other rights that emphasize that children deserve a voice and they deserve to be respected. (Flett, 2018a, pp. 295–296)

The overarching theme of this book is that every child must experience the benefits of having a sense of mattering to others. This right needs to be made explicit and used commonly and routinely as a metric to evaluate how children are faring in their lives. Of course, we learn daily of troubling examples of young people treated in ways totally at variance with this feeling.

Research findings on mattering are valuable and informative, but there is also much to be learned from case accounts of individual children and adolescents. Their life stories serve as reminders that the feeling of mattering or not mattering is exceptionally personal. Jean Peterson (1998) provided us with a perfect reminder through her account of six adolescent girls. These girls were at risk for various reasons, but it was not readily apparent because some girls outwardly projected an image of doing well. Mattering came into play in the description of one of the girls, Angela. She was clearly functioning at a high level, and mattering likely played a role. Angela was described as a problem solver who had benefited from having a relative who showered her with unconditional care and affection. Angela also found mentors who supplemented her capacity to receive attention and positive regard from others. Peterson concluded that the need to be known to others in positive ways was a strong desire shared by all six girls. This need to be known is, in essence, the need to be seen and heard and feel significant (i.e., to matter). Peterson observed that all six girls just needed someone to pay attention to them. As Chapter 4 of this book states, far too many young people lack this feeling of mattering to others.

This book would not have been possible without the growth of the mattering field over the past decade and the many significant research developments reported by various teams. The study of mattering has become much more international in scope and focus. Interest in the concept is spreading as scholars realize that feeling important to others is a core aspect of self and identity for people of all ages. This has impacted my own research opportunities. Scholars from various countries have contacted me and proposed key collaborations. It is rewarding to witness the growth of interest in research and theory on mattering and how mattering promotion may be implemented.

This book is the first to examine mattering in children and adolescents comprehensively. Three obvious questions arise regarding a new book such as this one. First, why write this book? Second, why write it now? Finally, how is this book unique? Each question is addressed next.

WHY WRITE THIS BOOK?

I wrote this book for several reasons. First, mattering is a unique construct with incredible power. It has exceptional resonance among most people. Mattering is the psychology concept I point to if someone questions whether what researchers study has any bearing on the daily lives of most people. It is also a window into understanding a person; you can find out a lot about someone simply by learning whether they feel like they matter and, if so, what has made them feel this way. Also, do they treat other people like they matter?

Perhaps the best way to become more aware of our shared need to matter is to reflect on whether you could truly be happy if you felt that you did not matter to other people or that other people seemed to matter more than you matter. Think about this as if there were a birthday party for you and nobody came. Stories of this happening to some children have been reported (ABC News, 2015), and the public response in support of these children has been enormous. Why? People know how they would feel if this happened to them.

Second, while awareness and understanding of mattering is growing, it is still arguably the best-kept secret in psychology. I continue to encounter many highly educated and accomplished people who either do not know about mattering or mistakenly see it as similar to the concept of belonging or some other psychosocial construct it overlaps with. This book represents an opportunity to summarize converging evidence indicating that mattering matters, and it does so in a way that shows how it is unlike any other factors, especially in terms of making a difference in the lives of children and adolescents and their families and in society.

Another reason is to create a resource for groups and organizations invested in making a positive change in the lives of children and adolescents in their local communities. I have been fortunate to work with school boards in Ontario and public organizations dedicated to promoting resilience and positive youth development, such as the Maine Resilience Building Network. Seminars and workshops are increasingly being punctuated by requests from some people in attendance for a book focused on mattering in children and adolescents. This book serves as a summary of what is known thus far, but it also includes suggestions for how to extend the vitally important applied work being done on the promotion of mattering among young people.

This book is intended to be a potential catalyst for further research and conceptualization about mattering in general and among children and adolescents in particular. The volume of research on mattering needs to be expanded considerably because key information that could be easily obtained is being lost. Opportunities abound to expand the scope of inquiry meaningfully. One illustration of the possibilities is the emphasis on giving youth a voice in participatory action research, which represents a platform for understanding how mattering is tied to hearing the voices of youth, as shown in a recent investigation by Renick and Reich (2023).

It is far too often that I read a new study on concepts such as self-esteem or social support and am left to wonder why mattering was not included or at least acknowledged as likely having played a key role in shaping the research findings. The following is an example of this.

A new line of research has been built around the concept of childhood family connection. This impressive work by Whitaker and colleagues (2022), with participants from 26 countries, established that higher levels of childhood family connection predict higher levels of flourishing among adolescents, continuing on to when they reach adulthood. Mattering is not mentioned at all in this article. However, its role becomes evident after examining the five scale items used to assess self-reported family connection. These five items are heavily laden with themes that directly or indirectly reflect mattering to one's parents (e.g., My parents listen to me and take what I say into account. There are people in my family who care about me. My parents and I make decisions about my life together). Given the themes in this measure of family connection, it is reasonable to infer that having a feeling of mattering to parents contributes to elevated flourishing among samples of adolescents from 26 countries. Accordingly, this study is revisited in Chapter 8 of this book, where the focus is on mattering, happiness, and flourishing in children and adolescents.

Of course, researchers are entitled to investigate whatever they choose to study. Moreover, of course, they can label their variables in accordance with their interpretations. I prefer that interested researchers simply include a measure that directly assesses mattering if they think it is relevant. In most instances, this decision will be rewarded.

WHY WRITE THIS BOOK NOW?

Here again there are several reasons for writing this book now, but I focus on two themes: the prevalence of mental health problems and the prevalence of feelings of not mattering.

First and foremost is the growing mental health crisis among young people. I am convinced that feelings of not mattering account for much of the distress that children and adolescents experience.

To what extent is there a mental health problem? One example is the alarming results that emerged 5 years ago from an epidemiological study in Austria involving diagnostic interviews. This study, with a sample of 3,615 adolescents from Austria, found that the point prevalence of any disorder was 23.9%, which is almost one in four adolescents (Wagner et al., 2017). The lifetime prevalence for any disorder was 35.8%. Anxiety disorders were the most common disorders identified; they had a lifetime prevalence of 15.6%. The three most common anxiety disorders were specific phobias, separation anxiety disorder, and social anxiety disorder. Overall, almost half of the adolescents (47%) with some disorder had two or more disorders diagnosed. Feelings and fears of not mattering are likely playing some role; I have discussed at length how mattering is associated negatively with anxiety in children and adolescents (Flett, 2019).

There is no doubt whatsoever that the COVID-19 global pandemic added to the stress, strain, and mental health challenges faced by children and adolescents. We owe a debt to the three Boston physicians who felt compelled to write a journal article about their experiences (see L. K. Lee et al., 2021). These three emergency room physicians reported that, as of the summer of 2020, an unprecedented five to 10 children and adolescents have been presenting daily to their emergency department with new mental health crises.

An impressive study by Racine et al. (2021) provided a broad view of how the pandemic was challenging for young people through a meta-analysis of 29 studies conducted during the pandemic. Overall, more than 80,000 participants were included in these studies. Racine et al. concluded that depression was evident among 25.2% of the participants, while anxiety was present in 20.5% of the participants. Thus, it can be estimated that one in four have diagnosable depression, and it is likely that for many children and adolescents, this depression is comorbid with anxiety. How much of this can be attributed to the pandemic? Racine et al. concluded that cases of anxiety and depression among young people doubled in comparison with prepandemic levels. This has serious implications for our schools and mental health treatment systems that already were short of resources, and it suggests that there is an urgent need for prevention. It also suggests that boosting levels of mattering among young people is now more urgent than ever, and action is immediately needed. This suggestion fits entirely with the original claim from Rosenberg and McCullough (1981) that the need to matter is highly salient among adolescents, and mattering is a construct of profound societal importance.

Unfortunately, none of the investigations described in Racine et al. (2021) included an assessment of individual differences in mattering. Thus, we can only infer but cannot establish that those young people without a feeling of mattering to others are overrepresented among children and adolescents experiencing depression and anxiety.

Support for this conclusion can be drawn from a 2018 document produced by UNICEF Australia, which was submitted to the United Nations Committee on the Rights of the Child: *The Children's Report* (Irani et al., 2018). It garnered considerable media attention because of what was said by the 527 children, adolescents, and emerging adults who were interviewed for this report. The contributors ranged from 4 to 24 years old. The children and adolescents interviewed for the report sent the clear message that they were tired of being made to feel invisible and irrelevant. In other words, they had had enough of being treated and made to feel as if they were insignificant and did not matter. These young people emphasized that they felt invisible to adults in government and also to adults in their families and communities.

The authors of the report concluded, "At a general population level, there remain serious questions about how Australians value children and young people" (Irani et al., 2018, p. 6).

Perhaps the frequency, intensity, and breadth of this message reflect, at least in part, the specific participants sampled. Care was taken to prioritize young people who are marginalized and with lived experiences that increase their vulnerability to abuses of their rights (Irani et al., 2018). Participants included Aboriginal and Torres Strait Islander children, children with disabilities, children who identified as LGBTIQ+, asylum seeker and refugee children, and children described as being from culturally and linguistically diverse backgrounds. As noted in the report, many of the young people interviewed had lived with neglect and abuse, addiction in the family, incarcerated parents, and homelessness, among other conditions. Not surprisingly, this also included children with mental health diagnoses and a history of attempted suicide.

Themes of feeling invisible and not heard are antithetical to mattering and represent what we have called anti-mattering themes (see Flett et al., 2022). As suggested earlier, anti-mattering is a sense of not being valued and living life feeling unheard and unseen. The unmet need to matter among these Australian children and adolescents came through in their messages (Irani et al., 2018). Each participant was tasked with writing the one message they wanted people to know. Consider a few examples. One participant wrote, "We matter, we are the future and living in the now. Understand us, our needs and our wants because wether [*sic*] you think it or not, it is <u>IMPORTANT</u>. We are important" (Irani et al., 2018, p. 5). Another young person emphasized the need for a sense of voice to matter:

> Everything that you are doing now is going to impact our future, and if we don't get a say then how are we going to fix anything? How are we going to be happy with the world that you left us? We have to start making a contribution now or we will never feel valid enough to try later in life. (Irani et al., 2018, p. 4)

Another girl emphasized the feeling of not mattering in society:

> I have a single mum who struggles to keep my brother and I alive but the government seems to just brush us away like we don't matter. I'm personally struggling, but no one knows, and no one knows how bad it is and how bad I want to be gone. And I don't know who is there to help me. (Irani et al., 2018, p. 47)

This contribution reflects how despair and demoralization and the pain of not mattering can ultimately result in suicidal thoughts and tendencies. These themes are explored at length in Chapter 8.

Mattering is not a panacea for all mental health challenges and life problems experienced by young people. Still, it must be noted that the Wellcome Trust in the United Kingdom highlighted its role in safeguarding the mental health of young people. In October 2021, the Wellcome Trust published a report on what scientific research has identified as "active ingredients of effective intervention" (Wellcome, 2021, p. 6) when seeking to reduce anxiety and depression among young people. In total, 27 "ingredients" were identified and included on the list, including instilling positive tendencies such as hopefulness and self-compassion and reducing destructive influences such as perfectionism and repetitive negative thoughts. The seventh ingredient on the list is "a sense of mattering." Where would mattering be listed if all 27 intervention ingredients were rank ordered? It deserves to be in the top 10, but for some children and adolescents, it is their biggest need.

The second reason for writing this book now is the prevalence of feelings of not mattering. This book on mattering is needed now to draw attention to the current reality that far too many young people do not feel like they matter to other people, their school, or their community. We will see in Chapter 4 that when the focus is on feelings of mattering in general, about one in three young people feel like they do not matter. The prevalence of feelings of not mattering is more widespread when the focus is on feelings of mattering versus not mattering in the community. It must be incredibly unsettling to live somewhere growing up without the feeling of being valued.

I conclude this section by noting that the reality for many young people is that they lack a sense of relational mattering to other people, and in more existential terms, they also lack a sense of mattering in society. They do not feel important to the people in their lives or in the big picture. Children and adolescents can be made to feel insignificant and marginalized on a broad scale. Children exposed to discrimination, prejudice, and stigma that makes them feel irrelevant or insignificant in society are desperately in need of feeling like they matter to the people in their lives who are important to them.

A focus on mattering has given me ways of reinterpreting historical events, such as the horrors faced by Canada's Indigenous people who were sent without consent to residential schools. This practice was a profound indignity that not only conveyed the message that they did not matter in society but also removed these children and adolescents from the significant people in their lives who could provide them with a sense of relational mattering. The sudden loss of mattering and prolonged lack of contact with loved ones was understandably highly traumatic.

Canada now observes Orange Shirt Day every year on September 30. This day honors residential school survivors and their families and remembers how their experiences reverberated through so many lives. Phyllis Webstadt is the creator of Orange Shirt Day. Orange reflects the color of the shirt she wore on the day she was removed from her community and sent to a residential school. One of the first things that happened to Phyllis at this school was that her new orange shirt was taken away from her. Phyllis has poignantly remarked that, as a result of her experiences as a young girl, she regards orange as the color that signifies not mattering (Croteau, 2016).

HOW IS THIS BOOK UNIQUE?

The final question pertains to how and why this book is unique. At present, there is no comprehensive book on mattering in childhood and adolescence. Elliott (2009) authored an important book focused on adolescents, but the focus of his book, as reflected by its title, was on mattering in the family. The book has not received the attention it deserves; accordingly, various key pieces of information and insights from it are highlighted throughout this book.

I wrote this book as a significant extension of my previous book on the psychology of mattering (see Flett, 2018a). The topic of mattering in children and adolescents merits the extended focus it receives here for various reasons, including those outlined earlier. Most notably, this book is in keeping with the original emphasis that Rosenberg and McCullough (1981) placed on mattering in children and adolescents. This book's focus on children and adolescents also reflects the strong belief espoused by scholars such as Missildine (1963), Bowlby (1980), and Ainsworth (1982) that early developmental experiences are vital in shaping the self-concept and developing the capacity to deal effectively with challenges and conflicts.

Who would argue with the contention that the young child who knows that they matter to significant others is a child who has had an exceptionally better start to life than the young child who feels unimportant and not appreciated? We frequently hear the term "adverse childhood experiences;" one of the greatest adversities some children face daily is that they simply do not matter to the significant others in their lives. The secure feeling of being home is similar to what mattering feels like. Contrast the feeling of growing up in a home with a caring and attentive family to living in a place where you are made to feel insignificant. The story of Mary that opened this book is useful to remember. As you read through the rest of the book, I hope you will keep in mind how it feels when you are treated as someone special versus when you are made to feel invisible, irrelevant, or insignificant.

ORGANIZATION OF THIS BOOK

This book summarizes existing knowledge and introduces many new themes and perspectives. The first two chapters are designed to give readers a clear sense of the nature of mattering. Chapter 1 considers mattering in terms of how it is expressed and experienced by young people with respect to their affect, motivation, and cognition. Chapter 2 examines mattering from a definitional and a conceptual perspective and reviews the components of the mattering construct, beginning with the elements proposed by Rosenberg and McCullough (1981).

Chapter 2 tells part of the story of mattering from a historical perspective. Chapter 3 adds to this historical account by analyzing the emphasis on mattering in the positive youth development field. A key theme emerging from the chapter is that young people need opportunities and roles to build a sense of mattering while developing other skills and capacities. Most notably, support for efficacy and mattering is central to positive youth development and the programs promoting it.

As noted earlier, Chapter 4 provides detailed information which shows unequivocally that far too many young people are vulnerable because they do not have a clear and stable sense of being important to other people. This leads naturally into Chapter 5 and my analysis of the keys to understanding children and adolescents who feel unseen and unheard.

Chapter 6 discusses the assessment of mattering. I describe existing measures and outline specific assessment issues relevant to individual differences among children and adolescents that need further scrutiny.

Chapter 7 considers the multiple factors that impact levels of mattering from a developmental perspective. Existing research is summarized, and the case is made for a complex model in keeping with the model proposed by Bronfenbrenner (2005).

Chapters 8 and 9 examine mattering as a force of good in the young people's lives. The key themes addressed include the role of mattering in happiness and flourishing (Chapter 8) and how mattering is central to developing resilience and the ability to adapt to transitions (Chapter 9). Chapter 9 also illustrates how adverse experiences that can add to feelings of not mattering can become a troubling element of the stress experience of children and adolescents.

If mattering is central to the lives and experiences of children and adolescents, it should be reflected in the significant activities in their lives. This premise is explored in Chapter 10, which uniquely examines how the need to matter plays a role in the rampant social media use of children and adolescents.

The emphasis on mattering as a force of good is a welcome contrast to the realities reflected in the subsequent chapters. Feelings and fears of not mattering can be highly problematic. Problems arise when the need to matter is not satisfied, especially when the need to matter has become excessive. Topics considered at length include addiction and substance use (Chapter 11), youth violence and aggression (Chapter 12), depression (Chapter 13), and suicide (Chapter 14).

The final chapter summarizes some key themes in the book and examines some key considerations when seeking to instill a sense of mattering in every child. This chapter builds on a recent article that examined how mattering can be put into action to address the growing problem of youth suicide (see Flett, 2024a).

Mattering is well-suited to community initiatives, and I hope this book will help provide the catalyst for new initiatives and meaningful extensions of existing programs and activities that have already been implemented and are underway. Impressive gains have been made. A greater focus on mattering is important in its own right, but it is also essential in showing how positive psychology can make the world a better place at a time when people need to see the possibilities for positive change and growth.

A central aspect of this introduction was to address the questions "Why write this book?" and "Why write this book now?" A related question I have saved until now that I have repeatedly asked myself is, "Why do I need to write this book?" If I had to describe my personality, I would focus on two tendencies. First, I tend to be a hopeful optimist, and this persists even during challenging times. My hope and optimism stem partly from the mattering concept and how the feeling of mattering and the possibility of mattering tend to inspire people. People can relate to the concept of mattering, which helps them connect with others who also understand how it feels. We can make positive change happen broadly by instilling a sense of mattering in people of all ages, especially young people. It represents a pathway to solutions that are much needed.

Another one of my personality features is a tendency to be protective, perhaps overprotective, especially when it comes to safeguarding young people. I maintain that anyone approaching the generativity stage described by Erikson (1968) will find the mattering construct quite appealing on multiple levels. Mattering needs to be put into action to promote the development and well-being of children everywhere, both now and in future generations.

PART I MATTERING: A COMPLEX CONSTRUCT

1 MATTERING AS A CORE FEELING AND A CORE NEED IN CHILDREN'S LIVES

This chapter and the subsequent chapter are designed to provide readers with a clear sense of what mattering is. Mattering is a huge life advantage when it is present but a huge burden when absent. This chapter focuses on how mattering is experienced, especially in terms of how it feels.

When analyzing psychological constructs such as mattering, it is useful to consider each construct in terms of affective, motivational, cognitive, interpersonal, and behavioral aspects. The various ways of experiencing thoughts and feelings of mattering are discussed next. Rosenberg and McCullough (1981) emphasized mattering as a feeling; indeed, most subsequent authors have focused on feelings of mattering versus not mattering to others. However, in their original article, Rosenberg and McCullough (1981) also proposed that mattering is a motive that exerts a powerful influence on our behavior. Mattering is complex in that it involves feelings, needs, and cognitive perceptions and addresses self and identity in relation to others.

We now examine the affective or emotional side of mattering. The overarching premise of this section is that the feeling of mattering tends to stick with us. Unfortunately, feeling insignificant also tends to persist.

https://doi.org/10.1037/0000449-002
Mattering as a Core Need in Children and Adolescents: Theoretical, Clinical, and Research Perspectives, by G. L. Flett

HOW DOES MATTERING FEEL?

As noted in the Introduction, mattering is an intense affect that seems broad and all-encompassing because it is a feeling tied to our sense of self and identity. Mattering is a feeling rather than an emotion because it involves perception and appraisal, which can entail considerable reflection as we get older. It is our perception of how we are regarded by others. The feeling of mattering to others includes feeling connected to people who likely also matter to us. While mattering is not an emotion, it is strongly connected with emotions in a child who has a sense of mattering rooted in the mutually warm and responsive exchanges and interactions that babies have with mothers, fathers, and other caregivers.

It has been my experience that mattering is a topic which evokes strong reactions from other people. It is deeply felt at an emotional level. It is not uncommon to see people become quite emotional as they first learn about the concept. Indeed, at one public lecture at York University in November 2019, I was distracted by a nice woman in the first row who was crying and trying to hide it. She later explained to me, as part of an unnecessary apology, that her many years of caregiving did not yield the appreciation she felt she deserved. In short, she did not feel what she hoped to feel. However, she realized how much it did matter after some further reflection when I made a point during my lecture of expressing appreciation to anyone in the audience who had been a caregiver and I encouraged people to express appreciation to themselves.

It is possible that for you, the reader, thinking about mattering evokes strong memories of someone with a caring presence in your life who created feelings of mattering in you but perhaps is no longer living. I like to think that when we link a lasting feeling of mattering to these people in our past, it means, in a sense, that these significant people in our lives are still with us.

The feeling of mattering to others is like no other feeling. People who are missed are missed, in part, because the feeling of mattering to these people is also missed. The feeling of mattering is highly rewarding, and it triggers other feelings. The person with a feeling of mattering experiences complex emotional blends of joy, happiness, pleasure, and pride. Conversely, the person lacking a feeling of mattering will feel as if something important is missing and life is incomplete. The feeling of not mattering is often accompanied by loneliness and unhappiness. A sense of despair may be accompanied by a deep resentment if the person feels no one cares enough to notice and that they deserve better.

Mattering in relationships is at its peak as an experience and feeling when the relationship with someone special is not something you have had in the past or other people tend to have in their past. Similarly, the important other is being with you in a unique way. When it is said that mattering is experienced in the moments, these are the most memorable moments. Mattering also involves doing things together and sharing things with each other, but to be fully impacted by them, doing and sharing must include being with others.

Once you have experienced the feeling of mattering to key people in your life, you will want to revisit it, and you will want to reexperience it. You will also seek this feeling in your other relationships. It is most likely that once we are used to having the feeling of mattering, we will turn toward people who elicit this feeling again but turn away from people who evoke little feeling or, worse yet, evoke what it feels like when you know you do not matter to someone. It is this aspect that makes mattering essentially a relationship meter. Any significant relationship is in trouble when interacting with someone is no longer special, and we start to miss the feeling of mattering to that person.

It is widely acknowledged and understood that everyone has a core psychological need to connect with others. Ryan and Deci (2017) are seminal theorists in the motivation field, and they have cogently summarized mattering from a motivational perspective. Specifically, they concluded the following:

> One of the primary goals of behavior is the feeling of belonging and of being significant or mattering in the eyes of others. There is a basic need to feel responded to, respected, and important to others, and, conversely, to avoid rejection, insignificance, and disconnectedness, a fact that applies not just to humans but other primates as well (see de Waal, 2009). (Ryan & Deci, 2017, p. 96)

Ryan and Deci (2017) linked the need to matter with the need to connect and belong, which should be highly salient in most transactions that make us wonder whether we matter and whether we belong. I envision mattering as more than belonging and connection. It reflects three Cs: care, closeness, and connection. All three are evident in the first relationship we have in life, which, of course, is with our mother.

The one affective state in mattering that does not get enough emphasis is the feeling of being cared for and cared about. Mattering is largely about the feeling of caring connections, and we have argued that an emphasis on feeling cared about must be included when assessing individual differences in feelings of mattering to others (see Flett & Nepon, 2024). When viewed through a mattering lens, loneliness is not simply a sense of isolation due to a lack of social connection, but rather, it is a sense of isolation shrouded in the feeling of not being important to others and not being cared about.

This emphasis on care in close relationships also distinguishes mattering from belonging. The combined feeling of mattering and being cared about by people close to us goes well past simply fitting in and feeling like there is a place for us.

How does mattering feel to young people? An article in *The New York Times* asked adolescents to respond to the question "When have you felt that you mattered?" (Proulx, 2023). Hundreds of adolescents commented on the feeling, and many expressed heartfelt and effusive sentiments. One adolescent stated, "This feeling of importance and being missed makes me feel loved and fills my heart with joy" (A. Rogers, 2023).

The accounts generously provided by these young people were instrumental in providing me with some new insights into the nature of mattering in terms of how it feels and what the feeling can do for young people. It was evident from several personal accounts in the article that the feeling of mattering for many leads to greater strength and self-confidence. The feeling of mattering is a source of personal growth and development and is in keeping with the notion of expanding a positive sense of self. It is reasonable to conclude that the feeling of mattering to other people lifts young people up and energizes them. One adolescent girl described her experience as feeling enlightened by knowing she mattered to people. Other people gave her reassurance and the feeling of being loved and cared for (see Mulderrig, 2023).

Why does mattering seem to matter so much to these young people? Rosenberg (1979) provided part of the explanation, stating, "Other people's judgments of us matter enormously. Indeed, there is probably no more critical and significant source of information about ourselves than other people's views of us" (p. 64). This observation fits well with David Elkind's (1988) views of the adolescent period. Elkind said that most young people are highly aware of being viewed by an imaginary audience, making them exceptionally self-conscious at a time when they are grappling with uncertainty about who they are and what they will become.

I often reflect on what Morris Rosenberg would say today about mattering and the experiences of young people. I am convinced that he would conclude that the need to matter among young people is more important than ever for various reasons, including the pervasive and insidious impact and influence of social media on young people. Rosenberg (1986) was acutely aware of the impact of social comparison on young people. As discussed in Chapter 10 of this volume, access to social media now makes it far too easy to make life comparisons with some people who portray themselves as having perfect lives. Two key observations from Rosenberg (1986) underscore the potential impacts on young people and how they see themselves: "The self is the reference point, the phenomenal center, of all perceptions" (p. 192). He further stated, "The individual tends to compare himself with those in the groups, statuses, or social categories that constitute his psychological world" (p. 192). There is no denying that the psychological worlds of young people have changed in this century in ways that pose additional challenges when it comes to self and identity.

The introduction to this book began with the story of my mother, Mary. I had many reasons for beginning the book this way beyond paying tribute to my mother. Family and home are key considerations relating to how mattering feels. When you think about the home you grew up in, what feelings are brought to the surface? The feeling of mattering is directly related to how it felt when growing up. Children who live in a home where they know they matter feel a sense of relaxation. They have the comfort of knowing and feeling that they are in a safe and secure place where they are valued.

The child who lives in a home where they are not sure they matter or who feels they matter only some of the time will be on guard for signs of approval or disapproval. They will have a prolonged uneasy feeling and must remain alert for indicators of how people are feeling about them on that day.

The most unfortunate child lacks a feeling of not mattering and never truly gets the warm feeling of being at home. There are two potential versions of this child. Some children have a feeling of not mattering dominated by the sense of never being seen and never being heard. They experience total indifference, as if they do not exist. This may involve emotional neglect with no apparent connection. The association between feelings of not mattering and emotional neglect is discussed at length in my previous book (Flett, 2018a). In it, I cite highly insightful work by Missildine (1963), who described children exposed to extreme indifference in the form of chronic emotional neglect that conveys the message "You don't matter."

The second type of child has directly received the overt message of not mattering to significant others. The message of being unwanted and not worth being considered often takes the form of emotional abuse. A troubling example came from the Canadian Broadcasting Corporation investigative news show *The Fifth Estate* in an episode titled "The Trouble With Evan" (Docherty & MacIntyre, 1994). Cameras placed in Evan's home captured actual family interactions. Early in the show, it is evident that Evan is oppositional and gets into trouble most of the time. Circumstances escalate when some of his mother's money goes missing. Evan is blamed for it despite his constant denials and claims that he did not take the money. Much later, we learn that Evan told the truth. His mother simply miscounted, and no money was missing. Before that was determined, Evan's stepfather responded with rage and eventually told him that as far as he and Evan's mother were concerned, Evan no longer existed. Evan's mother later apologized, but this could not undo what Evan had endured. Not surprisingly, this filmed display of verbal abuse sparked an outcry from television viewers. Ultimately, Evan and his sister were removed from the family home by authorities.

These children reflect prototypes. There are, of course, variations on these themes in the experiences of children and adolescents. In their work on the Black Boys Mattering Project, Roderick Carey (2019) described conditional mattering and marginalized mattering to others. These two versions account for those times when mattering is contingent on behavior or performance or the child or adolescent is valued because of a skill (e.g., a star athlete) but not for who they are as a person.

A prime example of this delimiting form of mattering was provided in a case account of a young woman named June who had diabetes and was reflecting on her childhood (Tilden et al., 2005). June was diagnosed with Type 1 diabetes when she was 10 years old. June described a childhood in which other people paid attention to her when it came to diabetes management but did not focus on her other needs as a young person. She concluded, "I don't matter ninety percent of the time" (Tilden et al., 2005, p. 317). Because she felt she did not matter and the people in her life did not care about her, June began to treat herself like she did not matter, ceasing to follow the necessary medical routines to take care of herself at times. It is important for anyone with a chronic illness not to feel like they are defined by their illness, which is only a part of the person they are. Children need parents who connect with them in mutually rewarding interactions that foster the sense of being cared about.

June experienced feelings that many young people also experience. Several young people commented spontaneously in *The New York Times* article (Proulx, 2023) about how horrible it felt when they felt like they did not matter. One adolescent remarked that mattering is a "bubbly warm" feeling, but not mattering is the feeling of being lonely and alone (Cho, 2023). Sadness and depression were also mentioned often in the extreme (i.e., feeling worthless), and in one instance, an adolescent described "feeling like I am not doing anything for the world" (Hailu, 2023).

When it is intense, the feeling of not mattering to others triggers a network of interconnected feelings that contribute to feeling estranged from other people and society. It can become overgeneralized, so it involves the feeling that no one cares and no one understands the young person. It also involves feelings of being alone, not belonging, and feeling like a failure; like someone who is a person of no value or worth to other people. If there are no pathways to mattering apparent to a young person, they also experience feelings of helplessness and hopelessness. The feeling of not having any value may also fuel a feeling of being a burden to other people.

Ideally, every child would have the opportunity to live in a home with a family that radiates the feeling of mattering and being cared for and about, but we know that in the real world, this is not the case. It is illustrative to consider the accounts of unhoused youth. These young people illustrate the phrase, "A house is not a home." Some unhoused young people have access to home as a living option but have decided not to use it. Toolis and Hammack (2015) reported a narrative analysis of case studies that emerged from interviews with 11 unhoused youth. A common theme identified by the researchers was the unmet need to matter and an overarching desire to be valued. One teenager recounted wanting someone to listen to her for a change. Her sense of mattering and belonging derived from being with other unhoused youth.

Kidd (2004) reported the illuminating results of a qualitative study of 80 street youth from Vancouver and Toronto and their experiences of suicide ideation. Overall, 20 participants clearly expressed themes of not mattering, typically in terms of feeling entirely alone because no one cared about them. Such feelings of not mattering and not being cared about are often internalized into a sense of worthlessness that is central to no longer caring about the self.

If the feeling of not mattering is part of the problem, it can also be part of the solution. We (Flett, Gaetz, & Fisher, 2024) recently started to consider how mattering can be a key element in preventing youth homelessness in an article that is part of a special issue on the prevention of youth homelessness. We believe that mattering should be at the heart of prevention efforts, and in recognizing its importance, we are simply reflecting what youth tell us. For instance, Darbyshire and colleagues (2006) conducted qualitative research with 10 youths experiencing homelessness from Australia. These adolescents described the substantial impact of small acts of kindness and human caring when somebody connected with them in ways that showed them they mattered. Another core theme was encountering people who listened to them; this reiterates the role of youth voices in the link between feelings of mattering and feeling heard.

Technology can also help convey the message "you matter." For instance, in their analysis of the use of technology to sustain long-term communication with youth experiencing houselessness, Bender and associates (2015) noted their participants emphasized that having someone check in on them made them feel important and helped them realize they mattered.

Mattering experienced as someone caring was expressed by all but one of 12 participants in a qualitative study of adolescents who had formerly run away or been without housing (see Lindsey et al., 2000). The theme of someone caring was linked to feelings of safety, support, understanding, and warmth. Another theme was being held accountable. This conveys mattering in terms of someone wanting the best by insisting that the young person live up to reasonable expectations.

HOW DOES MATTERING MOTIVATE US?

I noted earlier that Rosenberg and McCullough (1981) emphasized that everyone needs to matter. Samuel Laycock, one of Canada's foremost educational leaders and an early leader in educational psychology, was the first to acknowledge the need to matter in children and adolescents. Laycock (1962) proposed that the emotional needs of children must be addressed for them to thrive and be mentally well and that schools play a vital role in the mental health of children and adolescents. He observed,

> Every child needs to taste success. This is often denied to the dull and the gifted. Not only are their needs for achievement and recognition denied but their needs for mattering to others, to belong, and to have a sense of worth as well. (Laycock, 1962, p. 417)

Laycock argued that the aim of education should be to achieve the highest possible development of each student in accordance with the student's capabilities and needs. He explicitly included the need to matter and belong on the basis of his understanding of young people.

When it comes to mattering and motivation, there are many unanswered questions. For instance, when a broad view is taken of children who do or do not feel like they matter, how are motivational factors reflected in their behavior? The young person with a strong and certain feeling of mattering to others will be highly engaged, goal oriented, and willing to take on challenges. Their goals and activities will reflect their sense of being connected with caring others and, as such, may also include engagement in shared goals and activities. In contrast, the picture of the young person without a sense of mattering is quite bleak from a motivational perspective. The feeling of not mattering is reflected in a state of demoralization and a sense of helplessness and hopelessness if it is perceived that nothing can be done to develop a sense of mattering to other people. Given the social nature of mattering, helplessness and hopelessness can be experienced in general, but it is potentially domain specific in terms of learned social helplessness and social hopelessness.

Rosenberg and McCullough (1981) proposed that when young people lack the feeling of mattering to their parents, not surprisingly, their need to matter is not being met, and this need will grow. The need to matter will become outsized for some. Satisfaction of the need for some will mean turning to less-than-optimal sources, and this could involve affiliating with antisocial peers.

The need to matter is regarded as a universal need, and according to Rosenberg and McCullough (1981), it is a need that applies across the life cycle. In short, everyone needs to matter. Given that the need to matter is a part of everyone and whether it has been satisfied is a key part of personality structure as well as self and identity, it seems essential to integrate and incorporate the need to matter as a central component in broad models of human motivation.

When I discuss mattering with scholars unfamiliar with the construct, some mention and try to equate it with the seminal work of Carl Rogers (1951, 1961, 1980). Rogers based much of his work on the contention that we all need unconditional regard and acceptance from others. However, my close inspection of his work suggests that Rogers never explicitly considered the need for regard from a mattering perspective. The need to matter is a specific type of regard that entails being important to others and gaining their attention as part of feeling related and connected to them. Mattering in this context stems from mutuality. Mutual mattering is discussed at length in Chapter 7 on the development of mattering.

The published literature on mattering is focused almost entirely on the feeling of mattering or not mattering, and there is little to no focus on the need to matter. This also applies to the research on mattering in children and adolescents described throughout this book. True advances in fully understanding mattering from a psychological perspective will only come through research and theory on the need to matter. There is no published measure of the need to matter, which has resulted in this element of the construct being almost entirely ignored. Next, I provide some conceptual views about the need to matter and then consider how motivational aspects of mattering are reflected in the actions of young people.

Questions abound when it comes to the need to matter. For instance, what forms does it take in young people? To what extent is the need to matter experienced broadly versus specifically in needing to matter to certain people such as parents and friends? What situational factors increase the need to matter and make it more salient?

I propose that while all young people need to matter, there are discernible individual differences in the need to matter to others. It is reasonably safe to assume that the need to matter will be more important to young people who have a low level of mattering and who have not had their needs met versus young people who do have a feeling of mattering to others. However, it is plausible that among those young people who do feel like they matter, a subset of children and adolescents will require constant reassurance and evidence that they matter to others.

There should also be considerable heterogeneity among young people in how they react and respond to an unmet need to matter. Rosenberg and McCullough (1981) noted that some children and adolescents seek to satisfy their need to matter through affiliations with undesirable peers. However, there are other differences in the personal strivings of children and adolescents with a need to matter. Ideally, striving to matter will come in the form of engaging in positive prosocial activities such as volunteering and mentoring to make positive differences in the lives of others. But, more typically, this form of striving is focused on achievements.

The concept of striving to matter has potentially important connotations when seeking to understand achievement behavior. Many children and adolescents strive excessively and seem driven to be perfect. Our work indicates that perfectionism is highly prevalent among young people (Flett & Hewitt, 2022), and we have come to understand and emphasize that the need to be perfect is largely underscored by interpersonal needs (Hewitt et al., 2017). The notion of striving to matter among those who absolutely must be perfect is quite plausible, given evidence that feelings of not mattering are linked to strong negative reactions to imperfections among adolescents (see Hill & Madigan, 2022). Excessively striving to matter to others seems like a potential recipe for burnout and disappointment for those young people who realize that even perfection will not matter to a neglectful or self-absorbed and disinterested parent.

Once it is satisfied, is this need to matter ever quelled? If it is, it is only for the moment. The need to matter, while seemingly dormant, is reactivated whenever a young person experiences a loss of mattering. Schlossberg (1989) stated that experiencing transitions often makes people reflect on whether they matter. For instance, a transition such as moving from middle school to high school should reactivate the need to matter because the focus is now on mattering in high school. Also, the need to matter may be satisfied in one setting (e.g., at home) but not in other settings (e.g., the community), so it will remain salient in terms of other thoughts and feelings.

The need to matter has different levels of intensity and clearly becomes dysfunctional when it reaches an extreme level or becomes imbued with irrational importance. One clear indication of how the need to matter can become problematic is provided by research on the assessment of narcissism in adolescents. The Dirty Dozen for Youth measure (Muris et al., 2013), designed to assess the dark triad (i.e., narcissism, psychopathy, and Machiavellianism) in adolescents, has two items on the narcissism scale that tap into an excessive need or wish to matter (i.e., I want others to pay attention to me; I want that others think I am important). Higher scores on this narcissism subscale were significantly associated with parental reports of aggressive and delinquent behavior. These associations, at least to some extent, likely reflect the frustration of failing to have satisfied the need to matter.

The feeling of not mattering described earlier is often accompanied by other negative feelings, which, in turn, can further undermine motivation. Flett, Su, Nepon, Sturman, et al. (2023) found that among 242 Chinese high school students, feelings of not mattering, as assessed by the General Mattering Scale (Marcus & Rosenberg, 1987), were strongly associated with the feeling of being defeated and trapped. All three feelings (i.e., not mattering, feeling trapped, and feeling defeated) were associated with submissiveness and a tendency to compare oneself unfavorably with others. It is easy to envision how a feeling of not mattering at school and in general would make learning and achievement seem like an uphill battle. Thus, it is not surprising that the students who had these negative feelings also had a motivational profile linked with higher levels of academic burnout.

HOW DOES MATTERING GET REPRESENTED IN OUR MINDSETS?

How is mattering experienced and expressed at a cognitive level? It is difficult, if not impossible, to consider the feeling of mattering without also reflecting on the role of cognition. The feeling is based on our perception of whether we matter and are being noticed by others. Mattering is tied directly to cognitive appraisal, which is reflected in Rosenberg and McCullough's (1981) emphasis on the theme of "inferred significance," expressed in the title of their seminal article. His sage observations about mattering included Rosenberg's (1985) caution that mattering is highly subjective. Some young people overestimate how much they matter to others, while other young people underestimate how much they matter to others. One basic but untested prediction is that those young people who have an accurate sense of how much they matter have had extensive positive or negative experiences that are unambiguous. Certainty about mattering or not mattering is rooted in being shown how much or how little we are regarded by key people in our lives.

The importance of viewing mattering from a cognitive perspective is reflected by the fact that when children or adolescents are asked to complete a questionnaire that taps their feelings of mattering to others, the scale item responses represent cognitive appraisals. Few people publicly broadcast that they feel like they matter, so thoughts and appraisals are typically part of a young person's internal world.

The cognitive side of mattering can be examined in many ways. I keep returning to the fact that it weighs heavily on a young person's mind when they feel like they do not matter to others and the need to matter is unresolved. This should be reflected by extensive rumination and reflection marked mostly by ruminative brooding. Some initial research with adults has confirmed that feelings of not mattering are associated with the type of ruminative brooding discussed by Nolen-Hoeksema (1991). Rumination is a process that links feelings of not mattering with depression (e.g., Flett et al., 2021), and these same associations should be evident among children and adolescents. I propose that it should be the case that there is a mattering-specific form of rumination that dominates the thinking of young people who cannot escape the feeling of not mattering to other people. Rumination and mattering have not yet been examined in published research with children or adolescents as participants.

There is a significant cognitive price to pay when a young person's thoughts have become dominated by the feeling of not mattering to others and associated reminders of their apparent insignificance. When the feeling of not mattering has become highly cognitively salient, it is a strong source of cognitive interference that limits the young person's ability to learn and pay attention.

A newly developed measure for adults that examines self-recrimination from a cognitive perspective is centered on the notion that there is a negative internal dialogue, and one element of this dialogue is frequent and intense thoughts about not mattering to other people (Hewitt et al., 2024). When this type of thinking has been activated, it should create a cognitive orientation that may amplify the motivational and emotional aspects of feeling unimportant.

The child or adolescent who lacks a feeling of mattering may have projected this into the future: They feel insignificant in the moment, but there is also hopelessness about ever mattering to other people. This negative view of the future is particularly entrenched if held by a young person who has experienced considerable adversity. It should also be less amenable to change if the young person has a relatively fixed mindset about mattering (i.e., entity thinking). It can be extrapolated from the work by Carol Dweck (2017) that the feeling of not mattering will be worse for those with a fixed entity mindset.

A key intervention goal for clinicians and counselors, as well as parents and educators, is to address the appraisals of not mattering to others and the possibility of becoming someone who matters to others. There is extensive literature on the positive goals and motives of young people and how their ambitions and hopes can be magnified through a positive possible selves approach (see Markus & Nurius, 1986). The possible self should include an explicit emphasis on mattering and a view of what is possible in making a difference and being valued and cared about by others. Extensive evidence attests to the widespread benefits of making positive possible selves more salient, including academic benefits (see Oyserman et al., 2006). One study examined whether it was possible to counter the well-known finding that low parental involvement undermines academic success. This general pattern was confirmed among participants in the control group, but among those who received the possible selves intervention, there was no noticeable decline in school achievement over 2 years (Oyserman et al., 2007). Low parental involvement likely included a sense among the participants that how they did in school did not matter to their parents; countering this view should result in greater behavioral engagement, learning, and performance.

I proposed that low levels of mattering will bias the interpretation of ambiguous feedback (Flett, 2018a). A circumstance that is not clear and uncertain (e.g., why text messages are not being responded to) could be seen as a lack of care and interest rather than a reflection of something else having occurred in the other person's life.

I also suggested that feelings of not mattering are reflected in autobiographical memories (Flett, 2018a). Intense affect is centered around being made to feel special and important. However, being made to feel irrelevant and insignificant results in quick and vivid recall of these events and experiences. When these types of memories are predominant and quickly recalled, they significantly impact how children and adolescents feel in terms of their levels of happiness and life satisfaction.

Future research will almost certainly identify key elements of the mattering experience that go well beyond the affective, motivational, and cognitive elements outlined here. The cognitive manifestations of feelings of not mattering as a form of rumination have much potential for expanding our understanding of the cognitive side of feeling connected to others and how it can keep stress activated in ways that take a toll on our mental and physical health.

MATTERING AS A SOURCE OF SELF-EVALUATION

In the final section of this chapter, let us consider mattering and its role in self-evaluative processes. On the surface, mattering seems like common sense because it should be the case that we feel good and happy when we perceive that we matter to someone who matters to us. My response to anyone who might downplay the significance of mattering and its complexities is to point to an element that has not received much consideration thus far: In most instances and for most people, the feeling of mattering or not mattering to others is a self-evaluative cue. It is a source of self-evaluation that is highly salient. This may be especially true when vulnerable people become preoccupied with feeling unimportant. Typically, they turn the feeling of not mattering on themselves and evaluate themselves. Children and adolescents who are uncertain about themselves or are highly susceptible to information about themselves are particularly likely to judge themselves according to whether they have been made to feel important or unimportant to other people.

The feeling of mattering versus not mattering represents a key piece of information about the self, especially for those who have imbued their need to matter with extreme importance. Psychotherapists often discuss the relationship the self has with the self. Those who conclude that they matter to no one can come to believe that some aspect of the self is faulty, which is why they cannot capture the attention of and be of interest to others. The tendency to negatively judge oneself due to feelings and perceptions of not mattering to others can create and exacerbate feelings of self-criticism.

How would using mattering as a self-evaluative cue be represented as a questionnaire item? It would mean endorsing a scale item such as "I judge myself according to how much I matter to others." This element could be experienced in comparative terms as a form of negative social comparison. This likely entails an extended process of negative self-evaluation that includes repetitive negative thoughts about the self and can be triggered by the feeling of not mattering as much as a peer or classmate. This may be especially likely after coming across someone on social media who seems to have a perfect life.

The feeling of not mattering used as a negative self-evaluative cue fits well with a well-known phenomenon common among people prone to depression. Abramson and Sackheim (1977) introduced the depressive paradox. The essence of this paradox is the tendency to blame the self for things beyond personal control (i.e., feeling responsible for things you are not responsible for). A young person could be exposed to a parent who is excessively self-involved or personally incapacitated to the point that this parent is incapable of demonstrating interest and affection (Flett, 2018a). Nevertheless, the young girl or boy will perceive that the lack of interest and attention is due to some negative and perhaps defective or deficient aspect of themselves. The feeling and experience of not mattering is used here as a self-evaluative cue and a source of self-blame instead of being attributed to the parent's tendencies. This scenario is often real rather than hypothetical. It demonstrates how young people's cognitive development and social cognitive skills are important in how feelings of not mattering can easily be directed at the self.

Clearly, the tendency to use the feeling of not mattering as a source of self-evaluation can and should become a prime target in clinical and counseling interventions. Young people who negatively evaluate themselves due to the sense and feeling of not mattering can learn to stop making these judgments and to be self-compassionate. They also need to learn that they do matter, making negative self-evaluations particularly unwarranted. This was brilliantly portrayed in the movie *Good Will Hunting* (Van Sant, 1997) when the psychologist, portrayed by Robin Williams, revealed to Will that he, too, was abused as a child by his alcoholic father. Will was physically abused by his foster father. Dr. Sean Maguire repeatedly tells Will, "It's not your fault. It's not your fault. It's not your fault" (1:49:40), and this is precisely what young people who have internalized the feeling of not mattering need to realize about themselves.

SUMMARY

This chapter focused on elaborating the mattering construct by discussing it as a feeling, need, and cognition. The discussion included several new observations that represent testable hypotheses for future research. Mattering was discussed extensively in terms of how it is experienced at an affective level and how it is often intensely felt. I proposed that mattering matters greatly, especially for most adolescents, because of their self-consciousness and concern about how others see them, which contributes to intense affective reactions. From a motivational perspective, mattering was discussed as a core need, which is related to other core needs, such as the need to connect.

However, the need to matter has distinct properties. An unmet need to matter in people of various ages, including children and adolescents, is associated with dissatisfaction, unhappiness, and other affective states.

Mattering is clearly relevant to study as a form of social cognition. The cognitive aspects of mattering are evident in that the feeling of mattering is tied to a cognitive appraisal; however, there is much more to the cognitive side of mattering. I proposed that, at the cognitive level, various ruminations accompany feelings of not mattering to others. This likely comprises a specific type of thinking that includes ruminating about not mattering. When we collectively consider mattering versus not mattering in terms of affect, cognition, and motivation, feelings of not mattering are not simply the inverse of feelings of not mattering due to distinct cognitive tendencies and motivational orientations.

Finally, I provided a brief but important analysis of how mattering and feelings of not mattering are implicated in negative self-evaluations. I proposed that many young people who feel like they do not matter to others respond to this feeling by seeing themselves negatively, as if they are responsible for not being important to others. This tendency accounts for links between feelings of not mattering and self-criticism, including extreme judgments of being defective and worthless.

The next chapter considers the facets of the mattering construct introduced by Rosenberg and McCullough (1981) in their seminal work from over 4 decades ago. This analysis further contrasts feelings of mattering with feelings and fears of not mattering commonly felt when people feel marginalized.

2 DESCRIPTION AND CONCEPTUALIZATION OF MATTERING

This chapter introduces mattering in a more detailed way, according to how it has been classically described by previous authors. The components of mattering are outlined to paint a picture of how mattering is typically instilled in a young person. I begin by listing and describing facets of the mattering construct outlined by Rosenberg and McCullough (1981). Their work was an extension of earlier work that included a description of how the mattering construct was derived from earlier work by Rosenberg (1965), which showed that children fare better when they know their parents are actively interested in them. The benefits of parental interest are examined in Chapter 7.

THE COMPONENTS OF MATTERING

In their original work, Rosenberg and McCullough (1981) made some key observations about the overall role of mattering. They noted that although mattering is important for the individual, it is also important for society

https://doi.org/10.1037/0000449-003
Mattering as a Core Need in Children and Adolescents: Theoretical, Clinical, and Research Perspectives, by G. L. Flett

because it represents social obligation and is a powerful source of social integration. It is something we share, and according to these authors, it is a motive that "exercises a powerful influence on our actions" (Rosenberg & McCullough, 1981, p. 163). Importantly, the need to matter is broadly shared by people, and it is something that we have in common with each other.

The three facets introduced by Rosenberg and McCullough (1981) are outlined next. Additional facets have been identified as awareness and understanding of the mattering construct has grown. These facets are also described.

The Feeling of Getting Attention

The first facet is the feeling of being noticed by other people and getting their attention. This facet was identified as the most elementary facet of mattering (see Rosenberg, 1985; Rosenberg & McCullough, 1981). Mattering was not discussed in terms of the development of young children, but the salience and primacy of this aspect of mattering makes sense in terms of the worlds of young people. We notice at an early age whether people are paying attention to us. Some of this awareness is likely preverbal and reflects the responsiveness of care providers who react sensitively or fail to react to cues from infants and toddlers. By the time children reach preschool age, they are well aware of where they stand compared with the other young children vying for the attention of caregivers. I return to this theme in Chapter 7, which examines mattering from a developmental perspective.

The Feeling of Being Important

The second facet is feeling important to someone (Rosenberg & McCullough, 1981). The experience of feeling important is powerful, in part, because it is tied directly to the sense of self and the thought, "I feel important, so I am important." Once it is experienced, the person who feels important will want it to last.

Importance is highly central to overall feelings of mattering. Beginning in 2014, I partnered with two school boards in Ontario, Canada to conduct research on mattering and resilience in students. The results from this research were shared with me, in my capacity as a consultant on the project, and I use those data to evaluate issues and themes related to mattering throughout this book. Results from the school board project typically showed that when responses from thousands of students were correlated, agreement with the item "I feel like I matter to other people" was strongly correlated ($r = .80$ or greater) with agreement with the item "I feel like I am important to other people."

What is especially salient about importance is what Rosenberg and McCullough (1981) observed that links it with being cared about. Mattering in terms of feeling important is, "To believe that the other person cares about what we want, think, say, or do, or is concerned with our fate, is to matter" (Rosenberg & McCullough, 1981, p. 164). When we are in a reciprocal mattering relationship, the other person also cares about what we truly need so that it becomes about more than just what we want.

Rosenberg and McCullough (1981) further emphasized that mattering in terms of feeling important is not simply about getting the other person's approval. The person who they matter to is someone willing to tell a young person when they have messed up and need to try to do better. Mattering is not about looking the other way when someone acts in ways that are not in their best interest or someone else's best interests. When this is framed in terms of the person caring about what we need and what is best in the big picture, communicating something that may initially upset the young person is part of engaging and investing in them.

It is not difficult to imagine the personal attributes of someone who conveys to us that we matter. The person who lets us know we matter is someone who shrouds interactions in interpersonal warmth. We often know we matter to someone by their style of interacting with us; our mere presence seems to elicit and activate the expressive side of their personality in ways that set the stage for interactions that deepen the connection and bond between two people.

The adolescents who shared their mattering experiences in *The New York Times* article were clear in expressing many themes that support conceptualizations of mattering (Proulx, 2023). Both the attention and importance facets were represented in the many examples they gave of people who engaged with them and gave them their full attention without judging them. These people were portrayed as listening deeply to what the young person had to say. Attention here meant being fully seen and heard. By the same token, when people are openly dismissive and act as if being forced to listen to what the young person is saying, it evokes the feeling of not mattering. In many respects, the growing literature on providing young people with a sense of voice is highly relevant to the feeling of mattering to others. This need to be listened to and heard at a deep level is especially vital when a child or adolescent has a problem and needs to be understood without being made to feel irrelevant or like a burden. When the problem is serious (e.g., being bullied relentlessly), the listening needs to be followed responsively by actions so that the young person in distress feels cared for and about.

Being Depended On and Feeling Useful

The third facet is the feeling of mattering that stems from being depended on by others (see Rosenberg & McCullough, 1981). This element of the construct is distinct because it involves being relied on by others.

I have come to appreciate this facet of mattering more after reflecting on it and seeing how it is expressed and experienced in people's lives. The sense of being depended on can keep people going despite adversities. What seems to be at the root of this facet is the need to be needed. People put up with a lot if their need to be needed is satisfied or they have the hope of being needed and useful. The need to be needed is at a level that goes well beyond wanting to be liked by others or needing to be liked by others. There is a deeper sense of being valued when we know we are needed.

The first years of life are dominated by the need to feel safe, secure, and loved. But as we get older, we also need to feel needed. This need becomes increasingly important to children and adolescents as they begin to wonder about their place in the world and experience self-doubts. The children and adolescents with people in their lives who make them feel needed and convince them this is indeed the case are those who have a vital source of strength that will help them negotiate the process of developing a positive identity.

What related feelings are involved when mattering stems from being depended on? This element is tied to a sense of purpose and mission. It is most apparent to the individual child or adolescent when they feel useful. Consider, for instance, one boy's reply in the comment section of *The New York Times* article: "A time I feel like I've mattered most was when my parents needed someone to look after my brother and make dinner. So when they came home to dinner being finished and my brother being ok, they really appreciated me and it made me feel great" (Nordyke, 2023).

Another boy described in the comments section a tense situation that no doubt will never be forgotten: "I felt needed when I was riding motorcycles with my cousin and he had wrecked down the road and broke his leg and I had to take him the hospital. The reason that made me feel needed is because if I wasn't there to help him, he might have been hit by a car and been killed" (Mayes, 2023). I feel grateful to these young people and the other adolescents who replied to *The New York Times* article because they provided some valuable reminders of what mattering is all about.

Some children endure abjectly horrible family situations if they have a clear sense they are needed by a parent who is not functioning at a high level. A positive sense of worth can still emerge and be fully experienced if the parent acknowledges the child's contributions. Unfortunately, some people lack the capacity to be good parents, perhaps because they have some form of mental illness or addiction. The parent who lacks self-awareness and is focused on themself will not likely express much appreciation and may treat the child's contributions as obligatory rather than allowing the child to experience the warm feeling of mattering due to being needed. Instead, resentment and frustration will build up in the child or adolescent.

A recent study of a sample of late adolescents and emerging adults documented the mental health benefits of feeling needed and useful (Fuligni et al., 2022). It showed that feeling needed and useful predicted emotional well-being beyond the benefits of receiving social support.

Fuligni (2019) conducted programmatic research and described at length the strong need to contribute to others during adolescence, which can help adolescents fulfill fundamental needs related to autonomy, identity, and intimacy. However, being useful and feeling needed are related to the core need to matter, which is exceptionally salient in early adolescence.

Ego Extension

In keeping with the emphasis on having a deep connection with other people, Rosenberg and McCullough (1981) also discussed how feeling important to someone involves ego extension. When people in a relationship are ego extended, what impacts one person also impacts the other (i.e., Your pain is my pain; your joy is my joy). Ego extension seems healthy, but only up to a point; the parent who must live vicariously through a child's achievements has taken things too far. After further consideration, Rosenberg (1985) suggested that ego extension is distinct enough to be considered another separate facet of the mattering construct.

Being Missed

Rosenberg (1985) proposed another facet of the feeling of mattering: knowing other people miss you when you are not around. Some adolescents who shared their experiences of mattering in *The New York Times* article spontaneously added that they know they are valued because the people in their lives had made it clear they would be impacted if their adolescents were no longer around (Proulx, 2023).

Mattering in terms of being missed by others can have life-saving potential. The feeling of not mattering is highly aversive and painful when young people conclude that their absence will not be noticed. Far too many people have no idea how much they would be missed, underscoring that it is best to let people know their absence is felt. Extensive literature has shown that the risk of suicide is lower when individuals have many good reasons for living (Linehan et al., 1983). Some reasons for living in the Reasons for Living Scale (Linehan et al., 1983) sound as if they are taken directly from a mattering measure. Most items from this scale involve the theme of mattering through feeling needed (e.g., my family depends upon me and needs me; close friends depend upon me and need me; I have people who love me and who listen to me and understand me; I have a job in which I am involved and where I am needed; I make a contribution to society). The work on reasons for living has been extended to adolescents, and, here again, there is evidence of the protection of reasons for living (Pinto et al., 1998). One compelling reason for living is how much you would be missed and how much others would be impacted if you were no longer in their lives.

One version of the inventory developed for adolescents has seven items that tap a family alliance factor (Osman et al., 1998). Most items tap themes that reflect mattering to one's family (e.g., family cares the way I feel; family cares what happens; family takes time to listen). A peer acceptance and support factor is laden with mattering-related items (e.g., I can count on my friends; friends care; friends stand by me). Osman et al. reported that both the family and friends factors were correlated negatively and strongly with depression, hopelessness, suicide ideation, and the likelihood of suicide. Another study with adolescents by Gutierrez and colleagues (2000) suggested that the Reasons for Living Inventory for Adolescents is a reliable measure of adolescent suicide risk potential and has more predictive power than hopelessness. The research also examined sex differences and suggested that suicidal girls, in particular, may have lost the protection inherent in strong feelings of family alliance.

Being Appreciated

Schlossberg (1989) proposed that appreciation is another facet of mattering after interviewing caregivers of family members. They indicated that their feeling of mattering was rooted in having their contributions appreciated. As noted previously, if a child or adolescent derives a sense of mattering by fulfilling key roles in the family, a true sense of mattering will only come when they are acknowledged and appreciation is expressed.

Appreciation can operate at another level when it is centered not just on what we do but also on feeling appreciated as a person in terms of who we are in other people's eyes. Imagine the impact when someone expresses appreciation to a young person for who they are. The question in the young person's mind is, "Do they appreciate me?" The sense of mattering is blunted if appreciation is contingent on doing something or achieving something. This theme is revisited later in Chapter 7.

Gratitude is a positive emotion linked to mattering to others and feeling appreciated by them. Expressing gratitude is also a way to build a reciprocal relationship between two people who matter to each other.

The Feeling of Individualization

In Flett (2018a), I emphasized that mattering is more likely to be felt following individualization. Mattering is especially likely when a person feels they are with someone who recognizes and respects their unique qualities as an individual and sees the person's unique true self.

People covet attention from key people in their lives. This focus on feeling uniquely special in someone's eyes makes mattering feel personal. This sense of mattering in a way that distinguishes a young person from their peers and perhaps even siblings seems especially important, given the frequency of social comparison that occurs in young people's lives. The specific ways we matter to people can foster a life orientation that reflects a clear view of the self as a recognized and valued individual and a sense of being and feeling unique. In contrast, when we lack a sense of mattering to other people and the experiences that would normally go with developing a feeling of mattering, it is difficult to have a strong sense of oneself and develop a distinct conceptualization of being an individual with unique attributes.

This emphasis on individualized attention and interest fits with analyses of how educators provide relatedness support to students (Sparks et al., 2015). Individualized attention and interest from teachers promote engagement and self-determination among students (Sparks et al., 2016).

Gerald Adams and Sheila Marshall (1996) astutely linked mattering with interpersonal differentiation and the process that results in the eventual formation of an autonomous self. They proposed that socialization that leads to difference results in a feeling of significance as an autonomous and unique person. It addresses our shared need for uniqueness and a distinct identity.

Adams and Marshall (1996) also described how mattering and a heightened focus on how one is significant yet different from others can bring people together and be a source of integration. They proposed another pathway to mattering that frames the need to matter as a dynamic social need; in this instance, young people are influenced by socialization processes associated with a group identity, group affiliation, and being valued within the group.

Ideally, this involves mattering to a prosocial group, but it can also lead young people down a dark pathway that fosters affiliations with gangs in just the sorts of ways anticipated by Rosenberg and McCullough (1981).

Mattering and individualization have been discussed thus far in positive terms, likely reflecting the lack of focus on mattering as a psychological need. Mattering can become an excessive need for some young people (i.e., needing attention too much), and the quest to matter can result in significant vulnerability and irresponsible risk-taking behavior. For instance, how might an excessive need to matter come into play in developing an eating disorder such as anorexia nervosa? Some young people may place irrational importance on mattering and becoming someone who is special and seen by others as special. In such instances, the need to matter may be fueled partially by the dysfunctional belief that "If I am successful at starving myself and can achieve a more desirable appearance, other people will appreciate me and value me." This way of thinking was acknowledged recently in a personal account by Hadley Freeman (2023) of her experiences with anorexia in adolescence and early adulthood. Freeman acknowledged that it took her until her late 30s to realize that disordered eating was a "scratchy, self-made jumper of self-defeating destruction and I no longer believed that holding on to splinters of anorexia made me special" (2023, para. 31). Similarly, in her autobiography, actress Portia De Rossi (2010) described how her eating disorder was maintained by the positive attention she received for maintaining a dangerously low weight level of 80 pounds. When an excessive need to matter fuels eating disorders, such behavior amounts to "starving for attention."

HAVING VALUE AND ADDING VALUE TO OTHERS

The facet of being depended on has received more emphasis due to the important work of Isaac Prilleltensky, whose 2020 article outlines the key distinction between having value to others versus giving value to others or adding value to others. Someone who has become dedicated to adding value to others has acted on their need to be needed and has found ways to put it into action.

There are various ways to add value to others (e.g., helping a classmate, volunteering at a food bank). Open discussions about adding value to others are a way to share some key life lessons with young people. One key lesson is that worth should not be solely defined by achievement and performance; a sense of being valued and important can come through making a difference in the lives of others. Ideally, these efforts are deemed "selfless" in that they are altruistic and well-intentioned and make a difference to others (but note that some altruism is not so innocent). Another key lesson is that adding value to others also adds a sense of personal agency and control to the feeling of mattering. When young people engage in activities such as volunteering, they learn that they can affect whether they will feel like they matter to others. Feelings of mattering can be self-generated. The young person who says, "I matter to no one," should be encouraged to find a cause or someone they can benefit. It is important to add that the gift of your time is one of the most precious things you can share and donate.

Discussions of adding value typically focus on activities outside the family home, but as we will see in the subsequent discussion of mattering in positive youth development, adding value can also be in the family context. Children and adolescents can fill valuable roles at home that contribute to the well-being of all family members. Adding value and having value become fused when family members express appreciation for acts that add value. In this context, core differences between warm, authoritative parents and cold, authoritarian parents become evident. Contrast warm parents who signal their awareness and acknowledge and appreciate a child's efforts with harsh and controlling parents who demand that the child continue to do something (e.g., clearing the dishes) that they freely chose to do in the first place. This negative scenario often includes the parent criticizing the child because of how they did something.

Young people who get a sense of being valued by giving to others are especially likely to retain a strong feeling of mattering if they know that other people will continue to rely on them and depend on them. People of all ages need to feel useful and valued and they need to know that others are counting on them for advice and the tangible support they provide. The young person who is depended on can conclude, "I am needed" and "I am useful." When this occurs outside the home, they realize that "I am needed at school and in my community."

There is extensive literature on the benefits to young people of engaging in activities such as volunteering or mentoring (Ballard et al., 2021). We examined adding value to others as part of the mattering construct by isolating a four-item subscale with items from the Mattering Index (Somers et al., 2022). The four items in this subscale are shown in Exhibit 2.1. This subscale was labeled "giving value to others."

In our sample of 206 high school students, we found that giving value to others is highly beneficial to oneself (Somers et al., 2022). Higher scores on this subscale were associated with greater hope, a positive future orientation,

EXHIBIT 2.1. Mattering Index Items Tapping "Giving Value to Others"

When people need help, they come to me.
People count on me to be there in times of need.
People tend to rely on me for support.
Other people trust me with things that are important to them.

Note. Mattering Index by Elliott et al. (2004). Data from Somers et al. (2022).

and a mastery orientation. Most notably, higher scores were also associated with higher grades ($r = .44$). The association with higher grades can be an important lesson for parents who are always pushing their children to achieve. When relentless striving does not include some balance and engaging in activities that give value and add value to others, the child does not fully benefit from the positive feelings and sense of worth and self-efficacy rooted in making a difference in the lives of others. This sense of adding value is also a vital resource that buffers the impact of those times when it seems like other people are going out of their way to make us feel like we do not matter. This more negative theme is considered in the next section of this chapter.

THE FLIPSIDE: FEELINGS OF NOT MATTERING

Mattering has been described as a double-edged construct (Flett, 2018a, 2022). It is highly protective when young people feel a sense of mattering, and it is highly problematic when they feel that they matter only a little or not at all.

Research and theory on mattering is considered part of the positive psychology field, and it is important to retain and sustain this emphasis on mattering as a source of power, inspiration, growth, and advancement. Subsequent chapters on happiness and resilience underscore this positive psychology focus. However, it is also important to be realistic and capture elements of the construct relevant to people's lives and ways of perceiving the world, even if the focus becomes much more negative.

This section describes facets of the mattering construct that move it away from the realm of positive psychology and place it firmly in the realm of clinical and counseling psychology. Right from the beginning, the flipside or downside was recognized in addition to the positive aspects. Indeed, Rosenberg (1985) concluded that "Low parental mattering is a strikingly dysphoric disposition; sourness, resentment, embitterment, and depression follow in its wake" (p. 218). In recent years, this focus on the negative has been more explicit and reflected in new approaches to conceptualization and measurement.

Anti-Mattering and How Children Experience It

In this section, I consider the part of the mattering construct I refer to as anti-mattering. Anti-mattering is not simply the opposite of mattering. The distinction between mattering and anti-mattering is captured by the many differences between the feeling of being valued and the feeling of being unvalued. However, some people experience more extreme forms of anti-mattering that seem to have an added element; not only do they feel unvalued, but they also feel devalued.

Just as people know how it feels to matter and to be important to others, they also know how it feels when they perceive that others view them as unimportant or irrelevant. This feeling also arises from not being acknowledged by others. It is even worse when you realize that someone you care about is not listening to you because their attention has wandered to something or someone they are more interested in.

Aspects of anti-mattering can parallel the facets of mattering. The person who needs to be needed has intense feelings when treated like they are not needed. The person who derives joy from feeling appreciated will be strongly affected when their efforts are not appreciated or when people seem to minimize or ignore their efforts.

The anti-mattering concept was first proposed over 5 years ago (Flett, 2018a), and there are now indications that the concept is taking hold in public awareness. Many authors have referred to it in various settings and circumstances. I noted that just as mattering is such a powerful and positive feeling and orientation, the feeling of not mattering also strongly affects people of various ages, including young people (Flett, 2018a). The concept of anti-mattering was proposed to capture when people feel they do not matter to others (Flett, 2018a; Flett et al., 2022).

The anti-mattering concept has its roots in the original work by Nancy Schlossberg (1989) on mattering versus marginalization. Her seminal chapter captured themes that resonate with everyone. She opens by stating, "The polar themes of marginality and mattering connect all of us—rich and poor, young and old, male and female. Are we part of things; do we belong; are we central or marginal?" (Schlossberg, 1989, p. 5). Schlossberg noted that during transitions, it is natural for people to feel marginal and as if they do not matter. The concept of anti-mattering reflects the fact that feeling marginal is not a passing thing for many people. Their daily lives reflect a chronic sense of being unimportant and irrelevant in the eyes of certain people if not everyone. This feeling is a burden to carry around and is a weight on people that takes a toll not only in terms of mental health but also in terms of physical health.

Earlier, Rosenberg (1985) contrasted the feeling of mattering with the sense of not mattering and being insignificant. He noted, "The person low on mattering feels irrelevant, unimportant, or peripheral in the minds of others" (Rosenberg, 1985, p. 219). When this feeling persists, it might be better to feel entirely off the radars of other people than be peripheral in their minds, but in both instances, there is bound to be considerable emotional upset.

As suggested earlier, people have a high level of anti-mattering when they feel uncared for, unheard, or invisible. This feeling can involve the sense of not counting to other people. If taken to the extreme, it can involve feeling entirely insignificant because no one seems to care. When people feel insignificant, they overgeneralize their experience and feel that no one is listening or cares. This overgeneralized anti-mattering is an indication of considerable risk for the individual. One reason risk is amplified is that when a young person has thoughts and feelings of not mattering to anyone, this is a self-statement about how life is unfolding. Thoughts and feelings can easily be amended to "In my life, I don't matter to anyone." If there is a form of cognitive rumination about not mattering, as was proposed in Chapter 1, the rumination for people who feel a sense of not mattering to anyone and see this as characteristic of their lives will likely be highly ruminative about how life is going at present and how it is likely to go in the future. The most problematic form of rumination is becoming cognitively locked into thoughts that highlight the discrepancy between how life is going and how far it is from how it ought to be going or ideally should be going.

Chapter 10 considers how the need to matter is reflected in the social media use of young people. One of my chief concerns about this is that seeing crafted images of peers with seemingly perfect lives may fuel destructive rumination. This type of rumination focuses on how life is going for the vulnerable adolescent and how it seems to be going for their effortlessly perfect peer with the perfect life.

Anti-mattering is not simply the opposite of mattering to others (Flett et al., 2022). Mattering and anti-mattering differ in the affective, cognitive, and motivational orientations they capture. One way to consider this distinction is to contrast the person with an approach orientation, who seems fully engaged with other people and life, with the person who has an avoidance orientation and is disengaged from other people and seems to have a life of isolation. Mattering versus anti-mattering reflects the many ways of distinguishing between feeling connected to and disconnected from others.

Anti-mattering is accompanied by many negative feelings and typically precludes positive feelings. It is particularly impactful if young people who feel unimportant to others conclude that they are social failures or losers. One study of social media use versus face-to-face communication included a measure of perceived social success (Pea et al., 2012). This subscale was couched as a "social success index." It combined items such as "I feel like I have a lot of friends" along with "I feel like I am important to my friends" and "People my age understand me." When mattering to others is aligned with how a young person defines being a social success, the social pain that emanates from anti-mattering will weigh heavy on the young person who feels like an abject failure on the outside of social circles.

Anti-Mattering as the Experience of Prejudice, Discrimination, and Stigma

The anti-mattering concept is a way of framing the emotional experience of people of various ages when they have been made to feel small and less than other people. When people feel devalued, anti-mattering captures how it feels to be the target of prejudice, discrimination, stigma, and other blatant and subtle ways that people are mistreated. A feeling of anti-mattering often arises when feeling and being ostracized. Williams and Nida (2009) emphasized, "Ostracism makes a person feel invisible, nonexistent, and totally insignificant" (p. 280), which closely resembles the felt experience of anti-mattering. Given that no one wants to feel like they do not matter, a focus on anti-mattering may help some people realize they have something in common with people who have been stigmatized and discriminated against. We are similar because we all have a shared need to matter.

There has been little research on anti-mattering and the experience of prejudice and stigma, but our initial pilot research points to the value of programmatic research that ties these concepts together. Some new exploratory pilot data we recently obtained from a university student sample points to evidence of a strong link between anti-mattering and the experience of ostracism (see Su & Flett, 2023). Gilman and colleagues' (2013) ostracism measure for adolescents was used to determine that ostracism is linked robustly with social stress, depression, and low levels of global satisfaction.

Another new investigation is broadly documenting the link between feelings of anti-mattering and the experience of stigma, discrimination, and distress among international university students in Canada (Su & Flett, 2023). Another innovative study has documented a strong association between levels of anti-mattering and a phenomenon known as "stigma by association," which is all too frequently experienced by adults with a close family member with a history of mental illness (Goldberg et al., 2023).

As for adolescents, research conducted with high school students from Western Canada found that being targeted and overhearing homonegative comments was associated with lower levels of mattering to friends (Sotindjo et al., 2019). More generally, this research also documented the presence of an alarming level of homonegative speech in schools despite efforts to reduce discrimination and promote inclusion.

The sense of being devalued can detract from the potential positive feelings of mattering that would otherwise arise through activities focused on making a difference in the lives of others or contributing to the community. Important work by Fuligni and colleagues (2022) extended prior work on feeling needed and useful by documenting how youth can have their contributions undermined and downgraded by others simply because of the ethnicity or gender of the young person seeking to make a difference. This study of 296 late adolescents recruited participants online. Analyses indicated that devalued contributions were experienced most frequently by African American, Latinx, and Asian American females. The frequency of having devalued contributions was associated significantly with depression. Other results showed that many participants were able to overcome these anti-mattering experiences and were still able to feel needed and useful. However, the frequency of experiencing discrimination was associated significantly with feeling less needed and useful and with having a lower sense of meaning and purpose. Fine-grained analyses indicated that Latinx and Asian American youth reported that they were most likely to report feeling less needed and less useful by society.

Countless people have had the experience of trying to do something nice for someone and having the intent of their well-intentioned efforts criticized or questioned. This type of treatment evokes a feeling that is not soon forgotten. Imagine how it feels if this is a repeated experience rooted in prejudice and discrimination. Efforts that should be appreciated amount to a thankless task or effort that can undermine a sense of worth and escalate frustration.

Experiences with discrimination are important to keep in mind as reminders that feelings of anti-mattering can feel personal and involve frequent negative social interactions and considerable interpersonal conflict, both inside and outside the home. The feeling of anti-mattering is based once again on cognitive appraisals and perceptions. However, as people who have experienced prejudice, stigma, and other forms of maltreatment have discovered far too often, these feelings may be veridical and based on various adverse experiences. I discussed this possibility at length in my recent article (Flett, 2022). I suggested that the experiences of being victimized, such as being bullied, were much worse for the person who was already carrying a sense of being unimportant and unvalued. I noted that "Feelings of not mattering should also amplify reactions to bullying and be reflected in more intense experiences of loneliness, shame, and other negative emotions so often felt by bullied children and adolescents" (Flett, 2022, p. 23).

Constant and Chronic Anti-Mattering Versus Episodic Anti-Mattering

Feelings of not mattering can be experienced chronically by people who have daily experiences that heighten their sense of insignificance. Next, I describe two examples of extreme anti-mattering episodes.

The famous disability rights advocate, Judith Heumann, died in March 2023. Judy Heumann had a remarkable life, and her advocacy profoundly affected many people. Judy was and is referred to by many as "the mother of the disability rights movement." Her autobiography, *Being Heumann*, is a book everyone should read and reflect on (see Heumann & Joiner, 2020). It chronicles her adaptation to having polio at 18 months old and, as a result, needing to use a wheelchair as a young child for mobility. Why is Judy featured here? Unfortunately, her life includes an example of one of the most extreme and troubling anti-mattering episodes experienced by a young child. Judy longed to learn and be with the other children, but when her mother pushed her in her wheelchair to enroll her at the local school at the age of 5, Judy was denied the right to attend school. The school principal told Judy and her parents that because of her wheelchair, Judy was considered a "fire hazard" and deemed unsafe. We can only imagine what this would feel like in terms of not only being made to feel unimportant but also being portrayed as a risk to the well-being of other children. Next, her parents sought to enroll Judy in a local yeshiva, and the school principal told Judy's mother that this would be possible once Judy learned enough Hebrew to attend school. Judy documented the intense tutorials and work she did throughout the rest of the school year to learn Hebrew at an exceptional level. However, when Judy's mother phoned the yeshiva and told the principal that Judy could be enrolled at the end of the summer, the principal reneged. Eventually, the public school board provided Judy with 2.5 hours of instruction per week in her home while she watched each day as her friends on the street headed off to school.

Other anti-mattering experiences followed and ultimately led Judy to realize that adults outside her family viewed her solely as a child with a sickness. Eventually, as a young child, she concluded, "I wasn't expected to be part of the world" (Heumann & Joiner, 2020, p. 14). Fortunately, Judy sought to prove otherwise; she demonstrated throughout her life that she was a part of the world and had an exceptionally important and valued role to play. Her life story is a shining example of giving and adding value to others through her many accomplishments as a disability rights activist. Judy's activities as an adult included serving as the assistant secretary for the Office of Special Education and Rehabilitative Services in the U.S. Department of Education from 1993 to 2001 in President Clinton's administration. She also served as the World Bank's initial adviser on disability and development from 2002 to 2006. President Obama appointed Judy as the first special advisor for International Disability Rights at the U.S. Department of State. She served from 2010 to 2017.

Another anti-mattering episode occurred recently, and it, too, is troubling in many respects. The story was documented in *The Washington Post*. A group of dedicated LGBTQ+ students from E. C. Glass High School in Lynchburg, Virginia, followed all the necessary steps to put together a compelling application that resulted in being awarded a $10K grant from the *It Gets Better* organization (Dvorak, 2023). The funding was to be used to create a safe space and calming quiet room for all the students in the school. The students' initiative reflected their attempt to address the needs of all students at the school who were vulnerable to mental health issues, including possible suicidal thoughts. However, adults on the Lynchburg City School Board summarily rejected the funding. The *Washington Post* article noted that the adults had essentially "created a blueprint for how to belittle, betray and dismiss kids" (Dvorak, 2023, para. 1). When the student leaders pleaded for reconsideration at a public meeting, adults in attendance were described as "stone-faced" and nonresponsive to the point that one of the student leaders, Chester Lobb, said it made the student presenters feel like they were not even there (para. 13).

Background for Anti-Mattering

The initial indication of the strong emotions tied to anti-mattering thoughts and feelings came to me over a decade ago through a series of discussions I had with colleagues on the school board project mentioned previously. We added two items assessing anti-mattering to the broader survey we created for the purposes of internal research. I explained that they would be an important supplement to our positive focus on mattering. My colleagues agreed at one level, but some were concerned about the emotional impact on adolescents when asked to rate scale items. They suggested that reading items reflecting anti-mattering would evoke negative feelings and possibly stir up thoughts of self-harm. Others suggested that these feelings and thoughts already existed, and measuring them would be the first step in doing something about them. The result was that one item with moderate wording was inserted into the survey: "There are times when I feel like I don't matter." Our analyses of survey data confirmed that distress is considerably higher among students who agreed with this statement.

Subsequent research using brief subscales from the Mattering Index by Elliott et al. (2004) also provided evidence of the individual differences in anti-mattering among high school students. One of the two four-item subscales described in Somers et al. (2022) consists entirely of items worded in ways that reflect anti-mattering (see Exhibit 2.2). Note that the wording of some items was altered slightly to make them more suitable for children and adolescents. Imagine how it feels to agree strongly with scale items such as "People do not care what happens to me" and "No one would notice one day if I disappeared."

Unfortunately, events and experiences such as these are much more common than they should be. While people who are marginalized in general are more likely to have anti-mattering feelings and experiences, there will be times in most people's lives when they either receive feedback indicating they do not matter or will be left to wonder whether they matter to others. Our recent conceptual extensions focus on what I refer to as *anti-mattering reactivity*. How do young people characteristically react when they have experiences that make them feel like they do not matter? The most vulnerable young people are those with chronic anti-mattering feelings and frequent anti-mattering episodes and who respond in maladaptive ways to these feelings and experiences. Chapter 9 examines mattering and feelings of not mattering in resilience and adaptability. More resilient and adaptable youth develop the proactive tendencies and sense of resolve and mission that emerge when they remain determined to make a difference and do not let themselves be defined by attempts to make them feel unimportant and irrelevant.

EXHIBIT 2.2. Mattering Index Scale Items With Anti-Mattering Themes

Sometimes I feel almost as if I were invisible.

No one would notice if one day I disappeared.

People do not care what happens to me.

It is hard for me to get the attention of others.

Note. Data from Somers et al. (2022). Items are reverse-scored items in the Mattering Index (see Elliott et al., 2004).

Students who agree with the items in Exhibit 2.2 are clearly at risk. Results from the school board project indicated that they have less hope, a more negative future orientation, poorer executive functioning, and a greater propensity to exhibit behaviors that reflect school risks, signifying disengagement (e.g., skipping class, not doing homework) and social risks. Social risks were assessed with the Adolescent Risk-Taking Questionnaire (Gullone et al., 2000).

Research on anti-mattering among children or adolescents is limited thus far, but there are clear indications that there are meaningful individual differences in levels of anti-mattering among young people as assessed by the Anti-Mattering Scale (Flett et al., 2022). A recent study by Hill and Madigan (2022) with gifted and talented adolescents from the United Kingdom demonstrated that anti-mattering is a highly relevant orientation (also see Maftei & Diaconu-Gherasim, 2023).

The Fear of Not Mattering

The fear of not mattering is a core insecurity that reflects the possibility, if not the likelihood, of a personal future characterized by being, becoming, or feeling insignificant to others. In most instances, the young person with a fear of not mattering to others already has strong feelings of not mattering to others and is simply projecting these current feelings into a feared future. This orientation typically reflects an insecure sense of self that persists despite associating with people who provide a sense of mattering to others. However, fears of not mattering may be rooted in harsh parental criticism, including future-focused messages such as "You'll never amount to anything."

The fear of not mattering is conceptualized as a fear that links the self and social concerns; it is seen as related to but distinguishable from other interpersonal fears, such as a fear of missing out or separation fears (Casale & Flett, 2020, 2023). The young person with a salient fear of being or becoming insignificant to others is likely someone with an anxious temperament and a history of early experiences with caregivers who are not responsive or effective in providing comfort and care.

When viewed at a broad level, the fear of not mattering seems like a vital part of the construct in terms of identifying a component that can account for the link between anxiety and feelings of not mattering to others. An earlier analysis suggested a link with constructs such as the fear of failure (Flett, 2019). This follows from research on the fear of failure construct that includes a facet tapping the fear of becoming unimportant to others (Conroy et al., 2002).

There is extensive evidence linking deficits in mattering with higher levels of depression and lower levels of happiness and less evidence linking low mattering and anxiety (see Chapter 8 and 13, this volume). However, lower levels of mattering have been linked to general symptoms of anxiety and social anxiety (Flett, 2019). The tendency to be socially anxious and socially avoidant seems rational if there is a high likelihood of interacting with people who see a child or adolescent as unimportant or who interact in ways that provide a sense of not being seen or heard by others. The fear of not mattering symbolizes and reflects the overlap between the mattering and anxiety construct in general and the anxious arousal and evaluation apprehension that can accompany the feeling of mattering in particular. McComb et al. (2020) proposed that an abiding fear of not mattering to others may stem from a ruminative preoccupation with the threat of depreciating one's worth or value to others.

How does the fear of not mattering relate to other worries and fears? The fear of not mattering often does not exist in isolation and is accompanied and perhaps exacerbated by other fears. Research on early developmental schemas has indicated that feelings of not mattering in university students reflect a core early schema involving abandonment themes (Flett, 2018a). Some children may have abandonment experiences or threats of abandonment that have fueled their insecurities and anxious attachment. Given our abiding need to connect with others, real or threatened abandonment should accentuate an already established tendency to feel small and insignificant.

The fear of not mattering can also be fueled by imagined scenarios about what would happen if the child or adolescent makes a key mistake or fails to be accomplished and live up to expectations. This fear is underscored by the dysfunctional thought, "If I am not perfect, people will lose interest in me."

The fear of not mattering may also be rooted in concerns and perceptions of what it means to not matter to others. An intriguing analysis by Neel and Lassetter (2019) led them to propose that being interpersonally invisible and perceived as irrelevant constitutes a unique stigma. They noted that all of us will experience times when we feel small and insignificant; however, for some people, this is a regular occurrence and can easily define who they are in their own eyes or the eyes of others. People from various marginalized groups may be especially prone to being ignored and overlooked, which can become a significant source of social pain.

Neel and Lassetter (2019) did not connect their theory to the developing research on mattering, nor did they link it with the conceptualization of mattering suggested by Rosenberg and McCullough (1981). However, there are obvious reasons to do so, given that they couch invisibility in terms of others conveying their lack of attention or even awareness of the person's existence. As noted earlier, attention and awareness are central elements of how mattering is conceptualized (Elliott, 2009; Rosenberg & McCullough, 1981).

Experiences of being overlooked can fuel fears of not mattering to others. The fear of not mattering is especially prominent for anyone who has been neglected or interacted with historically as if they are nonexistent. This fear, combined with actual experiences, can fuel the kinds of resentment and frustration that boil over and become expressed in acts of rebellion, aggression, and violence.

Individual differences in the fear of not mattering have been documented in samples of university students (e.g., McComb et al., 2020). Research is beginning to explore the fear of not mattering among children and adolescents. Our initial analyses of newly collected unpublished data from a sample of over 1,200 children from China indicate that the fear of not mattering is linked robustly with anti-mattering and higher levels of loneliness.

At this point, some readers may long for a view of mattering that focuses on it solely as a positive psychology concept that inspires a focus on hopes and possibilities rather than problems and fears. This is understandable, especially for anyone who spends too much time watching the news and needs uplifting. However, an exclusive focus on the positive is not in keeping with what children and adolescents must deal with. The first step in addressing and removing feelings and fears of not mattering is acknowledging and measuring their existence. We are then much better positioned to do something about them and, to paraphrase the sage words of Yoda, "Do something we must."

It is appropriate to conclude this chapter with a few observations about how Rosenberg would likely comment on the life experiences of young people today. He doubtlessly would have some important things to say. I am confident that he would maintain that mattering has grown in terms of its relevance and its importance as a core need of young people.

SUMMARY

This chapter began with a description of the facets of mattering introduced over 40 years ago by Rosenberg and McCullough (1981). This was followed by an extended description of mattering that reflected new conceptual developments relevant to understanding children and adolescents, including the distinction proposed by Prilleltensky (2020) between having and giving value to others. I discussed at length how feelings of not mattering are distinguishable by feelings of not mattering. Work on the concept of anti-mattering was discussed, followed by an emphasis on another distinguishable aspect of the construct that focuses on fears of not mattering to others. The chapter provided a historical overview of key developments and how it has become increasingly evident that mattering is a complex construct with multiple elements.

3 THE ROLE OF MATTERING IN POSITIVE YOUTH DEVELOPMENT

This chapter tells a key part of the story regarding the historical role of mattering from a developmental perspective. Mattering in children and adolescents is a topic that should be considerably more prominent in the psychological literature, given its important role in positive youth development.

Three reasons typically come to mind when I reflect on how and why research and theory on mattering has lagged so far behind. First, the original article on mattering by Rosenberg and McCullough (1981) was not published in a mainstream source, so many scholars, counselors, and clinicians never noticed it. The situation today would likely be quite different if it had been published in a high-profile journal with electronic online access.

Second, the field has been set back because, for 2 decades, there was no easily obtained measure to assess individual differences in self-reported levels of mattering to other people. The first published measure appeared in 2001 (see Marshall, 2001). The most widely used measure is the General Mattering Scale (Marcus & Rosenberg, 1987; also see Flett, 2018a). Unfortunately, Marcus and Rosenberg (1987) did not publish their measure. Their scale items first appeared in print in a 1997 article on mattering among

https://doi.org/10.1037/0000449-004
Mattering as a Core Need in Children and Adolescents: Theoretical, Clinical, and Research Perspectives, by G. L. Flett

unhoused adults (DeForge & Barclay, 1997), but this is not where anyone would expect to find the scale.

The third reason is that scholars in the positive youth development field have failed to link their work with developments in the mattering field and vice versa. In this chapter, I seek to integrate these fields by establishing the links between mattering and positive youth development.

MATTERING AND OTHER KEYS TO POSITIVE YOUTH DEVELOPMENT

On behalf of the National Research Council and Institute of Medicine, Eccles and Gootman (2002) led a comprehensive evaluation of the key aspects of positive youth development (PYD) and effective ways to promote it. Exhibit 3.1 lists the eight key themes. One theme is support for efficacy and mattering.

How does mattering emerge within the context of PYD? Eccles and Gootman (2002) emphasized the need for youth to be exposed to settings that support efficacy and mattering. How important is this support? They regard it as constituting "necessary features for development in any setting. If adolescents do not experience personal engagement and a sense of mattering, they are not likely to grow personally" (p. 106). In short, to matter to others is to grow. Given this strong emphasis from the National Research Council and Institute of Medicine (2002) in the United States, it seems remarkable that the focus failed to significantly increase developmental research on mattering among youth.

Support for efficacy and mattering is especially beneficial for young people with low self-esteem. I stated earlier that mattering can be generated by giving and adding value to others. However, Rosenberg (1965) noted

EXHIBIT 3.1. Keys to Positive Youth Development

1. Physical and psychological safety
2. Appropriate structure
3. Supportive relationships
4. Opportunities to belong
5. Positive social norms
6. Support for efficacy and mattering
7. Opportunities for skill building
8. Integration of family, school, and community

Note. Adapted from *Community Programs to Promote Youth Development* (pp. 8–9), by the National Research Council and Institute of Medicine, 2002, National Academies Press. In the public domain.

that low self-esteem youth tend to turn inward rather than outward, so they are less likely to be interested and engaged in public affairs and community activities. These young people are disengaged and resist opportunities, partly due to low self-confidence in their ability to offer anything of value or anything that will be valued by others. However, youth programs that help them overcome this self-confidence deficit result in a greater willingness to engage in such activities as volunteering and mentoring younger children. I witnessed this in our local school where senior students built their sense of mattering and confidence by becoming the reading buddy of a student in Grade 2 or 3. Helping younger learners also built a stronger connection to the school.

Why are efficacy and mattering grouped together in this framework? The reason is not explicitly stated in the Eccles and Gootman (2002) report. Theorists in the self-efficacy field, such as Bandura (1986), have typically not included a focus on mattering; efficacy and judgments of personal worth are seen as distinct. However, one justification for pairing mattering with efficacy is that they are linked in empirical research (e.g., Somers et al., 2022). Moreover, descriptions of youth with a sense of mattering frequently refer to them developing a strong sense of agency and efficacy.

Mattering is typically associated with a constellation of other positive attributes. I illustrate this key point next and then return to discussing support for efficacy and mattering.

Haddock and associates (2020) conducted an investigation with 676 adolescents that evaluated the impact of their Campus Connections program using a pre–post research design. The broad array of measures assessed at Time 1 included six representative items from the Mattering Index (Elliott et al., 2004).

The correlations reported by Haddock et al. (2020) are shown in Table 3.1. Higher levels of mattering were significantly associated with meaning in life, self-efficacy, conscientiousness, aspirations, and having a positive future

TABLE 3.1. Mattering and Its Correlations With Developmental Assets

Developmental asset	Correlation
Conscientiousness	.29**
Aspirations	.19**
Belonging	.35**
Developmental assets composite	.37**
Future orientation	.37**
Meaning in life	.42**

Note. $N = 676$ adolescents. Data from Haddock et al. (2020).
**$p < .01$.

orientation. There was also a significant positive link between mattering and a composite measure of eight developmental assets: perceived support, empowerment, boundaries and expectations, constructive use of time, commitment to learning, positive values, social competence, and positive identity. Imagine young people with a strong sense of mattering to others who have most, if not all, of these other attributes. They would be poised to withstand stress and grow as a result of the challenges experienced throughout adolescence.

PYD and the programs that promote it enhance the lives of youths in tangible ways, such as reducing the risk of substance abuse and the propensity to engage in violence (Bonell et al., 2015). Feelings of mattering and efficacy grown through opportunities for development likely play fundamental roles in the prevention of substance misuse, aggression, and violence.

TRACING THE ORIGINS OF THE MATTERING AND PYD LINK

When I first learned of the emphasis in PYD on support for efficacy and mattering, I felt compelled to trace the origins of this specific focus. How did efficacy and mattering get paired together? This focus on efficacy and mattering came at a time when there had been little focus on mattering after the appearance of the seminal Rosenberg and McCullough (1981) article.

The emphasis placed jointly on mattering and efficacy in the PYD framework stems largely from insights derived from analyses of rural life and the lives of children in the United States. An illuminating book by Elder and Conger (2000) titled *Children of the Land: Adversity and Success in Rural America* examined resourceful farm families and the children of these families, as well as the community ties established in rural settings. The topics in this book were varied and covered an extensive range of themes. A key focus of the book was an analysis of pathways to high school success.

Much can be learned from a careful reading of the book, reflecting on how so many of its findings are still relevant today. The forward contains an introductory overview by Ross Parke (2000), former editor of *Developmental Psychology*. He emphasized that the book provides multiple illustrations of how mothers and fathers, as well as the extended family (i.e., grandparents), matter in the lives of children. Moreover, it is important for young people to locate themselves within a broader network of social ties and organizational relationships. An explicit emphasis on mattering comes in the form of children typically assuming key roles in the operations of the family farm. Their roles give them a profound sense of significance and importance, especially when it is clear that the family needs their contributions. Having a valued role and being appreciated are vital contributors to a child's sense of worth, as is sharing time with parents, which often happens in farming contexts where adolescents work side by side with their parents. One clear pathway to a mutual and shared sense of mattering is for children and parents to be frequently engaged in shared parent–youth activities.

Elder and Conger (2000) noted that children and adolescents in farm families are enmeshed in meaningful relationships with each other, but they are also connected to other people in the outside world of adult culture in the rural setting. They observed further that successful acts of "required helpfulness" (p. 66) on the farm and in the broader community build a unique sense of confidence and efficacy and a robust sense of mastery. This sense is what is typically referred to when people describe the experience of "empowerment."

To underscore how roles need to be filled in the lives of farm families, consider the unique and varied day for our daughter, who married into a farm family with a dairy operation. She has spent many early mornings feeding newborn calves at the farm; she then continues attending to her daughter's needs and finding time to lead online therapy sessions with clients as part of her doctoral training in clinical psychology.

The positive impact of meaningful roles for youths was the focus of a revealing qualitative study by Larson et al. (2019). They interviewed 73 youths who had meaningful work roles in youth development programs in the United States. The study considered the tasks and complex challenges facing these young people and how they learned to approach them. Larson and his colleagues identified three key developmental processes. First, youths experienced a sense of agency while learning how to invest their energies. They characterized their involvement as "good pressure." Second, these experiences helped the youth develop key competencies and skills (e.g., strategic thinking and problem solving). Finally, the young people learned about accountability and taking responsibility. The youths developed modes of thinking, feeling, and managing emotions across settings. When considering these accounts of their experiences, it is easy to envision youth development opportunities as a form of basic training for navigating through life and learning about relationships.

KEY LESSONS AND INSIGHTS ABOUT MATTERING FROM THE PYD LITERATURE

There are well over 100 articles that analyze and evaluate PYD programs and emphasize support for mattering and efficacy. Ideally, this work would have been integrated with more direct research on individual differences in mattering among youth, but this has yet to happen. However, much has been learned about what youth need and the contextual features and kinds of experiences best suited to building efficacy and mattering among young people.

The best PYD programs for building mattering provide young people with the types of meaningful roles discussed earlier. Ideally, they have an opportunity to take on a leadership role. However, these roles must be significant ones that resonate with adolescents. An opportunity to develop mattering can quickly turn into an anti-mattering experience if what should have been a meaningful role turns out to be cursory and insignificant or overseen by adults who are controlling and do not grant the autonomy that youth covet. One telling question is, "Does the PYD opportunity allow the young person to have a strong say in decisions that are reached?" The importance of voice is evident in numerous analyses of popular, high-impact PYD programs (e.g., Krauss et al., 2014). Mattering is also built through having access to mutually supportive relationships with caring adult leaders and leadership opportunities that support the adolescent's need for autonomy (Bean et al., 2017). Special importance is placed on programs providing youth with leadership opportunities (Sendak et al., 2018).

An evaluation of positive development leisure settings for LGBTQ youth showed that all eight elements in Exhibit 3.1 were detected and had some importance (Theriault & Witt, 2014). However, support for efficacy and mattering emerged as the most significant contributor to positive development.

Fine-grained analyses of the best practices of youth programs can yield important insights about how to relate to young people in ways that instill in them the sense that they matter. Analyses of after-school programs commonly emphasize the need to be culturally responsive and to include elements that enable youth to see their backgrounds and interests reflected in activities and initiatives. Analyses of PYD programs also typically affirm the need for youth to have a sense of voice and input into decisions.

One key overarching message emerging from work on PYD is that a sense of mattering can be built outside the home if young people are granted opportunities to matter to others, their community, and society as a whole. Do these opportunities for young people exist in your community? Ideally, this is the case because the young person without these opportunities is losing out in multiple ways.

It is ideal if young people can engage with people who care about them outside their home, and it is even better if they can routinely and repeatedly go to a place where mattering is consistently felt. Settings built around sending the message to young people that they matter yield many benefits. I refer to such settings as *mattering milieus*. The milieu concept includes the physical and social environment and atmosphere. The best example of this type of setting in the published literature comes from an article that describes the features of schools deemed to be *odds-beating secondary schools* (Kramer et al., 2020). A school is classified as beating the odds when graduation rates and levels of achievement go well beyond what is expected, especially when many in the school are disadvantaged and marginalized. Kramer and colleagues described seven odds-beating schools that were defined by how closely they reflected PYD themes. The first focus was building relationships with caring adults in ways that fit with an emphasis on building mattering and efficacy. These authors did not mention mattering per se, but clearly illustrated it their descriptions of students with relationships with close and caring teachers who saw their students as individuals and focused on their well-being and development. One teacher summarized the approach by emphasizing, "You need to let your kids know you care about them and that they come first. . . . They're important to us and we are invested in them" (Kramer et al., 2020, p. 306). Other key features of these mattering milieus were an emphasis on social–emotional development, giving young people a sense of voice, promoting youth-driven identity development and goal setting, and providing leadership opportunities and the structures and strategies to support these opportunities.

These schools resonate with me because they closely resemble the public school our daughters attended in our local neighborhood. The principal who opened the school, Peggy Morrison, made it part of the school's mission to create an environment where everyone was recognized and valued and had a voice. Remarkably, Principal Morrison spent enough time with each student to be able to greet them all (over 900 at one point) and converse with them about their interests and events. Staff members were carefully selected with this approach in mind. One important initiative, among many, was pairing older students with younger students so that each developing reader had a reading buddy. Peggy Morrison is still the master of the hand-written note or letter in which she warmly acknowledges people and shows her appreciation of and interest in them.

MATTERING AND POSITIVE YOUTH DEVELOPMENT IN SPORTS

Any book on mattering in young people would be missing a key element if there were no discussion of the role of sports in PYD. Several great insights about mattering come from work on the role of sports in PYD. Moreover, this is one of the few areas of inquiry in which mattering is discussed in the sports context.

The opportunity to take part in sports should not be underestimated; it is an arena for learning and building a sense of self-worth. Several authors in kinesiology and sports psychology, including my colleague Jessica Fraser-Thomas, have emphasized the important role that sports activity plays in the lives of young children as a catalyst for their growth and development (see Fraser-Thomas et al., 2005, 2010). These accounts clearly support efficacy and mattering.

The adolescents who expressed their feelings about mattering on *The New York Times* website (Proulx, 2023) in response to the article by Gail Cornwall (2023) made frequent references to how sports roles and outcomes were consequential in giving them a feeling of significance. These accounts are in keeping with the emphasis on having value to others and giving value to others (Prilleltensky, 2020). Some adolescents described how they did something that led their team to victory and how their triumphs resulted in receiving attention and appreciation that they would otherwise not receive (Proulx, 2023). It made them feel special. It is clear from these accounts that noteworthy achievements offer a pathway to feelings of mattering, at least in the moment.

Other adolescents in the Proulx (2023) article described how they effectively assumed a key role for their team that no one else was able to assume. Their efforts were appreciatively received. These accounts made it clear that these young people learned something valuable about themselves in terms of their capabilities and qualities.

There are many accounts of how athletes of any age in recreational, amateur, and professional sports need to feel valued not only for what they do but also for who they are as people. The most committed and engaged athletes are those who know that coaches, managers, and teammates see them as a person and have their best interests at heart.

A comprehensive analysis of sports-based PYD programs by Perkins and Noam (2007) identified numerous key components that relate to the themes mentioned earlier. The three main themes of note identified by Perkins and Noam were (a) nurturing positive relationships between youths and adults who were caring and supportive, (b) maintaining a task-focused emphasis on learning specific skills and developing specific competencies, and (c) focusing on individualizing and tailoring elements of the programs to reflect the needs and interests of the youths. The broader analysis identified additional elements that seem to be critical in developing a sense of mattering to others. Youth in sports-based programs did exceptionally well when they had the overarching feeling that the program represented a safe haven in terms of both physical and psychological safety.

Another key element was providing youths with opportunities to help each other and talk with each other about their experiences. This could involve finding ways to inspire and support each other.

Another salient theme involved youth engaging in meaningful community service activities that solidify links with the community and go beyond the sports context. This element is maintained and recognized by professional sports leagues. Most leagues emphasize encouraging and acknowledging the exceptional community contributions of athletes. Being meaningfully engaged in communities and charitable activities is a component of their lives that helps athletes cope with the stress, strain, and performance pressure that comes with their roles.

The literature on mattering and what we have learned thus far have clear implications for coaches. The most effective coaches are ones who show their athletes how invested they are in them as people. This can include having an emotional attachment and bond such that when the coach is highly demanding or critical, the athlete sees it as coming from a person who wants the best for them in terms of developing their talents.

The worst type of coach treats the young athlete in a way that fosters a feeling of not mattering. The young person who seldom gets into a game or is criticized, while the best players are not criticized when criticism is warranted, is receiving the message that they are insignificant or do not matter as much as star players. This treatment could be so extreme that the young person begins to wonder whether the coach would notice if they did not show up for a game or match. It is also vital that anyone who gets injured and cannot actively participate still receives attention and feels valued. Ideally, a feeling of mattering could be maintained and grown by finding a meaningful role for this individual that advances the goals of the team or the organization. Fortunately, a study of coaches found that they use unique approaches to address each theme in Table 3.1, but importantly, their primary focus was on strategies for supporting mattering and efficacy (Bean et al., 2020).

I have argued that mattering is distinguished from similar constructs because it has great potential for knowledge mobilization and exchange (Flett, 2018a, 2022). Mattering has a practical side and can be implemented to effect change and lift people up. This is evident in the impressive project described next.

MATTERING IN ACTION IN SPORTS: U MATTER AND YOUTH LEADERSHIP DEVELOPMENT

The U MATTER global human rights and well-being project in the United Kingdom is built around an emphasis on the role of mattering in PYD. This impressive project is led by Tony Ghaye. U MATTER embraces the right to matter as a human right in keeping with my earlier call for expanding children's rights to include the right to matter and be valued. In my previous book (Flett, 2018a), I proposed that the right of every child to matter and feel a sense of mattering must be added as one of the fundamental rights in the United Nations Convention on the Rights of the Child (1989). I reiterated this call in my article in the journal *Child Protection and Practice* (Flett, 2024a), where I noted that the original 54 rights include each child's right to care and protection, which needs to be supplemented with the child's right to matter to others and in society.

U MATTER's initial emphasis was on how mattering can positively affect the experience and performance of elite athletes at the youth level (Ghaye et al., 2021). One overarching objective was to promote and strengthen a feeling of mattering as a source of support when things go wrong. The development of a positive orientation to the self is in keeping with our emphasis on enhancing the relationship that people have with their selves (Hewitt et al., 2017, 2024). Athletes can be rigidly perfectionistic and self-critical (Flett & Hewitt, 2023) but benefit from opportunities to build up positive resources involving the self to combat the self-criticism and negative internal dialogue that can overwhelm them. Ghaye et al. (2021) argued that elite youth athletes benefit greatly when mattering is paired with self-compassion. They advanced the argument that mattering needs to be afforded a much greater role in sports, especially youth sports. This call is in keeping with the benefits that accrue from the focus on support for efficacy and mattering in PYD.

Ghaye and Horner (2023) documented how the U MATTER program joined forces with the Laureus Sport for Good Foundation and outlined the beginning days of the U MATTER initiative. This account is worth considering in some detail because it has many important elements and themes, and, of course, its central focus is on mattering. U MATTER began on a pitch in Kenya with 44 children from a small orphanage. The stated goal was to grow the capacity of these young children to rise above their challenging beginnings and become leaders capable of rising out of "the poverty trap." It is a wellness-based, youth-focused leadership-development initiative through sport, with mattering as the core process and principle.

Much of Ghaye and Horner's (2023) chapter is based on separate interviews with two young people from the program—Jill and Lebo. Jill was a participant in the program and eventually became the manager of the Laureus Youth Empowerment Through Sport Programme. Several key themes were evident in the responses provided by Jill and Lebo; their verbatim responses can be found in the Ghaye and Horner chapter. Both Jill and Lebo strongly endorsed the notion that mattering should indeed be a human right. An emphasis on mattering through finding a sense of voice emerged as a theme from the interviews. Participants also noted that mattering allows young people to be authentic and not hide their emotions. Mattering seems to combat the common tendency to stay hidden. Any factor that can reduce self-concealment and hiding behind a false front is worth considering, given the widespread tendency for young people to hide their distress behind a mask and project a false image of being perfectly fine (for an extensive analysis, see Flett et al., 2018).

Jill shared her view that mattering can reduce the threat inherent in vulnerability and play an important role in developing a feeling of psychological safety (Ghaye & Horner, 2023). Emphasis was also placed on mattering providing a sense of purpose and a needed source of energy. Perhaps the most telling observation was Jill's comment about how mattering can be transformational at the individual level. Specifically, in reference to the children and adolescents in U MATTER, she stated, "It will change the way they speak, it will change the way they walk, the way they talk about themselves and other people" (Ghaye & Horner, 2023, p. 273).

THE OPPORTUNITY TO MATTER

The U MATTER program represents an exceptional opportunity and experience for the young people participating in it. A point worth reiterating is that a central theme in PYD theory and research is that young people will best be able to develop a feeling of mattering to others when they have meaningful opportunities to build their sense of mattering. Mattering depends, in part, on having the good fortune to have supportive and encouraging people in your life and experiences that provide room for growth and building relationships with other people. This theme is also a key message to communicate to young people. It can be heartening to share with children who are not sure whether they matter the message that a sense of being valued will emerge in time by finding what works for them and accepting opportunities that give them a chance to be recognized and valued. Moreover, some of these opportunities will entail chances to make a difference in the lives of other children.

It should not be surprising to learn that the feeling of mattering is a reflection, in part, of who is included in the social environment. Mattering is about the self in relation to others, and the feeling of mattering is rooted in the perceived or actual feedback we receive from others. The child who has had repeated experiences of emotional neglect may still have the capability to have a positive and healthy sense of self-worth, but this will require eventually encountering people who prize rather than punish or overlook these young people.

This point is illustrated through the case account of Arthur. Murphy (1987) outlined Arthur's story while discussing how apparent vulnerability or invulnerability expressed by children depends, in part, on the situations and contexts they experience. Arthur was described as bewildered and anxious in his first-grade class because he had a teacher who was aggressive and tired. How much can a bad fit with the teacher affect a child? In this instance, Arthur became nauseated each school day morning while at home because of the prospect of spending his day with this teacher.

The family doctor learned of Arthur's situation when tasked with treating Arthur's nausea. His physician prescribed a key remedy for Arthur—that he be allowed to attend a different school known for its superb teachers. This cured Arthur. In fact, after just one morning in his new classroom, Arthur exclaimed, "This teacher understands children so much better, I want to stay there until I am 17!" (Murphy, 1987, p. 92). The feeling of being understood, wanted, and encouraged can have an enormous impact on a child. Arthur's story illustrates how relationships can have extreme impacts on children.

SUMMARY

This chapter described the PYD framework and how support for efficacy and mattering is enshrined as one of the eight keys to PYD, according to the framework provided by Eccles and Gootman (2002) on behalf of the National Research Council and Institute of Medicine (2002). The chapter illustrated how mattering is reflected in PYD programs and settings described as "mattering milieus." Important context was also provided in terms of what led mattering to historically being afforded a central role in PYD. Mattering among children and adolescents was also considered in sports contexts that have embraced a focus on PYD. The chapter concluded by emphasizing that we need to create opportunities to matter, such as the U MATTER program developed in Africa to foster a sense of mattering among young people who have had challenging starts to life.

PART II MEASURING AND INTERPRETING CHILDREN WHO FEEL LIKE THEY DO NOT MATTER

4 THE PREVALENCE OF FEELINGS OF NOT MATTERING AMONG YOUTH

Documenting an Epidemic in Children and Adolescents

This chapter considers the question, "Is there an epidemic of feelings of not mattering among children and adolescents?" The answer to the question depends mostly on how an epidemic is defined. The information summarized in this chapter will make it clear that far too many young people feel like they do not matter to others. Without a doubt, this is troubling. However, I hope that as readers wade through the statistics cited in this chapter, they will not lose sight of the implications for individual children and adolescents. One way to think about the children these numbers represent is to estimate how many classrooms in a school could be filled with kids who feel like they do not matter.

A second way of pondering this possible epidemic is to shift the focus to the feelings involved. One well-known phrase that taps into the feeling of not mattering is "I feel like a number," which is never a good feeling, regardless of your age. Older adults are well aware of feeling like a number or being treated as if they are, as was especially the case during the COVID-19 pandemic (Flett & Heisel, 2021). But imagine how it feels to be a young person surrounded by peers who are getting a lot of attention, whereas you

https://doi.org/10.1037/0000449-005
Mattering as a Core Need in Children and Adolescents: Theoretical, Clinical, and Research Perspectives, by G. L. Flett

are not. You feel like they count, but you do not. It might even start to feel like you will never count. This feeling illustrates why, when someone does give us the attention we need, it feels better and more personal if it is individual attention that is in keeping with being treated as someone special.

As stated earlier, this chapter summarizes the fact that far too many adolescents feel like they do not matter. The sad reality for young people who feel this way is that they feel quite alone and do not realize that so many of their peers feel the same. The alarming survey data presented next suggest that even by conservative estimates, as noted earlier, perhaps as many as one in three young people feel like they do not matter to others.

This chapter begins by considering prevalence when the focus is on mattering to mothers and fathers. The focus then shifts to mattering in general and mattering at school. Finally, we consider mattering in the community. Specific estimates of the prevalence of not mattering vary depending on whether the focus is on a specific form of mattering (e.g., mattering to parents or the community) or on general feelings of not mattering to others.

THE PREVALENCE OF MATTERING VERSUS NOT MATTERING TO PARENTS

Rosenberg (1985) provided the first valuable evidence about the number of young people without a feeling of mattering by reporting some summary data from one of the studies summarized in Rosenberg and McCullough (1981). Rosenberg and McCullough's work focused on feelings of mattering to parents. Rosenberg's (1985) chapter summarized descriptive results from the Baltimore Study conducted by Rosenberg and Simmons (1972). This well-known longitudinal study by Rosenberg and Simmons involved almost 2,000 participants, but Rosenberg (1985) reported results for the 1,115 adolescents who were 12 or older. Three items assessed mattering: (a) how much interest the mother had in the child, (b) how interested parents were in what their child had to say, and (c) how important the child felt as part of the family.

Rosenberg (1985) did not indicate what determined where he placed the dividing line to establish the number of adolescents without a feeling of mattering to their parents. The information provided by Rosenberg is summarized in Table 4.1. This table contains the percentage of girls versus boys who felt like they did not matter. The information represents three age categories—8 to 11, 12 to 13, and 14 to 18. Note that more boys than girls felt like they did not matter to their parents, with about three in 10 boys feeling that way.

TABLE 4.1. The Prevalence of Feelings of Not Mattering to Parents in the Baltimore Study

	Age		
Self-concept dimension	**8-11**	**12-13**	**14-18**
Mattering (% low)			
Total Sample	26%	29%	26%
Girls	22%	30%	21%
Boys	30%	29%	29%

Note. Data from Rosenberg and Simmons (1972).

Overall, about one in four adolescents in this sample felt like they did not matter, which has profound implications when considered on a broad scale (Rosenberg, 1985). If a high school had about 2,000 students, approximately 500 would not have a sense of mattering to their parents. This has profound implications, given all the negative correlates of low parental mattering summarized in the original article by Rosenberg and McCullough (1981).

MATTERING IN GENERAL AND MATTERING AT SCHOOL: ONTARIO STUDENTS

My initial concerns about the high prevalence of young people who feel like they do not matter stem from information from my research collaboration with school board partners. I suggested that we add the survey questionnaire item "I feel like I matter to other people" to the existing survey. Collectively, we were alarmed by the results when about 24,000 students responded. About two thirds of students (65%) agreed with this item. However, about one in five students (20%) disagreed or strongly disagreed with it, and the remaining 15% indicated that they were not sure they mattered to others. Presumably, a substantial proportion of this 15% would be able to develop a sense of mattering if they received some consistent and sustained feedback indicating they are indeed valued by others, especially if some of this feedback was experienced at home.

Subsequent results shared by another school board partner yielded comparable results for mattering at school when students responded to the item "I feel like I matter at school." In this instance, the findings were from over 30,000 high school students. Once again, about 30% of students indicated they either disagreed or were uncertain. Boys agreed more often, but the overall difference between adolescent boys and girls was not statistically significant.

Questions about mattering have continued to be included in the broad system-wide school surveys administered every 2 years. However, the wording and focus has changed, so direct comparisons across time are not always possible. The York Region District School Board (2017) survey item about mattering to people was made more specific by referring to mattering to people at home or in the community. Overall, according to the responses of over 25,000 elementary school students, 84% felt they mattered at home or in the community. While this is more encouraging, it still signifies that about one in six students lacked the feeling of mattering at home or in the community. It was worse at the high school level. The results from almost 19,000 students indicated that about one in five students (i.e., 21%) did not feel they mattered at home or in the community.

Surveys in 2018 and 2021 included the item "I feel like I matter to people at school," as described earlier and used by another school board. This item was written so it could be interpreted as mattering to other students, teachers, or people at school in general. Table 4.2 depicts the results for this scale item.

TABLE 4.2. School Survey Results for 2018 and 2021

Item	2018	2021
I feel like I matter to people at school.		
Elementary school students (Grades 7–8)	48%	32%
High school students	42%	21%
There is at least one caring adult at school who supports me.		
Elementary school students	82%	80%
High school students	77%	77%
I felt happy.		
Elementary school students	75%	64%
High school students	42%	30%
I felt nervous or anxious.		
Elementary school students	35%	45%
High school students	46%	62%
I felt sad or depressed.		
Elementary school students	20%	27%
High school students	26%	41%
I felt lonely.		
Elementary school students	19%	35%
High school students	24%	50%
I felt hopeful/positive about the future.		
Elementary school students	54%	34%
High school students	45%	28%

Note. Percentages reflect number of students who agreed with mattering and caring adult items. Data from York Region District School Board (2021).

The 2018 results showed that only 48% of the elementary school students and 42% of the high school students had the feeling of mattering at school. In short, given these results, it is normative to feel a sense of not mattering at school. Other results in Table 4.2 suggest that the specific wording of scale items matters, and providing some context makes a difference. Here, I am referring to other results from the 2018 and 2021 samples showing that most students at either school level reported having at least one caring adult at school who supports them. However, we should not feel too positive about these results because, at the high school level, only 42% agreed with the statement, "I felt happy."

The results for 2021 are also presented in Table 4.2. The sample size here was not revealed, but it is safe to assume that it was much smaller because of the pandemic. Of course, the degree of agreement was influenced greatly by the dramatic impacts and changes brought about by the COVID-19 pandemic and those times when it was decided to close the schools.

Table 4.2 shows a substantial drop among elementary students from 2018 to 2021, from 48% feeling like they mattered at school in 2018 to only 32% in 2021. As for high school students, mattering at school was previously 42% but dropped by half to 21% in 2021 (see York Region District School Board, 2021). Thus, most students felt like they did not matter at school despite the best efforts of teachers to adapt to entirely different modes of educating their students. This should not be seen as an indictment of the school board and its educators because they were required to adapt to an unprecedented global health emergency, and the school board would have benefited from more provincial support. However, the unmistakable conclusion is that for the students involved, the events and changes had a strong impact.

These data on mattering at school reflect the students' experience during the pandemic, including issues related to online learning. Survey responses from parents indicated that only around two out of five parents agreed with the statement that online learning worked for their children (York Region District School Board, 2021). The low level of mattering in the previous survey likely reflects the sheer amount of attention students received; in many classrooms, teachers had to undergo the divided attention task of simultaneously teaching the students who were physically present and online. It would have been easy for many students to feel they were not a priority and perceive that more should and could have been done to address their needs.

When all the results in Table 4.2 are reviewed, concerns about the well-being of younger people seem quite justified. There is a remarkable and troubling level of loneliness and depression evident among the high school students who responded to the 2021 survey.

The next section of this chapter examines feelings of mattering in the community. We will see that much applied work is needed, given evidence suggesting that the feeling of not mattering in the community is widespread.

PREVALENCE OF MATTERING IN THE COMMUNITY

A chapter in my previous book included a section that summarized survey results from various jurisdictions, with most of the results on community mattering coming from states in the United States or individual counties (Flett, 2018a). The overall conclusion was that, for adolescents, mattering in the community was essentially a fifty–fifty proposition: About one in two young people reported a feeling of mattering in the community. In some instances, the results suggested that about 60% felt they mattered in the community.

Table 4.3 contains the updated numbers after adding in more recent survey data made publicly available online. Overall, not much has changed,

TABLE 4.3. Percentage of Adolescents Who Feel They Matter in the Community

Location and date	Sample size and type of sample	Mattering prevalence
Arlington, VA, 2012	1,651 in grades 8, 10, and 12	40
Cleveland, OH, 2012	12,341 middle school	48.9
East Hampton, CT, 2019	389 middle school	50
Itasca, MN, 2014	2,307 in grades 7-12	66
Portland, OR, 1997	9,058 in grades 6, 8, and 10	38
Maine, 2019	28,538 high school 15,147 middle school	56.6 59.4
Monroe County, NY, 2019	1,828 high school	57
Norwalk, CT, 2019	1,976 grades 7, 9, and 11	41
Rochester, NY, 2019	3,280 high school students	49
Santa Clara, CA, 2010	1,085 high school	40.9
Stratford, CT, 2016	580 middle and high school	39
Sylvan Lake, AB, 2017	423 in grades 8-10	39
Texas, 2019 Texas, 2021	Not available	52.4 43.1
Vermont, 2019	18,613 high school 13,998 middle school	58 59

Note. Includes some data from Flett (2018a).

and the fifty–fifty proposition still holds, but it varies somewhat according to where the respondents live.

It is particularly important to note that the results in Table 4.3 represent the overall results for the samples. The rates vary considerably as a function of differences in race and sexual orientation. For instance, the public data from Texas indicate that the presence of community mattering in terms of race was as follows: Asian (33.6%), Black (47.7%), Hispanic/Latino (38.8%), and White (52.1%). Levels of community mattering according to sexual orientation were as follows: heterosexual (48.2%); gay, lesbian, or bisexual (26.9%); and other/questioning (23.2%). Note that these categories reflect verbatim descriptions found in the survey results.

There is much that can be said after reflecting on these alarming results. My initial reaction after seeing them was one of concern because of the established links between suicidality and feelings of not mattering in the community. This topic is considered in more detail in Chapter 14. My other main reaction was to reflect on how marginalized young people are made to feel when feelings of not mattering in the community are closely tied to discrimination, prejudice, and stigma.

THE PREVALENCE OF ANTI-MATTERING

Other data on the prevalence of general feelings of not mattering come from supplementary data analyses by Hill and Madigan (2022). This research was conducted with 308 gifted and talented adolescents from the United Kingdom who were assessed during the COVID-19 pandemic. The measures included in this study were the General Mattering Scale (GMS; Marcus & Rosenberg, 1987) and our Anti-Mattering Scale (AMS; Flett et al., 2022). The number of gifted and talented adolescents deemed to have low levels of mattering was not reported in the original article. There are no established cutoff points for the AMS or GMS. We felt it was reasonable to focus on how many adolescents had reported high levels of feelings of not mattering based on an AMS cutoff score of 14. This cutoff score was selected because it was much higher than established sample means, which range between 9 and 11 (Flett et al., 2022). A total score of 14 or higher is at least one standard deviation from the typical scale means. Moreover, 14 or higher can only be reached by agreeing with at least four of the five questionnaire items. One sample item is "To what extent have you been made to feel like you are invisible?"

Our secondary analyses showed that 84 gifted students (27.3%) had an AMS score of 14 or higher. Thus, once again, more than one in four students felt like they did not matter in general, but this was framed in terms of feeling unseen and unheard. When we substituted the more extreme AMS cutoff score of 15, 60 students out of 308 (19.5%) felt they did not matter according to the level of their anti-mattering feeling.

When we examined the individual responses of the adolescents in this sample, we found four students who achieved the maximum score of 20, the highest possible score on the AMS. All four students were gifted girls. Two of these adolescent girls also had low means on the GMS, while the other two adolescent girls had GMS scores closer to the sample mean.

It is impossible to overstate how much we should be concerned by the numbers from this sample and those reported throughout this chapter. Many gifted and talented students are under enormous pressure to achieve. The pressures faced by young people have been documented extensively by exceptional investigators, such as the late Suniya Luthar (see Luthar & Becker, 2002; Luthar et al., 2020) and the journalist Jennifer Wallace. Jennifer Wallace's 2023 book, *Never Enough: When the Achievement Culture Becomes Toxic and What We Can Do About It*, is based largely on interviews with students from high-pressure, high-achieving schools. Students who have been simmering in this pressure not only feel exceptional stress but also feel they do not matter at school or in general. Most reasonable people would endorse the position that students facing potentially overwhelming pressures and uncertainties deserve to feel like they matter. If they are able to have a sense of significance and establish a sense of mattering, Wallace maintains they will have a fighting chance to not only get through unscathed but also thrive and survive.

THE FEELING OF NOT MATTERING IN SOCIETY

Readers hoping to come across some hopeful information at this point are bound to be disappointed. This section concludes with recent findings focusing on mattering in society rather than mattering to others. While most of the literature on mattering focuses on interpersonal mattering, it is possible and meaningful to consider mattering from a broader perspective. Fromm (1941) introduced the concept of *societal mattering*. This is a sense of being someone who is seen as making a broader contribution and who has the satisfaction of feeling significant in society. The young person who feels a sense of mattering at both the interpersonal and societal level should be doubly protected, while the young person who feels insignificant and without a voice in their relationships and society will be in a risky situation.

Unfortunately, initial new data suggest that when it comes to today's youth, it may be normative to have a feeling of not mattering in society.

A collaborative project led by my colleague Mael Virat assessed societal mattering in 429 adolescents from France (Virat et al., 2024). Adolescents indicated their agreement or disagreement on a five-point Likert scale with a single face-valid item (i.e., I feel like I matter in society). Remarkably, only about one in three adolescents agreed with this statement. Overall, 35% agreed, while 39% disagreed, and 26% neither agreed nor disagreed. It is an open question whether these results can be generalized, but I suspect they are generalizable.

If this finding is replicated in future research, it will then be time for a deep and multifaceted analysis that identifies which young people are especially likely to feel they do not matter in society and why. The mattering versus marginalization described so eloquently by Nancy Schlossberg (1989) operates at the societal level, which is apparent to people confronted with challenging life situations, such as poverty. Isaac Prilleltensky and Ora Prilleltensky (2021) noted that mattering also involves issues of fairness and equity. Preventive interventions are especially needed wherever there is a preponderance of young people who feel like they do not matter to the people in their lives or society. Countless parents and grandparents who have had to live with prejudice, discrimination, and stigma at the societal level are highly aware of how important it is to instill in their children the feeling that they matter at home. It is not just a family matter, as illustrated when a caring adult in the community shows a young person that they matter to the adult, even if it might seem that society as a whole is less caring.

There is much still to be learned about mattering and its prevalence. For instance, future research with adolescents could consider the extent to which mattering is perceived as contingent on meeting certain conditions. This line of investigation would likely provide additional concern and even less comfort to those who worry about youth well-being. Feelings of mattering conditionally may be common. I base this prediction on survey results shared with me from my collaborators on the school board project mentioned in Chapter 2. One school board found that about four in 10 adolescents agree with the survey statement, "I feel like other people won't value me if I don't do well at school." The positive energy and power of the feeling of mattering is highly restricted when rooted in meeting conditions to feel valued.

I conclude this chapter by noting that the evidence cited here comes primarily from North America, and there is a clear and growing need to evaluate the prevalence of feelings of not mattering among children and adolescents in other countries, which will likely confirm that the prevalence of feelings of not mattering among young people constitutes a global problem. We know that research on mattering in young people warrants international attention based on research thus far in several countries (e.g., Canada, China, Great Britain, Italy, Kenya, and the United States; e.g., Fantinelli et al., 2023; Hill & Madigan, 2022; Kihia et al., 2024; J. C. Watson et al., 2022). A broader scope would be in keeping with the notion that everyone has a need to matter, and addressing this need is fundamental to the health, well-being, and development of children and adolescents everywhere.

SUMMARY

This chapter summarized evidence that there is an epidemic of feelings of not mattering among young people. The results that were reviewed indicated that an estimated 25% to 30% of young people have feelings of not mattering in general or to parents. Results from Great Britain suggest that about one in four gifted and talented youth are characterized by problematic levels of anti-mattering, as assessed by the AMS (Flett et al., 2022). Perhaps most alarming is the summarized evidence that indicates that 40% to 50% of adolescents in large surveys from the United States feel like they do not matter in their communities. Some evidence also showed that for marginalized youth, including LGBTQ+ youth, the feeling of not mattering in their communities is modal and typical. Collectively, the evidence summarized in this chapter suggested an urgent need to address the epidemic of feelings of not mattering, which should be a priority, given the costs and consequences accompanying the feeling of not mattering to others and the community or society as a whole.

5 UNDERSTANDING CHILDREN WHO FEEL UNSEEN, UNHEARD, AND UNIMPORTANT

The person low on mattering feels irrelevant, unimportant, or peripheral in the mind of others. He is the invisible man who passes through unnoticed, whose presence evokes no emotional response—either positive or negative—and whose absence is unremarked.

—Rosenberg, 1985, p. 219

This chapter focuses on key themes central to understanding children who feel like they do not matter to others. Observations in this chapter pertain not only to a sense of not mattering to specific people but also to the feeling of not mattering in the community or society. The topics and themes represented here reflect many conversations with parents and educators and insights shared by members of community organizations. Valuable input received from professionals must also be acknowledged. I am especially grateful for a brief chat with five social workers who attended a public lecture. Their collective message was that after having been to countless talks and presentations, mattering seemed to be the theme most relevant to the needs of young people.

https://doi.org/10.1037/0000449-006
Mattering as a Core Need in Children and Adolescents: Theoretical, Clinical, and Research Perspectives, by G. L. Flett

The attributes listed later do not capture all the important keys to understanding children who feel like they do not matter. However, the themes reflect existing research findings, case accounts, and life narratives of children and adolescents who have been made to feel insignificant and invisible. The narrative accounts that have proved especially useful are the individual stories of young people who have been neglected or shunned and left to feel isolated. Insights have also been gleaned from accounts of youths experiencing homelessness and those who have undergone many transitions as a result of their experiences in the foster care system.

Some themes in this chapter are introduced here for the first time. I hope to convey to readers that the young person with a sense of not mattering to others has vulnerabilities and unmet needs that should be urgently addressed by the people in their lives and perhaps mental health professionals. Ideally, this chapter will prove to be practical for clinicians, counselors, and educational experts seeking to assess, treat, and enhance the lives of young people who are suffering due to their profound sense of unimportance.

Loneliness is the first theme considered. The child or adolescent who seems lonely or expresses feelings of loneliness may have bigger issues due to a sense of not mattering to others. We referred to this combination of feeling alone and insignificant as a "double jeopardy situation" (McComb et al., 2020, p. 1). We further proposed that some established costs and consequences of loneliness, including the risk of early mortality, may reflect the chronic experience of not mattering to other people.

LONELINESS AND ISOLATION

Children and adolescents who feel like they do not matter often report profound feelings of loneliness marked by a sense of isolation and alienation from other people and society as is illustrated below. The young person without a sense of mattering to others feels alone and isolated and is also likely to be quite unhappy, distressed, and unsatisfied. This tendency is not specific to young people. It has been detected in people of various ages; however, given the prominence and importance of social relationships during adolescence, loneliness is felt strongly by adolescents.

Most theorists and researchers in the loneliness field and those seeking practical solutions to the loneliness epidemic have been largely oblivious to the key association that loneliness has with feelings of not mattering to others. Chronic and persistent feelings of loneliness and insignificance must seem unbearable for many young people who experience this combination.

This could signal potential health problems, given convincing longitudinal data that link loneliness with health issues and a heightened risk of death (Holt-Lunstad et al., 2015).

The association between mattering and loneliness has been studied primarily but not exclusively in university students. A study of adolescents by Somers and colleagues (2022) showed that lower levels of mattering in high school students were associated with greater loneliness as assessed by the Children's Loneliness Scale (Asher & Wheeler, 1985). As highlighted in Chapter 2 of this volume, this study included a four-item scale with items worded in the not-mattering direction (e.g., Sometimes I feel almost as if I am invisible). Scores on this factor had the strongest association with loneliness for both adolescent girls ($r = -.62$) and adolescent boys ($r = -.57$; Somers et al., 2022). These results suggest that many lonely adolescents feel invisible to others and perceive they would not be missed if they were no longer around. A mindset that includes a feeling of not being missed can signal current or future intentional self-harm and suicidal urges.

Two other investigations from China link feelings of not mattering and loneliness among young people. Flett, Su, Nepon, Ma, and Guo (2023) reported that lower scores on the General Mattering Scale were associated significantly with loneliness ($r = -.35$) among 172 early adolescents from China. A regression analysis found that both mattering and self-esteem were significant unique predictors of loneliness. Other results from a broader study in China (Cao et al., 2024) with participants from four age groups (students in Grades 4 to 6, Grades 7 to 9, high school, and college) also attest to the association between feelings of not mattering and loneliness. The results of our preliminary analyses follow. Two unique findings are represented in Table 5.1. First, this study represents the first evidence showing these associations exist among children as young as those in Grade 4. Second, to my knowledge, this is the first evidence linking loneliness with the fear of not mattering in children and adolescents.

TABLE 5.1. Correlates of Loneliness in Students From China

Mattering measures	Grades 4–6 (1,232)	Grades 7–9 (1,131)	High school (1,862)	College (3,594)
General Mattering Scale	–.09*	–.24**	–.21**	–.32**
Anti-Mattering Scale	.65**	.72**	.68**	.73**
Fear of Not Mattering Inventory	.48**	.43**	.44**	.46**

Note. Total participants in each group are in parentheses. Data from Cao et al. (2024).
*$p < .05$. **$p < .01$.

Other unpublished evidence comes from supplementary analyses of pre-test data from the school board project introduced in Chapter 2 designed to evaluate the promotion of resilience. Loneliness was included as a key focus after a survey administered to thousands of high school students found that the scale item "I feel like I matter to other people" was correlated significantly ($r = -.36$) with a self-rating of the frequency of loneliness.

Our research on the resilience project with school board partners with 536 early adolescents in Grades 7 and 8 included brief measures of mattering and loneliness. Loneliness was tapped by a single item (e.g., I feel lonely) taken from the Center for Epidemiologic Studies Depression Scale (Radloff, 1977). Feeling lonely over the past week was significantly and negatively associated with mattering in general ($r = -.32$) and mattering at school ($r = -.30$). Both mattering measures predicted unique variance. Thus, the young people who tended to feel the loneliest were the ones who felt like they did not matter in general, nor did they matter at school.

Lonely adolescents can and often do turn to social media to satisfy their need to matter while also seeking redress from feelings of isolation and loneliness. The role of feelings of not mattering in social media addiction is examined in detail in Chapter 10.

INSECURITY

Children who receive the message early and often that they do not matter to others have a deep-seated sense of insecurity that can color daily experiences. This insecurity is psychological and goes beyond the insecure attachment style linked with feelings of not mattering to others. The insecure child's level of functioning can be interpreted in the context of Maslow's (1943) hierarchy of needs. A strong sense of insecurity and inferiority translates into not satisfying the basic lower level need to feel safe. The feeling of not being physically or psychologically safe often fuels avoidant behavior designed to protect the self. When children feel insecure and like they do not matter, the association with feeling unsafe indicates a sense of alarm and being alert to possible sources of stress. One specific manifestation in a key context is the link between the feeling of not mattering at school and feeling unsafe there.

Maslow (1942) went to great lengths to document and understand insecurity as a syndrome or complex. His conclusions were based on multiple lines of inquiry. For instance, he conducted a psychoanalytic study of approximately 30 students, who provided him with autobiographical narratives that enabled him to compare the themes of students with high versus low insecurity. Maslow also consulted about the nature of insecurity through discussions with his mentors (Alfred Adler and Karen Horney) and with Ruth Benedict, Eric Fromm, Kurt Goldstein, and Max Wertheimer.

Maslow (1942) concluded that feelings of security versus insecurity represented a syndrome with many features. He proposed it as an insecurity syndrome rather than a psychological construct because he felt that most of the 14 core attributes he identified would be present in an insecure person. Maslow envisioned the 14 attributes as interconnected.

The potentially destructive effects for children with lasting feelings of not mattering and insecurity become clear when reflecting on these 14 core attributes. These are listed in Exhibit 5.1 in an abbreviated form. The attributes designated with an asterisk represent attributes I regard as likely to be present in the child who lacks a feeling of mattering to others. The complete descriptions of each attribute and the corresponding expression of security for each attribute are listed in Maslow's (1942) highly recommended article.

Some attributes in Exhibit 5.1 are reflected in other themes emphasized in this chapter. For instance, the second attribute in Maslow's (1942) proposed syndrome (i.e., feelings of isolation) fits well with the prior emphasis on loneliness. The first attribute in the insecurity syndrome (i.e., feeling

EXHIBIT 5.1. Core Features of the Insecurity Syndrome

- Feeling rejected, unloved, and treated coldly without affection*
- Feeling isolated, ostracized, and alone*
- Seeing the world and life as dangerous, dark, hostile, and challenging
- Perceiving other people as bad, evil, selfish, or threatening
- Having constant anxious feelings of threat and danger*
- Feeling suspicious, mistrustful, envious, or jealous of others
- Being generally pessimistic and expecting the worst*
- Being discontented and/or unhappy*
- Feeling tension and strain with physical and psychological consequences, which may include psychosomatic disturbances, fatigue, uncertainty, irritability, and emotional instability*
- Being acutely self-conscious and compulsively introspective*
- Feeling guilt, shame, self-condemnation, and self-recrimination*
- Having disturbances of the self-esteem complex, expressed perhaps in masochistic or narcissistic ways*
- Continually striving and hungering for safety and security*
- Being egocentric and selfish, and having low social interest

Note. *Reflects elements linked with feelings of not mattering.

rejected, unloved, and treated without affection) may be seen by some readers as synonymous with the intense, abject feeling of not mattering to significant others. The final attribute of low social interest no doubt reflects feedback that Alfred Adler shared with Abraham Maslow.

INVALIDATION

There are numerous case accounts of adolescents who not only feel invisible but also feel their experiences and feelings do not matter to others. Relevant examples come from case excerpts involving adults who emphasize that their issues reflect longstanding conditions that go well back into their childhoods. For instance, in one case study, a woman receiving cognitive-behavioral treatment had three core beliefs: (a) It is useless to express feelings to anyone, (b) no one believes me, and (c) I am not important (Milestone, 1993). These beliefs suggest an inextricable tie between emotional inexpressiveness, feeling isolated, and feeling insignificant.

Perhaps the lesson to be learned here is that when we know we matter to someone, it feels as if these people are tuned into our emotions and can feel what we feel as part of ego extension. However, it is exceptionally painful when others do not notice, discount, or reject our emotional experiences. Emotional invalidation occurs when someone is sent the message by others that their emotions are wrong or inappropriate or not what they are supposed to be feeling. This need might not be restricted to negative emotions. Is there a quicker way to lose joy than to have someone refuse to acknowledge it or question whether you deserve to feel it?

The perception that "My feelings don't matter, and my experiences don't matter" can be veridical when children are neglected and receive no attention from others. Unfortunately, in many instances, this sense of being invalidated is rooted in a family system that includes members who discourage and sometimes punish the expression of negative emotions. Such people may go out of their way to quash the hopes of young people.

Parental invalidation of emotions is potentially a key developmental pathway to feelings of not mattering (Flett, 2018a). Numerous clinical case studies have shown that feelings of insignificance and not mattering reflect the sense that personal feelings do not matter. In many instances, parents disregarded their children's emotions or openly discouraged their expression.

This tendency to invalidate emotions can have a strong negative impact on the child, a situation that is exacerbated if a parent also negates the identity and interests of the child. Identity negation is highly destructive because it often crushes the goals and aspirations of young people. There are far too many instances of parents violating the adolescent's need for self-determination by dictating what that adolescent must choose as a future occupation. I have heard too many stories of young people who were told they must become doctors or lawyers instead of following their hearts and pursuing what they are interested in for their lifelong careers.

THE INTERNALIZATION OF FEELING INSIGNIFICANT

The sociologist Charles Cooley (1912) introduced the notion of the looking-glass self. He maintained that our sense of self depends largely on other people's reactions, and seeing how other people treat us is akin to looking in a mirror that reflects the self. The term *reflected appraisal* was proposed to refer to the tendency to take this information and use it to make self-evaluations. People who see others reacting warmly to them can infer that they are likeable and appealing to others, but people who see others react negatively can infer that they are unappealing and perhaps flawed. By extension, the child without a feeling of mattering to others can internalize this in a way that the feeling "I don't matter to others" simply becomes "I don't matter." Ideally, as I discuss in the final chapter, young people internalize the sense of mattering and the value of people needing to matter after having positive role models.

The case account of an adolescent named Ben illustrates this tendency to internalize feelings of not mattering and insignificance (Gedo, 2011). Ben was a suicidal adolescent who vowed to his therapist that he would follow through on his self-destructive urges because he was determined to die by suicide. He was raised by his mother, who endured chronic depression and alcoholism. Ben's mother was described as lacking emotional availability and incapable of meeting his needs. Ben's assessment revealed two core themes: (a) a sense of not mattering due, in part, to being unable to emotionally reach others; and (b) a sense that his anger and rage had driven his mother into her bouts of depression. This sense of being to blame was furthered by Ben's awareness of being unable to do things that would help his mother overcome her depression. Unfortunately, his only sense of mattering was to see himself as someone who had contributed to his mother's poor well-being.

What indications are there that anti-mattering feelings have become internalized? We (Flett et al., 2022) showed in research with a high school sample that there is a strong link between feelings of not mattering and dispositional self-criticism. This finding is in keeping with the results of research conducted with university students that link feelings of not mattering with self-criticism (e.g., Flett et al., 2021; Joeng & Turner, 2015). Unfortunately, in some instances, this becomes a total rejection and disregard for the self.

In most instances, children and adolescents who have positive feelings of mattering will internalize mattering into a positive self-view. For instance, perceived mattering to parents is linked not only with self-esteem (Elliott, 2009; Rosenberg & McCullough, 1981; J. C. Watson, 2017) but also with reports of elevated self-efficacy (Wu & Kim, 2009).

THE SHAME OF IT ALL

Shame is an intense emotion, especially when experienced by adolescents with an intense self-focus and a cognitive preoccupation with how they are being perceived by others. Shame is a negative emotion that reflects a broad and sweeping negative view of the self, combined with the sense that personal attributes worthy of shame are publicly displayed (Tangney, 2002).

Erik Erikson (1950) focused on autonomy versus shame and doubt as one of his earliest psychosocial developmental stages. Erikson observed that shame can involve a sense of being exposed early in life when one is not ready for public exposure and can result in the young person wishing to sink into the ground and out of sight.

An abiding sense of shame is one of the predominant feelings of young people who lack a sense of mattering to others. Shame often results in intense humiliation among people who feel their lack of importance to others is visible and known (Flett, 2018a). Elliott and colleagues (2011) stated that the failure to matter is a fundamental source of shame, especially for young people who have failed to matter to their families; shame is rife among youth who have become so disregarded by their families. Billingham and Irwin-Rogers (2022) similarly noted that feelings of not mattering, shame, and humiliation frequently coexist. They emphasized the role of policies, systems, and institutions in eroding a sense of mattering among young people in ways that inevitably lead to a heightened experience of shame and humiliation.

There has been little clinical or empirical focus on the shame experienced by children with feelings of not mattering to others. Some evidence of a link comes from our initial study with 242 high school students from China (Flett et al., 2014). We found a significant link between lower scores on the General Mattering Scale (Marcus & Rosenberg, 1987) and characterological shame. A follow-up study established that lower levels of mattering are associated with shame in early adolescents from China (Flett, Su, Nepon, Ma, & Guo, 2023). Neither study included the Anti-Mattering Scale, which should have a comparatively stronger association with shame.

BURNING WITH RESENTMENT, ANGER, AND FRUSTRATION

Another issue in understanding children and adolescents who feel like they do not matter to others is that many young people are consumed with resentment and possibly anger, hostility, and frustration. This resentment and anger may build up for several years, especially if not expressed. It may have been suppressed or redirected at peers and classmates to alleviate the angry arousal and frustration for at least a little while.

Rosenberg (1985) introduced some of the best evidence to support the core significance of how a failure to matter relates to anger, resentment, and hostility. Table 5.2 summarizes the key results from over 2,000 adolescent boys in Grade 10 who completed a rudimentary measure of not mattering to parents. Rosenberg remained committed to differentiating mattering from self-esteem. In this instance, he emphasized that the correlations shown in Table 5.2 were virtually unchanged after statistically controlling for levels of self-esteem.

Shame and anger have been discussed in this chapter as separate keys to understanding young people who lack a feeling of mattering to others, but they may be fused in a complex and intense emotional blend. Elliott et al. (2011) proposed that rage is often concomitant with shame. They observed, "The rage that emerges from a failure to matter to one's family may be like no other" (p. 1009). Therapists and counselors need to assess whether feelings of not mattering are accompanied by dysphoria, shame, rage, or all these extreme emotions. The intensity of these complex emotional blends may be unleashed in clinical and counseling sessions or continue to simmer below the surface.

TABLE 5.2. Correlates of Feelings of Not Mattering to Parents

Item theme	Mattering
Overt aggression	−.25**
Impulse to aggress	−.26**
Irritability	−.29**
Resentment	−.36**

Note. Data from Rosenberg (1985).
**$p < .01$.

HOPELESSNESS AND A NEGATIVE FUTURE ORIENTATION

The experiences that have built up and contributed to a generalized sense of not mattering to others are especially destructive because they can strip a young person of a sense of hope. It is difficult to keep the faith and envision a positive future when present experiences are demoralizing and not what seems to be going on with peers perceived to have more ideal lives. Many impulsive and self-destructive behaviors seem to reflect no awareness of future consequences. A lack of restraint or impulse control may be steeped in feelings of not mattering and being unlikely to have a positive future.

The young person with the combined experience of feelings of hopelessness, not mattering, shame, and psychological pain will be at considerable risk for suicide. This is explored in Chapter 14. Hopelessness is both general and specific in the form of social hopelessness that can include envisioning an abject future marked by never mattering to others.

HIDING IN PLAIN SIGHT

The association between feelings of not mattering and feelings of shame has important implications when viewed from a self-presentational perspective. We have written at length in Flett and Hewitt (2013) about the tendency of many young people to hide their distress behind a calm exterior. Flett and Hewitt introduced this idea by describing how distressed, perfectionistic youth who are skilled self-presenters often go undetected and fly under the radar. They hide behind a facade of apparent invulnerability, which is an effective mask that conceals despair. Flett, Hewitt, Nepon, and Zaki-Azat (2018) extended this analysis in a subsequent chapter on adolescents who hide distress by flying under the radar.

Although they did not discuss the possibility that feelings of not mattering are connected with hiding distress, both Rosenberg (1965) and Elliott (2009) made independent contributions that advanced our understanding of the tendency of young people to put on a front. Rosenberg (1965) described data from more than 5,000 adolescent respondents. The tendency to put up a front was assessed by having adolescents respond to two items: (a) I often find myself putting on an act to impress people, and (b) I tend to put up a front to people. One in three adolescents agreed with both statements. These young people were about six times more likely to have low self-esteem than adolescents who did not agree with both statements. Given the consistent association between self-esteem and mattering (Rosenberg & McCullough, 1981), it can be inferred that many adolescents with low self-esteem who agreed to both scale items also had reduced levels of mattering. Rosenberg (1985) reported additional evidence based on a measure of putting on a false front. He characterized this tendency as the adolescent's sense of a fundamental discrepancy between the self shown to others (the presenting self) and the self that actually exists (the extant self; p. 237).

Elliott (1982) extended this focus by reporting analyses of data from 2,625 children and adolescents from the Baltimore Longitudinal Study (Rosenberg & Simmons, 1972). Elliott (1982) described the correlates of a five-item measure of "fabrication" that tapped a tendency to put on a front. One item tapped the tendency to hide negative emotions by smiling despite not being happy. This has been called *smiling depression* when it comes in more extreme forms. Elliott's main results indicated that putting on a front was linked with low self-esteem, engaging in fantasy, private self-consciousness, and social anxiety.

Current published research has not directly examined the link between feelings of mattering and hiding distress. However, survey data from the school board project I collaborated on suggest that it is indeed a core characteristic of young people who feel they are not valued and do not matter. Table 5.3 outlines the correlates of a plainly worded single item that asked our participants to rate the extent to which they "have to keep feelings inside and hidden." Scores on a brief assessment of mattering were correlated negatively with reports of keeping emotions hidden. However, as shown in Table 5.3, the magnitude of the association with hidden distress was greatest when participants rated the item that tapped being made to feel like you do not matter ($r = .56$). The tendency to keep feelings inside was also correlated with a brief measure of self-esteem derived from the Rosenberg Self-Esteem Scale (Rosenberg, 1965). Notably, the link between anti-mattering and keeping feelings inside was still significant ($r = .42$) after controlling statistically for individual differences in self-esteem.

TABLE 5.3. Correlates of Having to Hide Feelings Among Adolescents

Scale item	Hidden feelings
Being made to feel like you do not matter	.56***
Having people who do not listen to you	.43***
Feeling important to people	–.31***
Feeling like you matter to other people	–.32***

Note. Sample size varies from $N = 335$ to $N = 343$ students due to missing data. Students were in Grades 7, 8, or 9.
***$p < .001$.

The tendency to hide emotions and psychological pain and "present a front" by young people who feel like they do not matter has many implications. Unfortunately, when young people are good at hiding their pain, most people who can help them and provide support, encouragement, and attention may not know these young people need to be supported and feel valued. The common feeling, "No one notices me and wouldn't even realize if I were gone," could be due to being exceptional at hiding behind a front.

NEGATIVE HELP-SEEKING ORIENTATION

Mattering is built when significant others respond to cues and signals in ways that show they care. Their responsiveness builds a willingness to approach others, which is especially evident when help is needed. Unfortunately, it is likely that young people with a strong sense of not mattering will be unlikely to seek help as a byproduct of feeling unvalued and not cared about by others. Given that adolescents resist seeking help, parents and teachers should proactively check in and let them know that help and understanding are available to those who might need help but are hiding behind a front.

Empirical evidence is limited thus far but supports the contention that feelings of not mattering are antithetical to help-seeking behavior. Findings from college student research reflect a link between lower mattering and less help-seeking (France & Finney, 2010). Research led by my colleagues at York University has shown that lower levels of mattering assessed by the General Mattering Scale are associated with adolescents' greater self-stigma for seeking help for a mental health problem (Atkey et al., 2024).

This negative orientation may be due, in part, to less perceived available help. Fine-grained analyses of survey data from the school board project showed a significant association ($r = .44$) between feelings of not mattering and "feeling like you don't have anyone you can get help from." This finding is hard to dispute. It is based on the responses of over 20,000 students. The feeling of having no one to turn to is troubling, given that, in most instances, there are dedicated and caring people who are more than ready, willing, and able to help.

NO ONE CARES: THE OVERGENERALIZATION OF ANTI-MATTERING

This final theme is rooted in Beck's (1967) cognitive theory of depression and was mentioned earlier in the discussion in Chapter 2 (this volume) on anti-mattering. Beck also proposed a cognitive tendency he called *overgeneralization*, concluding that one negative aspect of the self represents the entire self. For instance, the child who overgeneralizes might say, "I failed my mathematics tests. I am a worthless person." The negative social exchanges that foster a sense of not mattering can become overgeneralized by saying to oneself, "I don't matter to them because I don't matter to anyone." This feeling can become further overgeneralized and internalized to foster the conclusion that "I don't even matter to myself."

Overgeneralization can also be reflected by thoughts such as, "I am entirely worthless" and "There is nothing about me that people value." This way of representing overgeneralization is a sad twist on the concept of "the whole child." In contrast, the child who is cherished and has a strong sense of mattering to others can feel valued as a whole person with a secure sense of self and identity that is accepted by people who matter to the child.

A study of children in the United Kingdom not attending school provided an example of overgeneralization. Harris and colleagues (2006) found that in interviewing children, some had an internal working model reflecting the belief, "I don't matter to anyone at school." However, once they attended a new school, teachers could make them feel valued and special in a variety of ways, including letting them choose the lessons they would receive or having a special lesson prepared specifically for them.

The thought "No one cares" is another everyday cognition that reflects the overgeneralization of not mattering to others. The clinical case literature is inundated with examples of people in dire straits who have reached the conclusion that they do not matter to anyone and no one cares about them. One prime case example is the story of an adolescent girl named Morgan, who had type 1 diabetes and attempted suicide by administering a potentially fatal overdose of insulin (McManama O'Brien et al., 2021). Morgan survived her attempt and later indicated that the triggering event was not anything in particular, but she had come to feel that no one cared about her anymore. This case example is useful for making a key point: Sometimes distress and pain go beyond a feeling of not mattering to include the lost feeling of having mattered in the past. The case of Morgan also reminds us that young people with physical health conditions need to know that they matter as people; interest in them must go beyond the safe management of their health challenges.

The sense of not being missed attests to the profound sense of isolation and aloneness felt by some young people. The internal and external worlds are considerably different for young people who feel like they do not matter compared with those who know they do.

THE IMPORTANCE OF CONTEXT IN UNDERSTANDING CHILDREN WHO FEEL AS IF THEY DO NOT MATTER

The themes identified in this chapter hopefully combine to reveal an image of children who feel like they do not matter, but an important part of the image has yet to be illustrated. Observations were provided with little to no mention of context because the focus was on the prototypical child who feels unimportant. However, context is important because the themes outlined earlier will become more or less salient depending on the situation the child experiences daily. The first key consideration is whether the child is being treated as if they do not matter or it is how life is perceived. Of course, even when it is largely a matter of appraisal, it is how the child feels, which is their reality.

The key contextual element that needs to be highlighted here is that some children have circumstances that make their lives uniquely challenging relative to the lives of other children. It is important to reflect on what life is like for the child without a feeling of mattering who is grappling with unique circumstances, such as poverty or prejudice and the inequities that accompany them.

For instance, some children and adolescents have bounced around from foster home to foster home, and some are unhoused. Multiple descriptions of the experiences of adolescents without housing align closely with the description of the anti-mattering concept. A qualitative study of 80 street youth from Vancouver found that about one in four participants felt they had no value to others (Kidd, 2004). They felt entirely alone because no one seemed to care about them. Kidd and Kral (2002) documented similar experiences in their interviews of 29 street youth with suicidal tendencies. One adolescent said, "I walked out at Christmas, and no one noticed" (p. 420).

There are also the realities and challenges faced by children with disabilities. They, too, need to belong and matter; this has been well documented (e.g., Foley et al., 2012). However, it is far too easy for these children to feel unseen and overlooked because they do not get the attention they deserve. As was described in Chapter 2, some children with disabilities experience profound indignities, as was the case when Judy Heumann was told that at school, she would be regarded as a fire hazard (Heumann & Joiner, 2020). Ultimately, we must proactively consider and identify which children in which situations most need to feel that they matter and then find ways to address their feelings of anti-mattering and unmet need to matter. Positive change is possible, as indicated by findings such as the role of perceived belongingness in buffering the negative impact of discrimination on the life satisfaction of Canadian youth with disabilities (Daley et al., 2018).

The good news that arises from the experiences of children facing real challenges is that there is no shortage of issues and causes for young people, or people of any age, to focus on if they want to become an advocate or activist embarking on a mission to make a difference. The good feeling of mattering through adding value will be needed to help cope and be resilient to the frustration and anger invoked when policymakers continue to look through and past people trying to make a difference. It is easy to become demoralized when the voices that need to be heard are not heard and fairness is not on the agenda. However, as with most things, persistence eventually pays off in ways that matter and, as the mission continues, the person dedicated to positive change is bound to develop close connections with inspiring people with shared concerns.

SUMMARY

The goal of this chapter was to paint a portrait of the young person without a sense of mattering by identifying key attributes and characteristics that define young people who feel unvalued or devalued. Many of these characteristics can serve as targets for counselors, therapists, or anyone in a position to try to increase the well-being of a child or adolescent who feels irrelevant and insignificant to others. The picture that emerges from the themes in this chapter is a young person who feels insecure and lonely and who may have a profound sense of shame but hides their internal struggles with a false front. Attributes that merit more attention than they receive include the anger and resentment that build in these young people and how the sense of not mattering to others can translate into a negative orientation toward seeking help. Feelings of not mattering are amplified when they become overgeneralized, and the sense of not mattering to anyone is seen as resulting from being someone who is without value and not worth caring about. Young people who have reached this point have a great need to matter and an urgent need to contact someone who truly cares about them.

6 THE ASSESSMENT OF MATTERING

Issues and Measures

Because good measures of mattering are not yet available, however, these conclusions are by no means firmly established.

—Rosenberg, 1985, p. 220

Forty years ago, Morris Rosenberg (1985) reflected on the limitations of how mattering was assessed. Rosenberg and McCullough (1981) described numerous key findings across four samples that emerged despite using sub-optimal measures of how much adolescents felt they mattered to their parents. The problems interpreting these findings were compounded by the varying ways mattering to parents was measured; a unique measure was used each time in each sample, thereby restricting comparisons across studies.

Are good measures to assess mattering in young people now available? The answer is an unequivocal yes. Are these measures perfect? This answer is an unequivocal no. However, this is one instance where good enough is good enough, and some currently available measures border on being excellent. Nevertheless, we will see later that there are concerns and considerations that readers should take into account when evaluating a measure. In some

https://doi.org/10.1037/0000449-007
Mattering as a Core Need in Children and Adolescents: Theoretical, Clinical, and Research Perspectives, by G. L. Flett

instances, when the focus is on the measures, researchers have used measures of less certain quality, and as emphasized earlier, there are measurement-based issues that restrict comparing findings across studies.

There is a larger concern regarding the general state of affairs when it comes to the assessment of mattering in children and adolescents. Research is based exclusively on self-report measures, typically in cross-sectional research, with no attempt to provide children and adolescents with information about the situational context. A criticism of personality assessment for children over the past 6 decades also applies here. Bronfenbrenner and Ricciuti (1960) noted critically that the personality assessment of children is limited by "Reliance on measurement by a single technique applied in a single situation often far removed from the context in which the variable appears in the day-to-day life of the child" (p. 812). Significant advances will emerge when mattering in children and adolescents is assessed using alternative modes. Interviews to assess mattering have not yet been created, but this is a way to learn more about individual experiences associated with mattering. In addition, the assessment of children and adolescents has not yet focused on gathering daily ratings in life contexts. Parent and teacher ratings also represent essential means of assessing individual differences in mattering. Moreover, given that there are bound to be discrepancies between self-reports and observer ratings, programmatic research that examines the nature of these discrepancies would be highly informative.

This chapter focuses primarily on the measures we typically use in our research. Other measures, such as the Mattering Index by Elliott et al. (2004) and Marshall's (2001) Mattering to Others Questionnaire, were discussed at length and are available in my first book (Flett, 2018a).

This chapter begins with an overview of some key assessment issues I have considered when conducting research on children in applied settings overseen by research partners. To some extent, the discussion in the first part of this chapter highlights the need to maintain a critical perspective informed by the practical realities that prevail in applied settings, especially when children and adolescents are involved. When considering how to assess a psychological construct, it is imperative to think about the nature of the construct in general and the people who will be asked to respond to questionnaire items. What is their experience of mattering?

HOW SHOULD MATTERING BE MEASURED?

The first consideration involves the distinction between categorical and dimensional assessment. Most individual difference measures reflect a dimensional approach, and individual difference measures are a matter of degree.

Categories are discrete and believed to reflect qualitative distinctions between personality types (e.g., introvert or extrovert). A dimensional approach reflects variations, with most people falling somewhere in the middle (i.e., ambiverts who are neither introverts nor extroverts).

Dimensional measures are invariably used and assess mattering along a continuum. However, there have been instances when a single-item continuous measure has been scored dichotomously (i.e., mattering or not mattering). It is likely that some children, especially young children, think about mattering in categorical terms, asking themselves, "Do I matter, or don't I matter?" If young people were interviewed and asked, "Do you matter to other people?" the answers would be "yes," "no," or "not sure." We know from our research with school board partners, which was summarized in Chapter 4, that about two thirds of the students will say yes and see themselves as mattering. In contrast, the other one third tend to select either "No, I don't matter" or "Not sure." A portion of young people who feel like they do not matter may see themselves as being in a category and having a host of other attributes that go along with not mattering to others. This may include feeling different from most other people their age.

The measures described here focus dimensionally on the feeling of mattering (i.e., How much do you feel like you matter?), but when it comes to the affective and cognitive experience, I believe that, regardless of age, most people think in categorical terms and say either "I matter" or "I don't matter." Perhaps this is in the form of "They care about me" or "They don't care about me." Two questions that likely follow, perhaps immediately, for those who perceive they do not matter are, "Why don't I matter?" and "Is it something about me?" A key distinction then emerges at this point for people who feel like they do not matter. Some will respond by telling themselves, "I do matter, and I will show them that I do matter," while others will say to themselves, "There is nothing I can do except get upset about it." These are key follow-up questions to pose in interview situations.

Young people in the "I'll show them" category can then express themselves through socially desirable acts (e.g., striving for significant achievements, dedicating themselves to making a positive difference) or undesirable and unacceptable acts (e.g., bullying, aggression, violence, terrorism). Relevant research supporting this possibility is summarized in Chapter 12. This last observation should be emphasized because it is important to focus not only on feelings of mattering or not mattering but also on the clear individual differences among young people when they have been made to feel like they do not matter. One of the most essential training goals for parents, teachers, and community leaders is to increase the tendency for young people to react positively to feelings of not mattering in desirable ways. There are three parts to our shared mission. First, we need to increase the number of children and adolescents who feel like they matter. Second, when they feel like they do not matter, show them how to respond appropriately and not overreact. Third, young people need to express and be encouraged to express how they are feeling. When they do, they can gain some sense of mattering if people listen to them and hear their voices.

Returning to our envisioned interviews of young people, the next question should be, "Who do you matter to?" This question reflects another important set of considerations that should be tailored to the child's family constellation and living conditions. A potential follow-up probe here is, "Do you matter to your mother?" and "Do you matter to your father?" and "Do you matter to friends?" It is natural to wonder whether we matter to certain key people. The measures described here focus on mattering overall, but we know from research and measures developed by Marshall (2001) that it is both possible and meaningful to measure mattering to specific people. Of course, Rosenberg and McCullough (1981) demonstrated earlier that it is meaningful to assess mattering to parents.

When seeking to truly understand and fully assess a young person, the focus at the individual level should certainly consider specific sources of mattering and the pattern of how broadly this young person does or does not feel a sense of significance. It must be unsettling and isolating for young people who have a clear sense of mattering at home to family members but not to peers, potential friends, and teachers. There has been no focus thus far on young people who are acutely aware of the discrepancy between their feeling of mattering to people at home but not at school or vice versa.

Sadly, as mentioned in Chapter 5, a substantial proportion of children and adolescents respond to a series of questions by saying, "I don't matter to anyone." This is the perception rather than reality in most but not all cases. The power of having even one caring person in our lives means no longer feeling and thinking, "I don't matter to anybody."

Mattering could be assessed somewhat crudely but would yield a powerful and meaningful measure by simply counting the number of people children and adolescents say they matter to and the number of places where they matter. When it comes to mattering, the maxim is "The more the merrier."

HOW IS MATTERING MEASURED?

The word "bifurcation" comes to mind when characterizing the current state of the art in measuring individual differences in mattering among children and adolescents. A substantial proportion of the literature uses well-known measures with multiple items. As is the case with the field as a whole, the most commonly used measure is the five-item General Mattering Scale (Marcus & Rosenberg, 1987), which is described in detail later in this chapter. However, a growing segment of the research is based on single-item measures. These measures are typically high in face validity due to an explicit reference to the feeling of mattering. However, they involve considerable subjectivity in terms of how an individual child or adolescent interprets and experiences mattering. General measures are also impacted by what a child needs to experience to feel a sense of mattering to others. Some children may require constant displays of care and reassurances of mattering, and if these are not received, they may report that they do not matter.

Single-item assessments of mattering are not always identified accurately by researchers. For instance, Waterman and colleagues (2021) accurately described a one-item measure of mattering at school in their study of stalking victimization (i.e., Do you agree or disagree that at your school you feel like you matter to people?). However, in contrast, Olcoń and colleagues (2017) labeled their variable "community belonging" even though they measured mattering in the community (i.e., Do you agree or disagree that in your community you feel like you matter to people?). Unfortunately, despite measuring mattering, some researchers have indicated that they have measured belongingness, relatedness, or social support. Flett (2018b), I stated that the four-item subscale developed by Furrer and Skinner (2003) is a mattering measure in disguise because three relatedness items assess either feelings of mattering (e.g., I feel like someone special) or anti-mattering (e.g., I feel ignored. I feel unimportant). The fourth relatedness scale item is "I feel accepted," which refers to the feeling that typically accompanies a feeling of mattering to others.

These same four items have been used to obtain separate measures of mattering to classmates, friends, teachers, and one's parents. Some illuminating research findings have emerged from research on mattering in disguise. R. B. King (2015) longitudinally showed that in 848 students from Manila, relatedness to parents, peers, and teachers predicted greater student engagement and higher grades. More recently, Kunyu et al. (2021) used these four items to assess relatedness to teachers and classmates. The participants were seventh-grade students of immigrant descent in Germany. The study evaluated predictors of acculturation stress. The results indicated that language-related hassles were associated negatively with both relatedness measures. Lower levels of relatedness/mattering to the teacher were also associated with lower levels of autonomy and competence, greater psychological distress, and poorer academic adjustment. Kunyu et al. referred to the relatedness/mattering subscales as measures of classmate and teacher belongingness but not mattering per se because the mattering themes that compose most items in this measure typically do not get acknowledged.

The use of one-item measures and other issues are discussed next. Brief measures are always subject to question. However, in their defense, their use typically yields the predicted findings.

THE USE OF BRIEF MEASURES

As with most measurement decisions, the reliance on single-item measures has clear pros and cons. The positive aspects are that these single-item measures tend to be highly face valid and are typically worded in plain language, which is less taxing for children and adolescents with limited reading ability.

Single-item scales typically require a self-rating of the feeling of mattering to others. As suggested earlier, using the term *matter* enables respondents to use their own understanding of the nature of mattering.

Using a one-item measure seems particularly straightforward when a specific context is mentioned (e.g., mattering at school). What problems could result in measuring mattering with one item? Some children may have a unique or mistaken view of what mattering means. Another potential issue is that by using a single item to assess mattering, ratings may be too affected by mood levels or sudden changes in mood level. Of course, a single item cannot reflect the nuances, complexities, and facets of the mattering construct (e.g., having value to others versus adding value to others).

However, a strong defense can be mounted to support using these single-item measures. Burisch (1984) considered the topic of questionnaire length and questioned the notion that longer measures are better. He concluded that in many instances, users essentially do not get what they pay for when they opt for longer measures, and at some point, longer measures become too lengthy and yield lower validity coefficients. The use of single-item mattering measures is also supported by the widespread and valid use of a single-item self-esteem scale introduced by Robins and colleagues (2001).

Pragmatics must also come into play. Any researcher who has worked with school boards and other research partners can attest to their continual need to have brief measures that reduce the reading load on students and take up less time. Time available for completing measures and reading difficulty level are important considerations. Most notably, surveys involving one-item measures have yielded key findings, such as the link between low community mattering and suicide ideation in adolescents (e.g., Olcoń et al., 2017).

Can lengthy measures be shortened and still be useful? Our research suggests this is the case. Somers et al. (2022) took the 24 items composing the three subscales of the Mattering Index (see Elliott et al., 2004) and developed a four-item subscale of having value to others and a four-item subscale of giving value to others. New insights about the mutual benefits of having value and giving value to others emerged from this research. Dixson and Scalcucci (2021) reported other analyses with this project's data. They used the full 24-item version of the Mattering Index. Unfortunately, their article inaccurately described the research as investigating school belonging. There was no mention in the abstract of their article of the specific focus on mattering. This same problem applies to a subsequent article by Bryce and Fraser (2022). Their research with children and adolescents in Grades 6 through 12 found that elevated hope before the COVID-19 pandemic was associated with higher levels of "school connectedness" during the pandemic. However, once again, mattering was implicated when school connectedness was measured with items such as "I feel like I matter in my school." This study shows that students with a sense of hope find ways to matter at school and can feel it.

USING MEASURES FOR ADULTS WITH CHILDREN AS PARTICIPANTS

Another concern is administering measures to children and adolescents that were created for use by university students or adults in the community. However, this is not a major concern in most instances, depending on the measure used. The brief five-item General Mattering Scale has item content suitable for children and adolescents. It could certainly be improved by making a version suitable for young children, but the psychometric evidence summarized later suggests that the General Mattering Scale is acceptable. More problematic is the full 24-item version of the Mattering Index (Elliott et al., 2004) mentioned earlier. It involves extensive reading with some language that could prove problematic for younger children.

THE DIFFICULTY OF COMPARING ACROSS STUDIES

I have already mentioned the concern about finding it difficult to compare research findings due to variability across studies in the assessment measures used. Some investigators have not used single-item scales or well-known, established measures but have instead developed their own unique measures. Two such measures are described next. Research with these measures has yielded some intriguing findings, but comparisons are problematic.

Hamby et al. (2019) created a five-item measure of general mattering. This and other measures were administered to 440 adolescents and emerging adults with a mean age of 16.38 years. This mattering measure had reasonable psychometric properties, including a reported alpha coefficient of .86. A factor analysis indicated that the five items were related to one factor. However, these five items vary considerably in their face and content validity. Three items clearly reflect mattering, and these items had higher factor loadings that ranged from .597 to .885 (e.g., I feel appreciated by my family and friends; I feel like I matter to the people around me; My family and friends care about what I have to say). One item tangentially reflects mattering (e.g., I know my family is proud of me), and another item reflects mattering but ties it to parental behavior that could be limited by time constraints and personal circumstances (e.g., My family comes to activities that are important to me). The specificity in this scale item may reflect its lower factor loading of .314. While this measure is not ideal, the overall scores are valid and associated meaningfully with a broad range of variables, including psychosocial strengths (i.e., group connectedness and relational motivation), family well-being, and sought and received levels of social support. The three items with the highest factor loadings and high face validity would constitute a suitable measure by themselves. This work by Hamby and associates has yielded a wealth of vital information regarding the correlates of this mattering scale. For instance, another article based seemingly on data from the same sample showed that mattering is associated with a higher health-related quality of life ($r = .41$; see Hamby et al., 2020). To my knowledge, this is the best evidence thus far for mattering playing a protective role in youth physical health.

Another example is a seven-item mattering scale used by Vélez et al. (2020). It has also been used extensively in related research from the same project (see Stevenson et al., 2014). This seven-item scale assesses levels of mattering to specific targets (e.g., mother, stepfather, biological noncustodial father), and it has item content comparable to the General Mattering Scale because the items were created to reflect the conceptual views of mattering expressed by Rosenberg and McCullough (1981). According to Vélez and associates (2020), the nine items that were originally created were scrutinized for face and content validity by a team of psychologists and sociologists. Two items were eventually dropped. This measure seems to tap one factor based on psychometric analyses, but one item refers directly to parents' love for the child rather than mattering per se. This scale has some unique items that couch mattering in comparative terms (i.e., another child or an object or activity perceived as mattering more to the target than their child), and this view represents another way to develop negative feelings about the notion of significance to others.

UNCERTAIN LONGITUDINAL STABILITY

It is generally assumed that mattering reflects stable individual differences in accordance with assumptions of a personality trait approach. However, mattering has been described as a feeling, a perception, and a need (Rosenberg & McCullough, 1981), and, as such, the mattering construct likely has both a trait and state component. There is limited information available about the longitudinal stability of mattering measures.

Evidence of the long-term stability of individual differences in mattering scores is accumulating among samples of emerging adults (see Etherson et al., 2022: Krygsman et al., 2022), but overall, there have been only a few empirical attempts to evaluate the temporal stability of mattering measures. Test–retest data for broad measures such as the General Mattering Scale have yet to be reported in the published literature. The two relevant published studies focused on the stability of mattering scores concerning specific targets (i.e., mothers, fathers, friends). Stevenson et al. (2014) conducted the first relevant study. Participants were children assessed in Grade 7 and again in either Grade 8 or Grade 9 and in Grade 10. The mattering measure was the scale by Schenck et al. (2009) described earlier. The adolescents completed the seven items at each point with reference to mattering to their mothers and fathers. The test–retest reliability for mattering to mothers was .55 from Time 1 to Time 2, and it was also .55 for fathers. Not surprisingly, test–retest reliability declines when the focus shifts from Time 1 to Time 3. The test–retest reliability was .32 for mothers and .46 for fathers. Thus, while there is some clear evidence of temporal stability, fluctuations over time are also evident.

Marshall and Tilton-Weaver (2019) also examined levels of mattering at two times. Their participants were 164 adolescents assessed in Grade 6 and reassessed 1 year later. The measure was an abbreviated four-item scale with three items taken from Marshall's (2001) Mattering to Others Questionnaire. The mattering measure was completed at each time to assess mattering to mother, father, and friends. The following 1-year test–retest reliabilities were mattering to mother ($r = .56$), mattering to father ($r = .67$), and mattering to friends ($r = .52$). Once again, there was modest evidence of stability.

The good news about the stability issue is that mattering is not entrenched. I have stated that mattering is modifiable, and as such, when we focus on the individual child or adolescent, it can be increased but, of course, can also decline (Flett, 2022).

SELF-REPORT SCALES THAT ASSESS MATTERING

The remainder of this chapter summarizes information about the psychometric properties of certain measures. The three measures described next vary considerably in what they measure and how much psychometric information is available. The two self-report scales developed in our lab were recent projects, so less information is available about them. We begin with the General Mattering Scale.

The General Mattering Scale

This five-item measure by Marcus and Rosenberg (1987) continues to be the most widely used in this field. As I noted in Flett (2018a), the General Mattering Scale (GMS) items originally appeared in an article by DeForge and Barclay (1997). A key aspect of the measure is its brevity. It is also evident that the GMS items correspond especially well with Rosenberg and McCullough's (1981) description of the components of the construct.

The GMS has four response options for each item (a lot, somewhat, a little, and not at all) and is intended to measure one dimension. The score is simply the sum of the five items. Possible scores range from 5 to 20. The scale items are shown in Exhibit 6.1.

Table 6.1 is a summary of some psychometric information. The means and standard deviations reflect scoring this instrument by summing across the five items. Some researchers have divided the sum by the number of items and instead have reported item means, but total scores are typical.

It is seldom the case that research has two or more mattering measures in the same investigation, so opportunities are lost to evaluate concurrent validity. However, Rayle and Myers (2004) examined ethnic identity, acculturation, wellness, and two mattering measures in 176 minority and 286 nonminority adolescents. The participants were in various grades ranging from 9 to 12. Rayle and Myers found that the GMS had an alpha of .73 when completed by minority students and .74 among nonminority students.

EXHIBIT 6.1. Items for the General Mattering Scale

How much do other people depend on you?

How much do you feel other people pay attention to you?

How important do you feel you are to other people?

How much do you feel others would miss you if you went away?

How interested are people generally in what you have to say?

Note. Higher scores reflect higher levels of mattering. From "The Internal Reliability of a General Mattering Scale in Homeless Men," by B. R. DeForge and D. M. Barclay III, 1997, *Psychological Reports*, *80*(2), p. 429 (https://doi.org/10.2466/pr0.1997.80.2.429). Copyright 1997 by Sage. Reprinted with permission.

Rayle and Myers identified a factor that consisted of mattering scores from both measures, thus suggesting the measures were positively associated. Regrettably, they did not report the magnitude of the correlation between the two measures.

The five GMS items tend to have high internal consistency. Vaillancourt et al. (2022) reported that Cronbach's α (Cronbach, 1951) was .86 for elementary students in the pandemic condition and .85 for elementary students in the pre-pandemic condition. Similarly, Cronbach's α was .87 for secondary students in the pandemic condition and .86 for secondary students in the prepandemic condition. Initial psychometric analyses supported the use of the GMS. Confirmatory factor analyses were conducted for elementary and secondary students within each condition using principal axis factoring

TABLE 6.1. Psychometric Properties of the General Mattering Scale: Norms and Reliability

Study	Sample	*N*	*M*	*SD*	Cronbach's α
Rayle (2005)	High school				.74
	Males	229	15.05	3.50	.73
	Females	233	17.80	3.25	.75
Dixon et al. (2009)	Adolesc. (U.S.) (Grades 6 to 8)	177	12.05	3.70	.85
Flett et al. (2014)	Adolesc. (China)	242			.77
	Adv. HS	111	13.08	2.69	
	Nonadv. HS	131	13.31	3.02	.77
Flett, Su, et al. (2016)	Children (China)	218	13.97	2.91	.69
	Grade 5 boys	109	13.62	3.34	
	Grade 5 girls	108	14.36	2.31	

Note. Adolesc. = adolescents; Adv. HS = advanced high school; Nonadv. HS = nonadvanced high school.

(see Vaillancourt et al., 2022). Results within each group indicated that one factor accounted for a large proportion of variance (ranging from 61.98% to 66.72%). Factor loadings for all items were high (min = .64, max = .81).

The respective means in the pandemic condition were as follows: 13.19 for elementary students learning in class and 11.53 for elementary students learning only online. For high school students, the respective means were 12.10 for students with blended learning (in class and online) and 10.89 for students learning only online.

Some differences have been detected based on group comparisons of GMS scores. We (Flett et al., 2014) compared the GMS scores of Chinese adolescents from advanced high schools with those from nonadvanced high schools. A significant group difference was detected between students from advanced high schools and students from nonadvanced high schools, who had significantly lower levels of mattering. Perhaps these lower levels of feeling important to others and being the object of their attention is a byproduct of greater achievement pressure on the students from the advanced schools and interactions with parents due to achievement outcomes.

Confirmatory factor analyses have provided consistent evidence that the GMS consists of one item and the items have acceptable fit. Collectively, the same general pattern has been obtained in samples of adolescents from Canada (e.g., Vaillancourt et al., 2022), the United States (e.g., J. C. Watson et al., 2022), and China (e.g., Flett, Su, Nepon, Ma, & Guo, 2023; Flett, Su, Nepon, Sturman, et al., 2023).

Mattering was included as a focus in the assessment battery administered to Alaskan native youth who attended a 5-day culture camp for young people in especially remote areas (see Barnett et al., 2020). Culture camps are believed to reduce suicide risk by promoting a sense of being culturally connected. This research using the GMS showed that adolescent boys, relative to adolescent girls, had significantly higher GMS and self-esteem scores. Some evidence of validity emerged from the correlations of the baseline data. Mattering was correlated significantly with self-esteem ($r = .37$). It was also correlated positively with mastery (i.e., problem-focused coping) and with lower scores on a measure of thwarted belongingness ($r = .55$).

While many issues remain to be addressed and replication is needed, the GMS appears to be a highly useful and valid measure in children and adolescents. We are currently conducting research with a six-item version that includes a new measure focusing on mattering stemming from the caring of other people. Initial research with university students who completed a six-item version supports adding a focus on feeling cared about (see Flett & Nepon, 2024).

The Anti-Mattering Scale

The second measure is one Flett et al. (2022) developed to reflect the premise that the negative feelings stemming from the perception of not mattering to other people are not simply the flipside of the positive orientation captured by measures such as the GMS. In other words, the Anti-Mattering Scale (AMS) item content reflects the notion that the presence of the negative is not equivalent to the lack of the positive. This distinction is akin to saying that a child who is bullied feels considerably different from the same child who simply does not receive support from family members when it is needed. A lack of support becomes anti-mattering when that nonsupportive family does not listen to the pleas of the bullied child and forces them to go to school where more mistreatment is certain to take place.

The AMS is shown in Table 6.2. It was developed primarily based on the responses of university students, but one sample in the original article consisted of adolescents (see Flett et al., 2022). However, the concept of anti-mattering was initially piloted in a provincially funded project focused on promoting resilience in children and adolescents. This first assessment

TABLE 6.2. The Anti-Mattering Scale

Choose the rating you feel is best for you and circle the number provided.

1 = Not at all

2 = A little

3 = Somewhat

4 = A lot

	Not at all	A little	Somewhat	A lot
1. How much do you feel like you don't matter?	1	2	3	4
2. How often have you been treated in a way that makes you feel like you are insignificant?	1	2	3	4
3. To what extent have you been made to feel like you are invisible?	1	2	3	4
4. How much do you feel like you will never matter to certain people?	1	2	3	4
5. How often have you been made to feel by someone that they don't care about what you think or what you have to say?	1	2	3	4

Note. From "The Anti-Mattering Scale: Development, Psychometric Properties, and Associations With Well-Being and Distress Measures in Adolescents and Emerging Adults," by G. L. Flett, T. Nepon, J. O. Goldberg, A. L. Rose, S. K. Atkey, and J. Zaki-Azat, 2022, *Journal of Psychoeducational Assessment*, *40*(1), p. 41 (https://doi.org/10.1177/07342829211050544). CC BY 4.0.

focused on a mixed sample of 350 elementary and high school students who completed a battery of measures, including one item tapping anti-mattering and two items tapping mattering. Anti-mattering was tapped by asking participants to rate their agreement or disagreement with the item "There are times when I feel like I don't matter." The two mattering items were "I feel like I matter to other people" and "I feel like I am important to other people." It is sufficient to indicate that there were clear individual differences in feelings of not mattering that were not redundant with the individual differences tapped by the two-item mattering scale. Moreover, anti-mattering was associated significantly with higher levels of sadness and fear and lower levels of happiness.

When creating the AMS, our shared mission was to develop a brief measure that would share similarities with the GMS to the point that they could be used together and compared and contrasted. Initially, a small pool of 12 items was eventually reduced to five.

The focus here will be restricted to the few samples of adolescents who have completed the AMS and related measures. The initial results with the AMS are promising, but much more research is needed, including a line of investigation with a pure psychometric focus.

The original article introducing the AMS concluded with a description of the first study with adolescents (see Flett et al., 2022). It was conducted with 134 Grade 12 high school students from Toronto. Participants completed the AMS and the GMS; measures of self-esteem, self-criticism, dependency, and self-efficacy; and the brief Marlowe-Crowne Social Desirability Scale (Crowne & Marlowe, 1960). They also completed a multidimensional measure of attachment style dimensions and domains of well-being. Psychometric analyses yielded a mean AMS score of 11.52 ($SD = 3.31$), and the five items had an internal consistency of .77. Adolescent girls had marginally significant higher levels of anti-mattering ($p < .10$). Concurrent validity was evident in terms of the negative association between AMS and GMS scores (r −.44). Higher AMS scores were linked with less self-efficacy ($r = -.43$), less self-esteem ($r = -.57$), greater self-criticism ($r = .48$), and greater dependency ($r = .41$). Several additional analyses indicated that anti-mattering has incremental validity in terms of predicting unique variance in other key variables after taking into account GMS scores and scores on the Rosenberg Self-Esteem Scale (Rosenberg, 1965). Importantly, there was a negligible negative association between AMS scores and social desirability ($r = -.20$), and the GMS and social desirability were not significantly correlated ($r = .11$).

Hill and Madigan (2022) conducted research with 311 gifted and talented adolescents from the United Kingdom. Participants had a mean age of 14.93.

These participants completed the AMS and GMS along with measures of academic stress, self-regulation of learning, and perfectionism (i.e., striving for perfection and negative reactions to imperfection). The mean AMS score was 11.20 (SD = 3.80). Once again, concurrent validity was evident in the modest association between AMS and GMS scores (r = −.52). Anti-mattering uniquely predicted academic stress, reduced effort regulation, and less time and environment management when entered as a predictor variable along with other measures it was pitted against (i.e., the GMS and perfectionism subscales). We obtained the data from this project and conducted additional psychometric analyses that went beyond the psychometric information provided by Hill and Madigan.

Analyses indicated that the AMS items had good internal consistency, with alphas of .81 and .84 for boys and girls, respectively. The GMS also had satisfactory internal consistency, with an alpha of .80 for the total sample and respective alphas of .77 and .81 for boys and girls. The respective AMS means for gifted adolescent girls and boys were 11.77 and 10.09, respectively. The respective GMS means for gifted adolescent girls and boys were 13.43 and 13.54. We conducted statistical tests to evaluate possible gender differences. The results revealed that the AMS mean scores were significantly higher in adolescent girls, but there was no statistically significant difference in GMS scores between adolescent girls and boys.

Confirmatory factor analyses (CFA) were then conducted. The first CFA of the five AMS items evaluated the replicability of the one-factor solution found in Flett et al. (2022) based on data from university students. The model was an adequate fit, with all AMS items having factor loadings (λ) of .63 or higher. Thus, this analysis showed that the AMS is a unidimensional measure among gifted and talented adolescents. A similar CFA was conducted with the five GMS mattering items. The model was an excellent fit; all items had factor loadings (λ) of .38 or higher.

Maftei and Diaconu-Gherasim (2023) evaluated the psychometric characteristics of the AMS in a sample of 480 Romanian middle school students with a mean age of 12.03 years. Psychometric analyses focused on the total sample and did not include a test of the AMS factor structure. The authors reported that the measure had adequate internal consistency (alpha coefficient of .84). The mean score was 10.76 (SD = 3.89). As noted in Chapter 10, the AMS also yielded some conceptually meaningful correlations with measures tapping distress, social media addiction, and motives for social media use.

Overall, initial results attest to the usefulness and psychometric properties of the AMS when used with middle and high school students. Once again, more psychometric research is needed, and the properties of the measure, when completed by children, still need to be established. In this regard, a current project conducted in China, described next, provides some additional support.

The Fear of Not Mattering Inventory

The final measure is still in the earliest stages of development, and there is not much psychometric information available if we restrict our focus to children and adolescents. Nevertheless, I include this measure so that researchers will be better able to access it and conduct research that examines its psychometric properties and correlates. More research is needed with children and adolescents linking this facet of the mattering construct with the various forms of anxiety and associated fears and worries. Given that feelings of not mattering are associated with anxious forms of attachment, there needs to be more of a focus on mattering and anxiety in people of various ages, including children and adolescents.

The Fear of Not Mattering Inventory (FNMI) was designed as a five-item measure to provide some balance when administered with the GMS and the AMS. The items that compose the FNMI are shown in Exhibit 6.2.

The FNMI has been used in research described in various journal articles, but these studies have been based on data from university student participants. Initial evidence has confirmed that the FNMI has one factor, and the items have acceptable internal consistency (see Besser et al., 2022; Chen et al., 2022; Liu et al., 2023; McComb et al., 2020). Moreover, the FNMI has been associated with concurrent mattering measures and measures such as distress, low positive affect, and loneliness, thus attesting to its validity.

We are in the process of examining the results of new research in China that includes administering the FNMI along with the AMS and GMS to samples of students in primary school (n = 1,232), middle school (n = 1,131), and high school (n = 1,862). Preliminary analyses shared with me by Ihua Chen suggest the FNMI is quite promising and that the measure will hold up to further scrutiny. In our analysis, the robustness of the three scales according to McDonald's ω coefficients was evident across various educational levels. Specifically, the GMS exhibited a range from 0.82 to 0.87, while the range for the AMS was from 0.84 to 0.91, and the FNMI had a range from 0.86 to 0.92. Correlational tests indicate that scores on the FNMI have small significant associations with lower levels of hope and self-esteem but a much stronger positive link with loneliness. Other evidence shows that FNMI scores are comparatively low in primary school students but higher in middle and high

EXHIBIT 6.2. Fear of Not Mattering Inventory

Please indicate your response to each of the following items by circling a number between "0" to "3" according to the response options shown below.

0	1	2	3
not at all	some of the time	much of the time	almost all of the time

How frequently:

Are you afraid that you will not matter to other people?

0	1	2	3
not at all	some of the time	much of the time	almost all of the time

Do you worry that as you get older you will be someone who no longer matters to others?

0	1	2	3
not at all	some of the time	much of the time	almost all of the time

Do you worry that others will see you as unimportant or insignificant?

0	1	2	3
not at all	some of the time	much of the time	almost all of the time

Are you afraid of becoming someone who doesn't seem to count to others?

0	1	2	3
not at all	some of the time	much of the time	almost all of the time

Do you worry that others will stop taking an interest in you?

0	1	2	3
not at all	some of the time	much of the time	almost all of the time

school students in China. Comparisons of the measures continue to indicate that the GMS, AMS, and FNMI tap unique parts of the mattering construct, each of which has a unique role to play in the assessment of mattering in young people.

It is worth reiterating at this point that information about other measures is summarized in Flett (2018a). It should be evident, according to the current summary, that it is indeed the case that mattering assessment has progressed considerably, and the concerns expressed by Rosenberg and McCullough (1981) no longer apply.

However, as stated earlier, there is considerable room for further advances because some basic information is still required. For instance, research on the measures created more recently (i.e., the AMS and FNMI) is needed to evaluate their psychometric properties with participants from various age groups (children, early adolescents, adolescents, emerging adults) and across cultures. Additional research is needed on key issues such as possible response sets and various types of validity (e.g., concurrent, incremental).

One key overarching goal is to evaluate the ecological validity of measures (see Brunswik, 1955) through methods such as using experiencing sampling to record feelings, thoughts, and behaviors that should be related to individual differences in levels of mattering.

More generally, several themes mentioned throughout this book merit being measured (e.g., partial or conditional mattering, the need to matter), but no measure suitable for children and adolescents seemingly exists at present. In many respects, conceptualization is more advanced than assessment, continuing a trend that goes back to the original article by Rosenberg and McCullough (1981), so there is still considerable room for additional progress in this area.

SUMMARY

This chapter is best regarded as a resource that summarizes the information available thus far about three measures—the General Mattering Scale, the Anti-Mattering Scale, and the Fear of Not Mattering Inventory. Initial results from samples of adolescents indicate that each measure has adequate psychometric properties, and each measure consists of one factor. The overarching premise that permeates our work is that each measure taps a unique element of the mattering construct, and in some instances, it is certainly merited to include all three measures. This is possible because all are relatively brief—each consists of five items.

Much of this chapter involved a discussion of key issues from a critical perspective. I noted that several investigations thus far have relied on single-item assessments of mattering, and these measures may not fully capture the essence of the mattering construct. Still, research with these measures has yielded useful information and unique findings. Most notably, this chapter illustrated the broad need for future research on mattering in children and adolescents, with a psychometric focus. The limited scope of existing research is problematic because statements and conclusions related to certain issues (e.g., the long-term stability of levels of mattering in children and adolescents) need to be qualified.

PART III

THE DEVELOPMENT OF MATTERING AS A RESOURCE IN THE LIVES OF YOUTH

7 DEVELOPMENTAL ASPECTS OF MATTERING

How does mattering develop? When it comes to the psychology of mattering, what would a comprehensive developmental model look like? Mattering is complex, and any attempt to explain its origins should incorporate multiple developmental processes and variables. Moreover, when seeking to understand mattering from a developmental perspective, key complexities within the construct (e.g., mattering vs. anti-mattering, having value vs. giving value) need to be reflected in the conceptual analysis.

This chapter is best seen as an expansion of the developmental chapter in The Psychology of Mattering (see Flett, 2018a). The central focus of this earlier work was how parental characteristics and behaviors relate to feelings of mattering versus feelings of not mattering in their children. This chapter revisits parental influences and considers child influences and external influences. We have already seen in Chapter 3 how positive youth development opportunities outside the home can support mattering in ways that can transform youth.

In addition, significant new issues are considered in this chapter. For instance, one unique focus is the issue of timing and developmental stages.

https://doi.org/10.1037/0000449-008
Mattering as a Core Need in Children and Adolescents: Theoretical, Clinical, and Research Perspectives, by G. L. Flett

Is there a critical or sensitive period for developing a persistent feeling of mattering? Similarly, the discussion of parental influences includes themes not addressed in previous work (e.g., the role of attention, the child's feeling of being accepted by parents, and the mutuality of mattering).

An ideal version of this chapter would be filled with descriptions of extensive new research on the developmental aspects of mattering and a broad conceptual model informed by key investigations. Unfortunately, however, the field, at present, is lacking in key respects. Most notably, there is a lack of observational research on the specific actions and tendencies of key people (e.g., the child and parent) that contribute to feelings of mattering and not mattering to others. Instead, in this chapter, I review what is known thus far and introduce some unique themes that could become the subject of observational research.

THE ESSENTIAL ELEMENTS OF A DEVELOPMENTAL MODEL OR THEORY

My best advice to the scholar who will eventually craft this developmental model is to never lose sight of some fundamental realities about the nature of mattering. First, mattering is relational. Thus, the developmental experiences that involve interactions with significant others need to be emphasized in any developmental theory or model. A reasonable assumption is that, given that it is possible and meaningful to assess mattering in terms of specific people (e.g., mother, father, friends), as illustrated by Marshall (2001, 2004), it stands to reason that the development of mattering is affected by these various relationships; they all have some role to play in the generalized sense of feeling important or unimportant. Many specific relationships can be implicated beyond the ones already mentioned. For instance, it has been demonstrated that mattering to a mentor can be reliably measured (see Kelley & Lee, 2018), and there is a wealth of data indicating that caring mentors can transform the lives of certain young people.

Second, mattering has its origins in multiple locations. Given that mattering is experienced at home, at school, and in the community and can be assessed with respect to these contexts, it should ideally be reflected in a comprehensive developmental model. Mattering also unfolds in face-to-face and online social media interactions, especially for adolescents.

Third, mattering is cumulative. Children or adolescents have multiple experiences that result in feeling significant and insignificant to others. This is vital to keep in mind when conveying "you matter" to a teenager who may have had a long history of experiences suggesting the opposite is true. As I noted, the "you matter" slogan may be an empty slogan for certain youth (Flett, 2024b).

Fourth, the core facets and other significant nuances that contribute to the complexity of the mattering construct need to be represented in complex developmental accounts (e.g., having value vs. adding value to others). This advice is reflected in the emphasis on parental interest and attention.

The extensive focus on positive youth development and support for efficacy and mattering in Chapter 3 has obvious implications for developmental models. What is needed is a broad model of the kind espoused by influential scholars such as Urie Bronfenbrenner. His ecological model of human development incorporates immediate settings such as the family but "also the larger social contexts, both formal and informal, in which these settings are embedded" (Bronfenbrenner, 1977, p. 513). His framework allows for and emphasizes how individual development is a product of the mesosystem, the exosystem, and the macrosystem (see Bronfenbrenner & Morris, 2006). This theme is represented in Exhibit 7.1.

What else should be included in a broad developmental model? Exhibit 7.1 lists additional themes that ideally will be reflected in a model. There is a strong emphasis on child factors in Exhibit 7.1. Some child-related influences are considered in the next section. The focus then shifts to identifiable sensitive periods in development in early childhood and adolescence. Next, the parent–child relationship is reconsidered, focusing on these two proposed sensitive periods.

EXHIBIT 7.1. Core Themes in the Development of Mattering

1. The feeling of mattering is influenced and affected by factors inside and outside the home. External factors can involve broad systems. By extension, mattering needs to be experienced in the family and the broader social environment.
2. Mutuality between children and their parents and being attuned and committed to each other are fundamental to feelings of mattering to others. Mutuality, reciprocity, and synchronicity are reflected in infant-parent interactions (see Bornstein, 2013).
3. Hyperresponsive and hyporesponsive parental behavior expressed toward the child fosters insecurity, self-doubt, and feelings of not mattering.
4. Feelings of mattering in children and adolescents reflect developmental processes that operate in infancy, childhood, and adolescence and must include unique characteristics of the child that influence the nature and course of development.
5. The sense of reassurance, safety, and connection that accompany a certain and unwavering feeling of mattering is relied on during periods of transition and challenge.

CHILD FACTORS

A developmental model of mattering must reflect a key transformation in conceptualization that occurred in the developmental psychology literature in the 1960s and 1970s. Many early developmental models focused exclusively on parents and their unidirectional influence on the child. This notion of development and socialization essentially treated socialization as "a one-way street" dominated by parental influence. For several years, this was reflected in the perfectionism field by developmental interpretations centered around the roles of parental expectations and criticism in the emergence of perfectionism in children and adolescents (see Flett & Hewitt, 2022; Flett et al., 2002).

A major change in emphasis can be traced to a seminal paper by Bell (1968). Bell questioned why children from the same family and parents can be so different in personality, temperament, and behavior. Much variability stems from differences among children in temperament, but self-socialization is another key influence. Children vary in the reactions and behavior they elicit from parents and other people. This statement would not come as news to anyone who has spent an afternoon with a child with a difficult temperament compared with one who has an easygoing temperament.

One indication of the child's role in the self-socialization of mattering comes from the work of Werner and Smith (1982). They noted that children in their sample who thrived and overcame adversity were differentiated by their tendency to have interests and hobbies and a capacity to connect with other adults that often came from engaging together in these activities. The notion that children vary in their capacities in ways that contribute to connection or social disconnection is intriguing, especially when viewed in terms of possible routes to mattering.

When it comes to child factors, one key issue is whether the child or adolescent has the opportunity to assume a role and add value by making a difference. The discussion in Chapter 3 of children in farm families and the roles they have filled illustrates how children differ in their opportunities to build their sense of mattering. Research with 252 Chinese American adolescents cast in the role of language brokers for their families revealed that they reported higher levels of mattering to parents, which, in turn, was associated with higher self-efficacy and lower levels of feeling like a burden (see Wu & Kim, 2009). More generally, the advantages of an adolescent having a role have been extensively documented (see Larson et al., 2019).

Any discussion of child factors must include individual differences in temperament. Theory and research on temperament derive from the seminal work of Thomas and Chess (1981) as part of their work on the New York Longitudinal Study. Rothbart and Putnam (2002) defined temperament as constitutionally based differences in reactivity and self-regulation. Temperament often refers not to the "what" but the "how" of behavior. Temperament differences are often reflected in differences in the style of expressing behaviors. Even in cases where two children exhibit the same general behavior, their outward expression of behavior (the frequency, intensity, and tempo or speed) may be different due to temperamental differences.

Thomas and Chess (1981) originally identified nine temperament dimensions that were then used to distinguish three types of children: (a) the easy child, (b) the difficult child, and (c) the slow-to-warm-up child. The easy child represented about 40% of their sample of infants. The easy child is described as even-tempered and typically in a positive mood. This child is open and adaptable to new experiences and has predictable habits. About 10% of their sample was composed of difficult children. The difficult child is described as active, irritable, and irregular in habits. They often react vigorously and negatively to changes in routine, and they are relatively slow to adapt to new people and circumstances.

The nine temperament dimensions were reduced to five for two reasons. First, some dimensions have limited variability among children. Second, the expression of temperament was too situationally specific for some dimensions and did not generalize across contexts. Subsequent research (e.g., Goldsmith et al., 1987) described five main temperament dimensions: (a) activity level, (b) irritability or negative emotionality, (c) soothability, (d) fearfulness, and (e) sociability. Later work by Rothbart and colleagues (2001) reduced 15 temperament dimensions to three broad dimensions: extroversion or surgency, negative affectivity, and effortful control. The effortful control dimension has been extensively studied. It reflects a cognitive tendency to focus attention and not respond impulsively.

Some caveats regarding hypothesized links between temperament and feelings of mattering must be emphasized. First, children with a similar temperament can experience dramatically different life outcomes. Thomas and Chess (1989) attributed these outcomes to goodness or poorness of fit in terms of the child's characteristics and environment. Second, if the need to matter is universal and exists among all children, even children with oppositional tendencies who push people away still need to matter.

One obvious prediction that needs to be tested is that children with an easier temperament marked by extraversion and effortful control will engage in more rewarding interactions that lead to a high and stable sense of mattering. In contrast, in addition to children with oppositional tendencies, children high in shyness and low in sociability stemming from behavioral inhibition (see Kagan & Snidman, 1991) have lower levels of mattering and more fears and insecurities. Indicators of behavioral inhibition include a lack of spontaneous interaction with others and an unwillingness to approach unfamiliar people.

Temperament is likely to be most relevant in terms of individual differences in reactivity to times and situations that can arouse feelings of not mattering. Emotional reactivity and diminished effortful control will likely translate into more prolonged and intensive negative affect and cognitive rumination centered on being made to feel unimportant. This reactivity is partly a byproduct of the reactive processes implicated in temperament (see Derryberry & Rothbart, 1997).

Temperament differences involving levels of emotionality and characteristic levels of shyness and social inhibition should also be relevant to differences among children and adolescents in the capacity and willingness to engage in activities that add value to others and generate feelings of mattering. Children and adolescents who are agreeable and outwardly oriented toward people should be advantaged in this regard.

Adolescents will likely be more invested in dedicating themselves to the well-being of others and adding value to others if they have had the opportunity to witness and imitate parents who model this behavior and frequently display it. Parents who are warm and responsive and experience positive outcomes are especially likely to be imitated and have their tendencies internalized by young people.

The focus now shifts to early childhood and adolescence as sensitive periods for developing mattering in young people. The emphasis on these periods does not indicate that other periods, such as childhood, are not important. These periods were selected because of the benefits of early experiences of mattering and the transformative benefits of having a sense of mattering as children adjust to the many challenges inherent in the transition to adolescence.

PARENT FACTORS AND THE EARLY YEARS AS A SENSITIVE PERIOD

While multiple experiences and factors affect the development of feelings of mattering, the child's earliest experiences in the first years of life are highly influential. A strong case can be made for the first 3 to 4 years of life as a sensitive period when it comes to the development of mattering. However, as is emphasized later, experiences in childhood and adolescence are also important and arguably just as influential. Age-related advances in cognitive and social-emotional development and the focus on self and identity that peaks during adolescence point to early adolescence as a sensitive period. However, even if this is the case, there is a need for an extended developmental model that leads into emerging adulthood.

Because mattering is largely about the degree and quality of connection with significant others, it is not surprising that theorists in the field have focused extensively on the attachment bond between children and their parents and how mattering relates to individual differences in attachment style (see Elliott, 2009; Flett, 2018a; Prilleltensky, 2020). The limited research on mattering and attachment styles indicates that feelings of not mattering are linked with insecure attachment in adolescents (see Flett et al., 2022). Programmatic new research is needed on mattering and attachment style. Ideally, this research will go beyond self-report and assess attention style through standardized interviews and by gathering behavioral data.

While the void in research is problematic, it seems safe in the absence of research to presume that our needs for connection and to matter are closely linked. When it comes to the healthy development of a child or adolescent, it is common for a secure attachment style and a strong and certain feeling of mattering to go hand in hand.

Although it is decidedly unfair to the countless good fathers in the world and their roles in their children's lives, I have often noticed and now feel compelled to mention the remarkable similarities in the words "mothering" and "mattering." These two words begin and end the same way, and seven of their nine letters are identical. Of course, at one level, this is just a coincidence, albeit a remarkable one. However, it is worth noting that the behavior typically associated with warm and responsive mothering, regardless of who displays and expresses it, is a route to the feeling of mattering. When this behavior is expressed consistently toward the child, mattering becomes more than a feeling because it now has certainty and stability built into it.

Research has shown that one key contributor to feelings of mattering is the amount of time spent with a parent. Parents who wish to matter need to spend time with their children (see Stevenson et al., 2014).

What parental behaviors foster feelings of not mattering rather than mattering? Feelings of not mattering result from parental indifference and neglect, especially emotional neglect (Flett, Goldstein, et al., 2016). Overcontrol and lack of autonomy are also problematic and not conducive to feelings of mattering (Kakihara & Tilton-Weaver, 2009). Our pilot data from a project that included a measure of helicopter parenting administered to high school students showed that higher mattering was associated with the factor that taps parental autonomy support.

If a parent needs to be fully engaged and present for mattering to be experienced, certain parental characteristics reduce the capacity for the parent to be so. Rosenberg and McCullough (1981) discussed the emphasis that Karen Horney (1950) placed on parental egocentricity, which precludes focusing attention on the child because it is focused on oneself. Parents may lack the capacity to fully engage due to mental health problems (e.g., postpartum depression) or personality disorders. Parents may also experience low mattering themselves, as shown by research linking low mattering with postpartum depression in a large sample of mothers from Portugal (Caetano et al., 2022). An example of diminished parental capacity was provided in Chapter 4. Recall that Ben internalized the feeling of not mattering because of his experiences of being raised by a mother who suffered from clinical depression and alcoholism.

It may also be the case that parents who are exceptionally burned out may lack the energy and time to engage in ways that promote mattering. One compelling example is the autobiographical account provided by Herbert Freudenberger, the originator of the term "burnout." He worked excessively at his clinic for up to 20 hours a day and was burned out (see Freudenberger & Richelson, 1980). A restorative family vacation with his wife and children was planned. Unfortunately, Freudenberger was too exhausted to get out of bed on the day of departure while his wife and children were waiting for him in the car she had packed.

When considering mattering and parenting, it should also be evident that the infant with a far-from-optimal parent, especially the mother, is at a profound disadvantage in becoming an adolescent or young adult with a strong sense of mattering. Fortunately, there are myriad routes to mattering and multiple influences, and having had a strong positive relationship with the father or responsive grandparents and other caregivers can also set the stage for a feeling of mattering to others.

Positive youth development settings can also compensate. The report by Eccles and Gootman (2002) included a list of key positive features of settings that support positive relationships and feelings of mattering and efficacy. The positive factors resemble the attributes of an ideal parent in several respects. They are summarized in Exhibit 7.2.

Bridges to the Development of Mattering: Parental Interest

Rosenberg (1985) pointed to research on parental reactions to report cards as part of his justification for the need to consider mattering to the parent. Of course, children prefer a positive parental reaction. Rosenberg further stated

EXHIBIT 7.2. Features of Positive Youth Development Settings Related to Mattering and Positive Relationships

Mattering

Youth-based empowerment practices

Efficacy that supports autonomy

Making a difference in one's community

Being taken seriously

Practices that include enabling, responsibility granting, and meaningfully challenging

Practices focused on improvement, not relative current performance levels

Supportive Relationships

Warmth, closeness

Connection, caring

Good communication

Secure attachment and responsiveness

Note. Data from Eccles and Gootman (2002).

that a negative reaction is better than no reaction because at least the parents with negative reactions care enough to express their displeasure and concern.

Rosenberg's extensive earlier work on parental interest and the impact of significant others on the child set the stage for the eventual focus on individual differences in mattering to others. Rosenberg (1965) wrote a chapter on parental interest in his classic book *Society and the Adolescent Self-Image*. He discussed at length how a child's view and awareness of parental interest are based on many interactions over the years. Rosenberg emphasized the destructiveness of low parental interest. He observed,

> Very likely such lack of interest in the child goes along with lack of love, a failure to treat the child with respect, a failure to give him encouragement, a tendency to consider the child something of a nuisance and to treat him with irritation, impatience, and anger. (Rosenberg, 1965, p. 146)

He concluded that feeling important to a significant other is essential to developing a feeling of self-worth. Rosenberg noted that 20% of the young people in his samples experienced total parental indifference.

Rosenberg (1965) also observed that, to some extent, a sense of the parent not being interested in the child is rooted in the child's reality. The child has interacted with family members thousands of times, and

> he has thus been exposed to innumerable signs as to whether others are interested in what he has to say: the stifled or open yawn when he speaks, the interruption or changing of the subject, the look of distractedness when he expresses an opinion. (p. 143)

Rosenberg then contrasted this with "the light of interest" that is sparked when a parent is animated in conveying interest and then shows encouragement.

When people describe important relationships with others that give them a strong sense of mattering, they often describe people who seem to shine their full attention on them. One of the strongest superpowers is the ability to shower others with attention and demonstrate the capacity to fully listen to people while showing a key interest in understanding them. This tendency to sustain this attention and interest in others is akin to investing considerable time and energy into them. It is worth it for people who enjoy being with other people and feel the embrace of mattering to these people.

One concern I have when I reflect on the importance of parental interest and its relevance over the years is that too many young people today are not getting the interest and full attention they crave because their parents have become mesmerized by their cell phones. I first witnessed this about 15 years ago while waiting with my daughter in line to go to a movie. A father and his daughter were in line ahead of us. We waited for 30 minutes, during which the father had an animated conversation on his cell phone while his daughter looked up at him, hoping to get his attention, to no avail. This lack of attention could easily escalate already existing feelings of not mattering.

Phubbing refers to the tendency to disregard signals from someone nearby or being unaware of this person because of a preoccupation with a cell phone or some other screen. We know that being phubbed undermines feelings of mattering. There is now a burgeoning line of inquiry on how being phubbed by parents has a profoundly negative impact on the mood states of their children (see Wang et al., 2020). The phenomenon is widespread enough to result in the recent development of the Parental Phubbing Scale (see Pancani et al., 2021). Research with this measure on a sample of over 3,000 adolescents showed that perceived parental phubbing was associated with feelings of social disconnection from parents.

Parents who become fully absorbed in using their cell phones and tend to do this often send a regular message that vulnerable children and adolescents will regard as a sense of not having an interest in them. Of course, youth are just as capable of phubbing their parents in ways that can undermine the need for parents to matter. With these scenarios in mind, we now turn to a more detailed analysis of the key role of parental attention.

Bridges to Mattering: Parental Attention

The first years of a child's life require parental attention. This alone is sufficient to make it the first sensitive period for developing the feeling of mattering to others. Rosenberg and McCullough (1981) stated that when it comes to attention, "The most elementary form of mattering is the feeling that one commands the interest or notice of another person" (p. 164). The initial key is how babies respond when they receive loving attention and how they signal to the mother, father, or grandparent that attention and care are needed. A baby knows when a parent is paying close attention, and loving attention is a great reward and comfort. Babies also know how they feel when not getting the attention they need. Given the reinforcement value of attention and how it is linked with survival and development, it is no wonder that children learn multiple ways to get attention; indeed, some young attention seekers need constant attention from the people they are around.

Early experiences give us a strong orientation toward whether we are or are not getting the attention we need. The presence or absence of attention is a strong elicitor of emotions. The young person not getting enough attention cannot help being strongly influenced by this in terms of how they think and feel about themselves. This will certainly be the case if they notice that others in their family are getting the attention they need or notice while accessing social media that others their age seem to be getting a great deal of attention.

Some influential research by my late colleague Maria Legerstee must be noted here. Our labs were beside each other for more than 15 years, and she used to tell me how and why there is much more going on inside babies' heads than most people realize. Her experimental work demonstrated that babies have a social brain, and by the end of their first year of life, they are aware of the attentional state of the people around them and whether this attentional focus is on them (see Legerstee & Barillas, 2003). This, of course, has profound implications for the early development of mattering, with its emphasis on other people making it clear that they are paying attention to us. Other work indicates how affect mirroring of mothers influences the social expectancies of 3-month-old infants (Legerstee & Varghese, 2001). We can extrapolate from this work that infants have already begun cognitively encoding how people have or have not responded to them. They can process whether others are showing interest and attention, which extends to tracking responses when they signal for their need to be met.

MATTERING IN CHILDHOOD

Rosenberg and McCullough (1981) believed that mattering is relevant to children, but they did not address how old children are before they engage spontaneously in cognitive appraisals involving assessments of their importance to others. This topic is useful to consider in terms of mattering being described as a feeling state, a need, and a perception, along with age-related changes in cognitive development and the capacity for social cognition. The feeling of mattering versus not mattering is likely relevant in early childhood as a function of the quality and quantity of parental engagement with the child and the degree to which parents are sensitive and responsive to the child's cues and signals, especially those that reflect the child's needs. This feeling of mattering is closely linked with the affectional bond that emerges from having a secure attachment style and the types of interactions that promote feeling close and connected to parents who can be relied on.

As children age, they progress from concrete to more abstract forms of self-understanding (Damon & Hart, 1982). As cognitive development continues, they are increasingly focused on the feeling and perceptions of mattering or not mattering to others. A growing awareness of certain aspects of the self as stable and constant will raise the psychological stakes associated with feelings of mattering or not mattering to others. Feeling and perceiving a lack of importance to others is much more upsetting when one realizes that certain aspects of the self are enduring characteristics.

The limited focus that Rosenberg and McCullough (1981) had on children versus adolescents is reflected in the research on mattering in younger people. Most research is focused on adolescents and not children. The youngest research participants thus far are the Grade 4 children in Vaillancourt et al.'s (2022) research. The failure to conduct research evaluations on mattering in younger children is troubling, and it is evident that there is a growing need to address core issues, such as establishing the age at which clear and meaningful individual differences in mattering can be identified among young children.

Rosenberg and McCullough (1981) made an intriguing observation about mattering in children. They proposed that mattering may be relatively high among children and adults but low among adolescents and older adults. They suggested that young children feel they are the center of the universe and the world revolves around them. This statement referred to children with typical circumstances and not young children dealing with early and chronic adversities and profound neglect. However, if children have an inflated sense of mattering, research on early childhood should reveal a preponderance of children with inflated levels of mattering. This prediction is important to test, and the outcome of this research should have key implications for many developmental models.

MATTERING IN ADOLESCENCE AS ANOTHER SENSITIVE PERIOD

If Rosenberg and McCullough (1981) are correct, and children have an inflated view of their sense of mattering to others, there is another significant implication, a key reason early adolescence is a sensitive period. A developmental challenge for most children, as they move from childhood to adolescence, is that they experience a perceived loss of how much they matter as they learn they are not as special and important as they imagined. When do children come to this realization as they age? The timing likely differs depending on individual circumstances, and some narcissistic children will defensively deny it altogether. When this loss of mattering is acknowledged and acutely felt, it can contribute to significant distress. Chandler (1994) suggested that continuity loss leads to depression for those young people who experience it as a loss of self and a discontinuity they cannot recover from.

The notion that children in late childhood need to know they matter to their parents is at variance with the image of early adolescents who seemingly want little to do with their parents and want to be left alone and free from interference or control. These young people in late childhood or early adolescence need a close and warm connection with one or more parents with certain attributions. Most notably, in addition to parents maintaining their interest and attention by staying engaged with adolescents and spending time with them, three characteristics are essential: (a) a mutual sense of mattering to each other, (b) parental engagement in terms of emotional availability, and (c) the adolescent having a sense of being accepted and appreciated unconditionally by their parents. Each of these factors is discussed next.

Mutuality of Mattering

Research has documented that just as children of various ages need to matter to their parents, it is also true that parents need to matter to their children (see Marshall & Lambert, 2006). Indeed, in their chapter on socialization as a dynamic process, Kuczynski and colleagues (2015) proffered a strong case for how the reciprocal nature of mattering is best interpreted from a relational, dynamic perspective. Their analysis refers to Sameroff's (1975) transactional, dialectical model of human development and the central notion that we cannot reduce causes to particular cognitions, behaviors, or dispositions of temperament and person of the parent or the child. They noted that because children and their parents matter to each other, they are interdependent and receptive to and respond to each other.

The strongest benefits and greatest comfort should come from a relationship that combines mattering with mutuality. There is extensive literature on mutuality between parent and child and how its presence is an exceptionally protective resource for adolescents (Deater-Deckard & Petrill, 2004; Funamoto & Rinaldi, 2015; Laursen & Collins, 2009).

Mutuality is a strong affectionate bond between the parent and child that makes them highly responsive to each other's needs in ways that reflect care and close contact. I propose the term mattering mutuality to refer to mutuality marked by the parent and child mattering to each other. This is particularly evident when both parent and child find ways to spend time with each other and have unique things they share.

When mattering mutuality exists, two people are connected to the point that they are willing to share inner worlds. The best relationships are ones in which one person wants to know what is happening inside the other. This can involve showing empathy and actively reflecting on what it is like to be the other person. This likely happens when a young person indicates they know they matter because the other person is trying to understand them.

The concept of mattering mutuality seems essential in accounting for truly special relationships that develop. Scores on mattering measures such as Marshall's (2001) Mattering to Others Questionnaire tend to be skewed so that mean levels of mattering are quite high. This skew applies to reports of mattering to mother, father, and friend (e.g., Marshall et al., 2010). However, whether the high level of mattering to mother, father, or friend resembles mattering mutuality has not been determined. Heterogeneity likely exists, such that only a subset of young people have a deep sense of mattering mutuality.

Although they did not refer to mutuality, Rosenberg and McCullough (1981) did mention conditions in the parent–child dyad that reflect these more ideal relationships:

> We suggest that the child whose parents are concerned with, and interested in, his inner thoughts, feelings, and wishes is more likely to feel that they are really interested in him as a person than the one whose parents are primarily concerned with his external appearance and behavior and overt behavior. Unfortunately, the data to test this interpretation are unavailable. (p. 176)

This observation is important because it reminds us that when someone is truly interested in us, they will express a desire to know what is happening inside us and get beyond the surface. This seems essential when considering the number of young people who successfully hide behind a front. This tendency was identified in Chapter 5 as a key to understanding children who feel like they do not matter. The parent who provides a safe atmosphere for revealing hopes, aspirations, self-doubts, and self-recriminations can deepen the relationship with their child. Ideal relationships are those in which both parties can be honest and forthcoming about their internal worlds and have someone who is patient and wants to know what is happening inside.

Urie Bronfenbrenner was highly attuned to the type of relationship I outlined and how it relates to the needs of children. He often repeated that every child needs an adult who is "crazy about the kid" (see Bronfenbrenner, 1990). He once told a U.S. Congressional Committee, "Some adult has got to be crazy about the kid, and truly be there for that kid, and let that kid know that his life is important and has meaning" (141 Cong. Rec. S5543, 1995). The emphasis on being there and conveying importance indicates that someone has to let the child know they matter.

This concept is included in the section on adolescence because mattering mutuality is especially important at this stage in the young person's life; Bronfenbrenner (1990) prescribed just this type of relationship. Adolescents may seem like they are pulling away from their parents, but natural exploration outside the home and in other relationships will be more successful if mattering mutuality between the adolescent and one or both parents already exists.

It is also included here to reflect that mattering mutuality ideally also exists with friends. There are clear individual differences among adolescents regarding mattering to friends (e.g., Marshall, 2001), but a more refined approach that directly assesses mattering-based mutuality with a best friend should yield better insights into how protective it is to have this relationship. This emphasis on mutuality means that we need to ask young people not only how much they matter to others but also how much other people matter to them.

How important is it to have a close friendship with someone who is regarded as a confidant? A vast literature attests to the significance and profound benefits of best-friend relationships in adolescence (e.g., Oswald & Clark, 2003; Richey & Richey, 1980; Wilkinson, 2010), and the time is nigh for programmatic research that examines mattering in these best-friend dyads.

It leaves an unmistakable impact on self and identity when there is someone like this in the life of a child or adolescent. In addition to parents and friends who may have mattering mutuality with the child or adolescent, grandparents often fill this role and have a special relationship that meets the needs of grandchildren and grandparents. The presence of people like this in young people's lives is evident in research on people designated as "cherished children" (see L. O. Lee et al., 2015). Cherished children have a highly favorable profile of early experiences that do not reflect the realities other children face.

Parental Emotional Availability

If there were a recipe for developing a cherished child, one key ingredient would be having parents who are emotionally available and responsive to the child's needs. How might parental emotional availability translate into specific actions and orientations that can promote feelings of mattering? Vital insights come from research by Lum and Phares (2005). They created the Lum Emotional Availability of Parents Scale (LEAP), which has 15 items and can be completed by adolescents to obtain separate ratings of the emotional availability of mothers and fathers. The scale can also be modified so that parents can rate their degree of emotional availability.

The link between parental emotional availability and mattering in children will seem evident to most readers familiar with mattering after even a cursory examination of the LEAP items. These items ask young people to rate the extent to which their parents showed a genuine interest in them, supported them, showed understanding, were available to talk anytime, showed they cared about the child, and remembered things that were important to their children. Higher levels of emotional availability were associated with parental acceptance, positive involvement, and emotional warmth. Importantly, according to Lum and Phares (2005), there was considerable agreement regarding child and adolescent ratings of parental emotional availability and parents' ratings of their own emotional availability.

Research with adolescents across various samples indicates that many positive outcomes are associated with having a mother, father, or both parents deemed high in emotional availability. The LEAP has been used in several investigations. Adolescents who perceive greater emotional availability in their parents have been shown to have higher levels of self-esteem and lower levels of depression (Babore et al., 2016). Other research has shown that adolescents with higher parental emotional availability have fewer internalizing and externalizing problems (Clay et al., 2017). Parents of adolescents with anorexia nervosa who report elevated levels of their own emotional availability also tend to report greater family functioning across multiple indices (see Criscuolo et al., 2023).

What is most unfortunate about this important line of investigation is that it has proceeded without any attempt to relate parental emotional availability to mattering among young people. However, as noted earlier, links have been established between parental emotional availability and self-esteem. An obvious important next step is for this research to include measures of general mattering and mattering to parents. A key question is whether mattering in children and adolescents relates to parents' ratings of their emotional availability.

Parental Acceptance and Appreciation

Consider how you feel when you are with someone who accepts and appreciates you for who you are, even if you are far from "a finished product." The sense of being fully accepted and appreciated versus not being accepted and appreciated by others, especially one's parents, is a key defining element of the developmental context that bears on the feeling of mattering to others.

A general atmosphere of feeling accepted and appreciated is especially beneficial during adolescence when there is conflict between the parent and child. A starting position of mutual mattering should defuse conflict situations, especially if they can be cognitively reframed as a conflict that reflects that parents care and choose to engage because that is what you do if someone matters to you.

While the focus here is on parental acceptance, feeling accepted and appreciated is vital to why mentors can play life-altering roles in young people's development. Mentors must often provide feedback that could be viewed as criticism but instead is seen as constructive. Why? It is constructive when offered by someone who accepts and appreciates you for who you are; accordingly, it is seen as instruction and coaching rather than denigration and humiliation. Criticism offered within this context can also be seen as another indication that the mentor truly cares because the young person matters to the mentor. Similarly, if you truly matter to someone, they will hold you accountable when you need to be held accountable instead of being avoidant and looking the other way.

A home is not much of a home and does not feel like a safe and secure environment if it is a place where you feel unaccepted. This observation is supported by results from Vélez and associates (2020) and supplementary results from further analyses of the pilot data. Vélez et al. studied mattering in 392 early adolescents in Grade 7. Half the participants were from intact families without divorce, and half were from families with a stepfather. Participants completed a 7-item mattering measure developed by the authors and a multifaceted measure of parent behavior as rated by children. The mattering measure tapped mattering to one's mother, biological father, and residential stepfather in families with a stepfather. The parenting measure provides adolescent ratings of parental acceptance and rejection and the consistent use of discipline. The acceptance subscale tapped such themes as an understanding parent who projected enjoying being with the child. Vélez and associates (2020) reported strong associations between mattering and higher levels of acceptance and consistent use of discipline and lower levels of parental rejection.

Levels of mattering, acceptance versus rejection, and parents' consistent use of discipline were so intercorrelated in their sample of families undergoing divorce that Sandler and colleagues (2013) combined these three variables into an index of "positive parenting." Positive perceived parenting from the mother only was associated negatively with children's mental health problems.

Key insights relevant to feeling accepted can be gleaned from research from the school board project I collaborated on (summarized in Chapter 2 of this volume). Participants in our sample of 344 middle and high school students were asked to indicate the degree to which they did not feel accepted at home. This feeling of not being accepted at home was associated robustly with being made to feel like they did not matter ($r = .46$).

Table 7.1 summarizes other correlates of "Not feeling accepted at home." The correlates indicate other factors associated with not feeling accepted and not mattering. Pertinent themes from a mattering perspective are "Not having enough contact with parents" and "Having people who do not listen to you."

This feeling of not being accepted at home is likely salient among sexual minority youth who feel like they do not matter to certain family members. It was noted earlier in this book that survey results focusing on LGBTQ+ youth show that they have significantly lower levels of feeling like they matter in their community, and this feeling is likely common among those youth who are living at home.

The emphasis on not being accepted at home is a commonly expressed theme among unhoused youth who have made the momentous decision to leave home. It seems reasonable for a young person to want to be elsewhere

TABLE 7.1. Correlations With Lack of Acceptance Among Adolescents

Scale item theme	Not feeling accepted at home
Feeling like you do not matter	.46
Not having enough contact with parents	.55
Not being trusted by parents	.54
Parents being too strict or demanding	.54
Having no one to get help from	.52
Feeling put down by a family member	.54
Being rejected by someone	.32
Having people who do not listen to you	.28
Having to keep feelings inside	.32
Feeling sad	.38
Feeling lonely or disconnected	.31

Note. All correlations are at $p < .001$ or greater. Sample size varies from $N = 335$ to $N = 343$ due to missing data.

if their daily living conditions make them feel like they do not matter and are unaccepted.

Of course, when feeling accepted is present and accompanied by a feeling of mattering, it is associated with other fabulous feelings. Data from the school board project showed that among tens of thousands of students, mattering at school was associated with feeling accepted by students ($r = .70$), feeling accepted by staff ($r = .61$), and feeling safe at school ($r = .62$).

The feeling of being accepted should be unconditional. It is important to reiterate the phenomenon of conditional mattering identified by Carey (2019, 2020). One of the many benefits of being unconditionally accepted by others is that it typically leads to unconditional self-acceptance. The goal is to have a healthy sense of mattering to oneself, and this internalized mattering should preclude engaging in risky behavior. Acceptance by self and others without preconditions should ultimately lead to valuing and caring for the self.

SUMMARY

This chapter selectively summarized some of the research findings available on the development of mattering, but as in the mattering field, more questions were raised than were answered. Accordingly, this chapter outlined numerous important directions for future research. The goal of this chapter was to provide a framework for a multifaceted model that includes multiple systems but still retains a central focus on the development of mattering in the family context with a primary emphasis on the parent–child relationship. Some key themes were underscored (e.g., examining mattering and its development in adolescence), and various key concepts (e.g., mattering mutuality) and hypotheses were proposed. One overarching point worth reiterating is that future work should include a central focus on the facets of the mattering construct to address the distinction between mattering and anti-mattering. Other issues were not addressed, such as the developmental course of mattering and whether developmental trajectories in childhood and adolescence are fundamental and merit programmatic research. Any broad future initiative is bound to be informative and yield vital information that can help harness the considerable power of mattering and provide insights that help us advance our understanding of mattering in relationships.

8 MATTERING IN YOUTH HAPPINESS, WELL-BEING, WELL-DOING, AND FLOURISHING

Hearing that someone actually thinks you matter and have a purpose is one of the best feelings to ever exist.

—Beneus, 2023

It is important to keep in mind when contemplating life and its ups and downs that the goal is to be happy, healthy, and wise and not just avoid or limit bouts of anxiety and depression. This focus is in keeping with the need to embrace the principles and tenets of positive psychology. The epigraph is a reminder that mattering and feeling useful can be at the heart of happy and mentally healthy youth.

The premise of this chapter is that mattering is fundamental to the happiness of children and adolescents. This applies to mattering in general and to one's parents. As noted by Rosenberg (1985), mattering is important to human beings, and the adolescent who feels a sense of mattering to their parents will have "a richer fuller more satisfying life" (p. 219). There is growing support for this link between mattering and life satisfaction in young people.

https://doi.org/10.1037/0000449-009
Mattering as a Core Need in Children and Adolescents: Theoretical, Clinical, and Research Perspectives, by G. L. Flett

This chapter examines the role of mattering among children and adolescents in well-being and flourishing in life. Although relatively brief, it addresses one of the most fundamental themes in the mattering field. Extensive analyses of mattering and happiness are in short supply, but it is a key topic in a relatively new book on mattering (Prilleltensky & Prilleltensky, 2021). However, long before this book and others like it appeared, William James (1889/2001), the founder of modern psychology, made clear the extent to which happiness and well-being are based on being important to others. James gave a series of lectures to teachers to help them better understand their students and how best to educate them. The link between happiness and feeling important to others was emphasized in a segment James subtitled, "What Makes a Life Significant." He described the intimate relationship between Jack and Jill and how they mattered to each other. James stated,

> Jill, who knows her inner life, knows that Jack's way of taking it—so importantly—is the true and serious way; and she responds to the truth in him by taking him truly and seriously, too. May the ancient blindness never wrap its clouds about either of them again! Where would any of us be, were there no one willing to know us as we really are or ready to repay us for our insight by making recognizant return? We ought, all of us, to realize each other in this intense, pathetic, and important way. (para. 2)

The reference to Jack and Jill realizing each other in a "pathetic" way might cause some readers to wish nevertheless that they could be a member of a pathetic couple if they too could have the happiness and joy that come from being in a relationship with someone who sees us as intensely important.

The New York Times article on the mattering experiences of adolescents elicited many comments from young people about the potential joy that comes from living a life built around the feeling of mattering (Proulx, 2023). A sample of their descriptions of how mattering feels is provided in Exhibit 8.1. These accounts make it clear that mattering is linked with well-being, happiness, and associated feelings and perceptions. The experience of mattering can also be a strong source of motivation and positive engagement.

A summary of research findings on mattering and happiness in young people is provided later. First, however, some context is provided by considering some ways of viewing happiness and flourishing in young people.

WELL-BEING AND WELL-DOING IN CHILDREN AND ADOLESCENTS

A timely analysis by Clarke (2023) revealed the nature of well-being for young people and its determinants. This qualitative study of well-being was based on interviews with 22 adolescents from the United Kingdom. The study documented how the feeling of doing well is framed almost entirely

EXHIBIT 8.1. Descriptions of How Mattering to Others Feels to Adolescents

I always feel wanted and safe.

It makes me feel like I have an important role in their lives.

I feel as though people respect me and appreciate me.

I feel like I am on top of the world, and no one will weigh me down.

They really appreciate me and make me feel great.

Some days, it is a breath of fresh air knowing I am wanted and heard.

Realizing you matter to someone is the best feeling in the world.

Feeling like you matter is a great happiness.

It can be incredibly motivating, boosting your confidence and making you believe in yourself even more.

I feel really important to others; this is what drives me forward over the course of the day.

Note. Data from Proulx (2023).

in academic terms. Clarke noted that *hedonia* refers to feeling well, and *eudaimonia* refers to doing well. The reality for most adolescents is that they are under considerable academic pressure and equate "well-doing" in life with doing well in school. This strong theme emerged from the qualitative interviews, and it fits that well-being is conditional on meeting expectations, including expectations dictated by other people (i.e., teachers and parents). While this study did not mention mattering per se, it did yield evidence suggesting that the need to matter is salient among adolescents and is clearly not being met. Specifically, Clarke emphasized that the adolescents in her study mentioned repeatedly that they craved interactions with teachers who treated them as people rather than as students who needed to perform well. Moreover, some students recounted incidents that involved teachers treating students in humiliating and insensitive ways that are antithetical to their desire to be cared for and cared about as people. The picture that emerges from their descriptions is one of resentment and frustration due to well-doing being defined primarily in terms of achievement outcomes. These accounts fit well with the description of anti-mattering (Flett et al., 2022).

In the well-being framework, there is a clear role for emphasizing interpersonal needs and social relationships when delineating pathways to well-being. When adolescents become too invested in achievement goals, any sense of fulfillment and satisfaction will be limited if there are important unmet social needs, such as the need to matter to others.

DOMAINS OF WELL-BEING AND FLOURISHING

A central focus of this chapter is the conceptual framework and empirical work of Carol Ryff and her colleagues. This work is widely cited and has been exceedingly influential. The essence of it, as first introduced by Ryff and

Keyes (1995), is that well-being is complex, and six key well-being domains are closely tied to what it means to experience well-being and flourish. The recent advances in the psychological literature on flourishing reflect this model outlined by Ryff. In fact, her multidomain measure of well-being is now regarded by many authors as a representative index that represents the essence of flourishing in life. Whether we are focused on happiness or flourishing, it is hard to imagine any young person being happy and flourishing if they lack a sense of being important and valued by others.

The nature of the flourishing of children and adolescents and the correlates of flourishing among young people is a topic of growing importance. Keyes (2006) drew attention to the many young people with high well-being. He surveyed a national sample of 1,234 adolescents in the United States between 12 and 18. Keyes sought to establish that the failure to assess positive functioning in research was overestimating the mental health problems of young people. He used multiple measures, including various measures of social and emotional well-being. Four of the six dimensions proposed by Ryff (1989) were assessed. The results indicated that 48.8% of 12- to 14-year-olds were flourishing, but only 39.9% of 15- to 18-year-olds were flourishing (i.e., two out of five young people). It is a safe bet to propose that if this study were repeated today, these estimates would be substantially lower, given current circumstances, reports of growing mental health problems, and the destructive impact of exposure to social media. However, it is important to underscore that this work signifies that if adolescence is a period of storm and stress, as was suggested by G. Stanley Hall (1904), many adolescents are nevertheless effectively navigating the storm and are functioning well.

It is also important to reiterate that while our focus here is on children and adolescents, the concepts, principles, and associations involved have clear implications for the future life experiences of young people as they navigate their lifespans. The domains of well-being resonate with people of all ages because they relate to key things in their lives.

What is known thus far about mattering in happiness and well-being in young people is summarized next. The evidence consistently shows that mattering is associated with happiness, positive affect, and well-being and should be if mattering is a core need that must be satisfied to experience happiness and life satisfaction.

MATTERING AND WELL-BEING

A check of the historical record indicates that Rosenberg (1985) provided us with the first evidence linking mattering with positive functioning in adolescents. Regrettably, this key aspect of his vast contributions is often overlooked. He summarized the results from broad surveys and indicated that higher levels of parental mattering were significantly correlated with happiness ($r = .32$) in the 2,213 adolescent boys in the Youths in Transition Study.

An association between happiness and mattering among young people was also evident in the results of our school board project that was conducted decades later. The results are summarized in Flett (2018b). Research on students in Grades 7, 8, and 9 confirmed a link between mattering and happiness ($r = .33$) when both were assessed with brief measures. Similarly, in another sample of over 1,000 high school students, happiness was associated with brief measures of mattering to others in general ($r = .46$) and mattering at school ($r = .48$).

This association with happiness likely reflects deeply ingrained attributes that go back to early infancy and childhood and the capacity to experience joy. Carroll Izard's (1993) classic work on the psychology of emotion identified joy as one of the 10 primary emotions. In addition, Izard stated specifically that the emotional worlds of infants and toddlers are dominated by two positive primary emotions (i.e., joy and interest) and two negative primary emotions (i.e., anger and anxiety). The types of relationships and early interactions that foster happiness, joy, and interest likely help establish an early association between feeling valued and cared about and feelings of joy and happiness. Infants who responsively receive the attention they need should be happy with how things are going.

What is the link between mattering and well-being in general? The next section summarizes existing evidence that links mattering with measures of positive affect, flourishing, and well-being.

Mattering as Family Connection and Flourishing

A recent study of family connection and flourishing is remarkable because it involves survey responses from 37,025 adolescents from 26 countries (Whitaker et al., 2022). The data came from the International Survey of Children's Well-Being. Flourishing was assessed as a total score based on six items, each representing one of Ryff's (1989) six well-being domains. Analyses focused on the total score based on the sum of the six items. It is worth noting that when analyses focused solely on levels of flourishing, a cutoff point was used to determine that the prevalence of flourishing across these countries was 65.8% (Whitaker et al., 2022). This key statistic signifies that about one in three adolescents were not flourishing at the time of assessment.

Mattering was not directly measured in Whitaker et al.'s (2022) study, but the family connection measure had item content typically associated with elevated mattering. The themes assessed included having a voice (e.g., My parents and I make decisions about my life together), being listened to (e.g., My parent(s) listen to me and take what I say into account), and being cared about (e.g., There are people in my family who care about me). Analyses with scores on this measure established that flourishing increased in a graded fashion as the level of family connection increased. The reference to graded means that as family connection levels increased, levels of flourishing also increased at a consistent rate. This can be envisioned as walking up a set of stairs, and the higher you go, the better you feel (parenthetically, the act of going up the stairs is a theme that will be revisited at the conclusion of this chapter). Whitaker et al. found that this graded pattern held after controlling for several factors, including age, family structure, and family finances. The pattern of results was comparable for adolescents across all 26 countries. Extrapolating from the results of this study shows that adolescents in families with a high degree of family connection have a clear sense of mattering in their family and associated elevated levels of flourishing.

Mattering in Positive Affect and Wellness

The results described next come from studies that have the advantage of using a direct measure of mattering but involve various approaches to assessing well-being. This research is based on broad measures of positive affect and wellness, with wellness being a form of maximum human functioning among adolescents.

The first study is based on Time 1 preassessment data from 81 adolescents in a pilot study that evaluated the extent to which taking part in cultural camps increased the wellness of Alaskan native youth (Barnett et al., 2020). The participants completed the General Mattering Scale (GMS; Marcus & Rosenberg, 1987), the Rosenberg Self-Esteem Scale (Rosenberg, 1979), an abbreviated measure of positive and negative affect, the Interpersonal Needs Questionnaire (Van Orden et al., 2012), and a measure of multicultural mastery. The Interpersonal Needs Questionnaire assesses feelings of thwarted belongingness and feeling like a burden. These feelings have been implicated in the risk of suicide. Positive and negative affect were assessed with an abbreviated 10-item version of the Positive and Negative Affect Schedule (PANAS; D. Watson et al., 1988). Unfortunately, the researchers combined the 5-item positive affect subscale and the 5-item negative affect subscale into one global measure of affect over the past week. The results revealed a positive association between mattering and a preponderance of positive affect ($r = .37$). Mattering was also linked modestly with multicultural mastery ($r = .40$) and less thwarted belongingness and feeling like a burden ($r = .55$).

The second study is a recent investigation of mattering in early adolescents in China. We (Flett, Su, Nepon, Ma, & Guo, 2023) had a sample of 172 adolescents complete the GMS, the Rosenberg Self-Esteem Scale, and another version of the PANAS, the Positive and Negative Affect Schedule for Children—Short Form (Ebesutani et al., 2012). This measure has two five-item measures of positive affect (e.g., happy, proud) and negative affect (e.g., afraid, sad). Higher levels of mattering were correlated significantly with higher positive affect ($r = .39$) and lower negative affect ($r = -.27$). Comparable correlations were found with the measure of self-esteem. Importantly, a regression analysis showed that mattering and self-esteem were both significant unique predictors of positive affect. Collectively, they accounted for 24.1% of the variance in positive affect.

Other research has examined the links that mattering has with wellness domains. The first two studies from Rayle and Myers (2004) and Rayle (2005) seem to involve the same data set of 462 high school students (229 adolescent males, 233 adolescent females) from the southeast United States. Rayle (2005) had participants complete the GMS and Marshall's (2001) Mattering to Others Questionnaire (MTOQ). This instrument taps mattering to mother, father, and friend. The participants also completed a 105-item measure known as the Wellness Evaluation of Lifestyle—Teenage Version (Myers & Sweeney, 2005), which assesses wellness across six life tasks (i.e., friendship, leisure, love, schoolwork, self-direction, and spirituality). Rayle (2005) reported separate correlational results for adolescent boys and girls but only with respect to total scores on the wellness measure. The results for adolescent boys suggested only a weak association. Mattering had a small association with overall wellness ($r = .14$), while the correlation with the total MTOQ score and overall wellness was even smaller in magnitude ($r = .12$). In contrast, adolescent females had stronger links between overall wellness and scores on the GMS ($r = .26$) and the MTOQ ($r = .32$).

Rayle and Myers (2004) provided additional information after conducting supplementary analyses involving ethnic identity and acculturations. They indicated that their sample of 462 high school students consisted of 176 minority adolescents and 286 nonminority students. Analyses showed that there was a remarkably strong negative association between acculturation and mattering ($r = -.89$). It was also found that mattering was associated positively with a positive ethnic identity ($r = .47$). Importantly, Rayle and Myers reported comparisons of minority and nonminority students indicating that minority students had significantly lower levels of mattering. The mattering variable was associated with wellness in terms of self-direction, schoolwork, and friendship. This pattern was seen as a reflection of the salience and importance of schoolwork and friendship in adolescents' lives.

Finally, sophisticated multivariate analyses indicated that the interrelations among the various constructs differed for minority versus nonminority students. Most notably, among nonminority students, ethnic identity status rather than mattering predicted their wellness when all variables were considered within the same analysis. Overall, Rayle and Myers (2004) advocated for school counselors to find ways to facilitate improvements to enhance mattering and wellness among all students and ethnic identity development and acculturation among minority students.

General Mattering and Wellness

Lemon and Watson (2011) examined mattering and wellness to identify high school students with an elevated risk of dropping out of school. This study used a modified and updated 95-item version of the Five Factor Wellness Inventory—Teenage Version (Myers & Sweeney, 2005). The wellness subscales were now identified as tapping the coping self, the creative self, the social self, the essential self, and the physical self. Mattering was assessed with the GMS (Marcus & Rosenberg, 1987). Perceived stress and dropout risk were also assessed with questionnaires. The participants were 177 high school students. Correlational analyses showed that mattering was associated with higher scores across all wellness subscales. Mattering was also linked negatively with the risk of dropping out ($r = -.23$) and stress ($r = -.28$). Given that all the wellness subscales were associated with less risk of dropout, the results seem to point to a potential meditational model—mattering is related to wellness, which, in turn, is associated with less dropout risk.

A subsequent study by J. C. Watson (2017) investigated mattering, self-esteem, school connectedness, and wellness in 254 students in Grades 5 through 8. Mattering was assessed once again with the GMS. The Wellness Evaluation of Lifestyle—Teenage Version was also used. The correlational analyses found that mattering was associated with overall wellness ($r = .48$), self-esteem, and school connectedness. Importantly, when all these variables were used simultaneously in a regression analysis, significant unique variance in wellness was predicted by all three variables. Thus, it can be concluded from these results that mattering is associated with wellness in middle school students, which is not explained by its links with self-esteem and school connectedness.

Mattering, Anti-Mattering, and Domains of Well-Being

Our recent research (Flett et al., 2022) investigated mattering, anti-mattering, and the Ryff domains, as assessed by an 18-item abbreviated measure proposed by Ryff (Ryff & Keyes, 1995). We also compared and contrasted positive feelings of mattering with negative anti-mattering feelings. Our sample was 134 high school students (72 adolescent girls, 62 adolescent boys) who were referred to in the original Anti-Mattering Scale (AMS) development paper (Flett et al., 2022).

The Flett et al. (2022) correlations with well-being are shown in Table 8.1. As expected, higher levels of mattering and lower levels of anti-mattering were associated broadly with flourishing in the form of well-being. However, a nuanced approach is needed because the results varied as a function of the well-being subscale being considered. Higher GMS scores were linked significantly with all subscales except perceived purpose. In contrast, scores on three of the six well-being subscales had significant negative associations with levels of anti-mattering. This pattern indicates that it makes sense in this sample to consider the separate well-being domains rather than treating them as one broad hierarchical second-order well-being factor with six well-being facets.

Both mattering and anti-mattering had strong associations in the expected direction, with the subscale tapping environmental mastery. It is difficult to overstate the importance of having a strong sense of environmental mastery, given the complexities that most adolescents face in their daily environments and experiences. Our results indicate that a young person with a sense of mattering can move forward and function effectively in the environment. However, it is the opposite for a young person with a high level of anti-mattering who feels insignificant and invisible to others. It is far too easy to envision a scenario in which this type of young person is reluctant to

TABLE 8.1. Correlations Between Domains of Well-Being and Mattering and Anti-Mattering

Well-being domain	GMS	AMS
Well-being–Total	.55**	–.45**
WB–Autonomy	.24**	–.17
WB–Environmental mastery	.40**	–.46**
WB–Growth	.35**	–.13
WB–Positive relations	.54**	–.43**
WB–Purpose	.12	–.09
WB–Self-acceptance	.47**	–.41**

Note. $N = 134$. AMS = Anti-Mattering Scale; GMS = General Mattering Scale; WB = well-being. Data from Flett et al. (2022).
**$p < .01$, two-tailed.

venture out into the world. There were many reports later in the pandemic and recently of young people unwilling or unable to go to school labeled as having school avoidance or refusal (e.g., McDonald et al., 2023). Perhaps many of these young people's avoidance stems from low perceived environmental mastery and an accompanying sense of feeling insignificant in the broader social environment.

We also found that mattering was positively associated with self-acceptance, and anti-mattering had a negative association with self-acceptance. These associations signify that relational mattering is often internalized as self-acceptance in the self-concept. Self-acceptance is regarded as a core component of well-being and emotional health among adolescents; it is a highly effective buffer in stressful situations, and programs have been developed and implemented to boost it (Bernard et al., 2013). A young person with self-acceptance and a feeling of mattering to others should adapt well to many uncomfortable situations. Bernard et al. described teacher training exercises to assist students in developing self-acceptance. These exercises should be more effective if delivered by teachers who convey to students that they are valued.

We performed extended analyses of the data for this book by calculating partial correlations to determine how mattering related to well-being after controlling for anti-mattering. GMS mattering scores still correlated significantly with all the well-being dimensions, except purpose in life. When the AMS was the focus, controlling GMS scores showed clearly that mattering rather than anti-mattering had a stronger link with well-being, as should be the case when the focus is on positive life experiences and associated affective experiences.

Ryff (2018) pointed to schools as a promising context for promoting well-being among young people. Some noteworthy attempts have been made to implement well-being training among young people, and some modest increases have been reported (Ruini et al., 2006, 2009).

A case can be made for adding a separate focus on mattering promotion into these programs or finding ways to pair mattering themes with existing components. The program implemented by Ruini and associates (2009) emphasized developing cognitive appraisals to cognitively restructure situations so that they would be less threatening and could lead to personal development. There were other elements designed to target specific well-being domains. For instance, in one session, students were asked to compliment each other to promote positive interpersonal relationships and self-acceptance. Next, they were asked to write about it in their diaries so that they could reflect on their experience and have more positive interactions. From a mattering perspective, it would be more effective to provide students with the opportunity to mentor younger students so they could experience the significance of giving to others. This should be reflected in greater well-being in interpersonal relationships and a stronger relational self.

SUMMARY

This chapter presented and evaluated the contention that mattering is linked to flourishing and life satisfaction for young people, and the evidence summarized supported this contention. As noted, the sheer volume of research on this topic is limited when we focus on research conducted with children and adolescents. I hope this chapter will serve as a catalyst for considerably more research.

I end this chapter by returning to the observation expressed earlier that the association between feeling like you matter and flourishing is stepped in a way. Imagine walking up a set of stairs and discovering that the higher you go, the better you feel. This example fits exceptionally well with a picture sent to me by an educator in York Region. The photo depicts a staircase at a school. Students at the school were asked to respond by completing the item stem "I feel like I matter at my school when ______." Student responses were gathered and written on large pieces of paper. Next, one school staircase in a key location was made into a mattering staircase by taking the students' responses and affixing them to the steps. This staircase enhanced the feeling of being at a school where students matter and projected the message that mattering will lift you up. Happiness awaits them at the top.

Exhibit 8.2 lists the statements provided by students. It is helpful to keep this staircase and these themes in mind to keep in touch with what children need to feel like they matter and experience joy and happiness.

When it comes to physical locations, if there is such a thing as "a happy place," you can be reasonably certain that the people who are fortunate to be in it tend to palpably sense that it is a place that makes people feel welcomed and valued. It is logical in such places that people develop a strong place attachment that makes them want to maintain it.

EXHIBIT 8.2. Staircase Themes for Mattering at School

I feel like I matter at my school when

someone really listens.

I can trust someone.

someone says something positive like "Good job."

someone helps me (solve a problem, when I am hurt, with homework).

someone smiles at me.

I help someone out.

someone notices that I'm down.

I make someone smile or laugh.

people accept differences.

someone says kind words.

people are positive.

you respect my space.

people respect my stuff.

9 MATTERING, RESILIENCE, AND ADAPTABILITY

What I was so grateful about in having the opportunity to play Juan was playing a gentleman who saw a young man folding into himself as a result of the persecution of his community and taking that opportunity to uplift him and tell him that he mattered and that he was okay and accept him. And I hope that we do a better job of that.

—Mahershala Ali, *Screen Actors Guild award speech*

Few would argue with the claim that today's children will need all the resilience and adaptability they can muster. Without question, the most glaring omission in the voluminous literature on resilience is the lack of a programmatic focus on mattering and resilience. Mattering is almost entirely absent as a focus among resilience researchers. I realized this a decade ago when I assumed the role of research lead on a resilience promotion project initiated by a local school board partner. They had sought and received over $600K to design, implement, and evaluate a resilience initiative focused on the well-being and academic success of middle school and high school students. A particular focus would be the transition from middle school to high school.

https://doi.org/10.1037/0000449-010
Mattering as a Core Need in Children and Adolescents: Theoretical, Clinical, and Research Perspectives, by G. L. Flett

The need for this project and similar initiatives is beyond question. Children and adolescents need to build up their resilience and actively play a role in strengthening themselves. This view reflects a significant change in how resilience is viewed. Initial work on resilience saw it as stable, relatively fixed, and ingrained. It was evident in children classified as resilient or not evident and lacking entirely in children deemed the "undercontrolled" or "overcontrolled" type (Block & Block, 1969/1980). In contrast, more contemporary views (e.g., Masten, 2014) see resilience as a resource that can be developed and grown. This makes sense because ongoing life experiences inform our self-understanding and capabilities to adapt and bounce back from adversities.

The list of constructs to be considered in our school board project (summarized in Chapter 2 of this volume) was extensive. I proposed we include mattering because I had seen its impact in our research on students transitioning to university. Students without a sense of mattering do not thrive and typically remain disengaged. The mattering concept also seemed to resonate with educators at the school board who were familiar with the literature and case examples showing how one caring adult, often a teacher, can have an enormous positive impact on a struggling student.

Strong support for including mattering came from a group of experienced school principals who were part of the school board project. They evaluated 15 psychological constructs under consideration (e.g., growth mindset, self-compassion, emotion regulation) and ranked them in their relevance to children. The feedback we received was clear. They agreed unanimously that mattering was the most relevant construct under consideration. It resonates and is relevant to students and also teachers, parents, and the community. I had seen mattering in action at our local elementary school, where it had been put into practice by the amazing leader of the school, Principal Peggy Morrison, and her teaching staff.

Shortly thereafter, I realized there was an enormous disconnect between the principals' feedback and the psychological research literature on resilience. Our initial search revealed no published research studies evaluating the role of mattering in resilience. This was shocking and demonstrated to me from another perspective that the research literature on mattering is plagued by enormous gaps.

In light of these observations, this chapter considers at length the role of mattering in resilience and adaptability. It reflects the core premise that mattering is arguably the psychological construct of greatest relevance in relational approaches to resilience and adaptability. Mattering is essential in coping with adversity and challenges and doing so in adaptive ways.

Conversely, when young people express that they are not coping and are consumed by helplessness and inertia, it may reflect a feeling of being insignificant, irrelevant, and ineffective.

This chapter begins by revisiting perhaps the most famous longitudinal study of resilience in children and adolescents because of the role that mattering played in this seminal investigation. The analysis then shifts to a discussion of how mattering relates to resilience and why mattering must become a much greater focus in research, theory, and practical applications pertaining to resilience and adaptability. The final main section of this chapter summarizes relevant research, including some results from our resilience project.

THE RELEVANCE OF MATTERING IN THE FAMOUS KAUAI LONGITUDINAL STUDY OF RESILIENCE

The Kauai Longitudinal Study led by Emmy Werner was the first to study children from birth through midlife (Werner & Smith, 1982). It is summarized retrospectively in Werner (2000). Werner and Smith (1982) studied a cohort of 698 children born in Hawaii on the island of Kauai in 1955, about 14 years after the bombing of Pearl Harbor. A team of investigators assessed these children as 1-year-olds and followed up when they reached ages 2, 10, 18, 32, and 40. These particular ages were selected because they coincide with key stages in the life cycle that usually involve transitions.

About three in 10 participants in the Werner and Smith (1982) study were raised in financially impoverished families. Children who experience poverty and inequities typically face innumerable risks because these living conditions are strongly associated with many other risk factors. Werner and Smith (2001) noted that children raised in poverty in their sample often were distinguished by having to contend with psychosocial stressors (e.g., divorce of parents and family conflict) and a range of other stressors and challenges (e.g., perinatal complications).

There is no denying the stress and strain on children who are faced with living in financial poverty and associated inequities. It becomes much worse when inequities exist at the psychological level as well. There is a much greater risk for children who are impoverished psychologically and disadvantaged because they feel they do not matter to the people in their lives.

One clear finding reported by Werner and Smith (1992) is that two thirds of the children who experienced four or more risk factors by 2 years of age had behavioral or learning difficulties when assessed at 10. Moreover, by the age of 18, they often had significant issues in terms of delinquency or mental health problems. However, most striking was the realization that one out of three children defied the odds and became healthy, competent, and caring adults. What factors distinguished these children?

Werner and Smith (1992) strongly emphasized the role of relational factors. They observed that among the many contributing factors, one vital key element was having at least one warm, competent, and emotionally sensitive person within the family who was attentive and attuned to the individual needs of the child.

These people fit the description of optimal parenting for mattering discussed in Chapter 7 of this volume. Werner and Smith (1992) noted that this nurturance often came from relatives in the extended family, such as grandparents or aunts and uncles. They further noted that the girls deemed resilient came from families that provided consistent support, and this support was similar to what was later identified as autonomy support. Autonomy support is highly beneficial in psychological development (Ryan et al., 2006). The boys in the study by Werner and Smith (1992) seemed to benefit from living in homes with clear structures and expectations.

Emphasis was also placed on the important support and nurturance provided by people in the community. This could be an adult in the community or teachers who fit the description of caring adults who could be counted on during difficult times. In many respects, Werner and Smith (1982) identified people with many of the same attributes and tendencies as adults in established relationships with children characterized by mutual mattering.

Although the power of mattering was being harnessed and fueling resilience, mattering was not explicitly mentioned or identified in published accounts of this project, partly because the term did not exist for most of the data collection period. Early research on mattering had a low profile for many years.

However, this all changed in 1980 when Emmy Werner participated in a National Institute of Mental Health conference along with Morris Rosenberg and other innovative leaders (e.g., Albert Bandura). It is worth revisiting her observation in 1980 about her groundbreaking longitudinal study. According to the conference proceedings published a year later, Werner closed the conference by stating,

> The most optimistic thing we have seen in our study is that, even under adverse circumstances, change is possible if the older child or adolescent encounters new experiences with people who give meaning to his life and who tell him that he matters. (Moore, 1981, p. 140)

This important observation about the role of mattering in resilience by a luminary in resilience research is unknown to most resilience researchers.

I was unaware of this remarkable conclusion by Emmy Werner until I came across it about 5 years ago.

Although, to my knowledge, Werner never again made an explicit reference to mattering, the essence of mattering is reflected throughout her subsequent work on the role of caring others. For instance, Werner and Johnson (2004) compared the lives of children who did or did not adapt well to having a parent with alcoholism. They examined the lives of these children, including how they fared in adulthood. Many participants thrived because they had not just one adult but many caring adults in their lives, including other family members (i.e., caring siblings, grandparents, aunts, and uncles) and caring people in the community. Werner and Smith (2001) emphasized that these caring adults did not attempt to remove children from stress and adversity, including adversities such as having a parent with alcoholism. Instead, they helped them through challenges that proved instrumental in building competence and confidence. These young people also built a lasting sense of work rooted in the security of having close relationships with people invested in their well-being and development.

Parenthetically, it needs to be noted that the focus in this chapter is mostly on the resilience of the individual child. However, resilience is also a family matter, and families vary in their resilience. Froma Walsh (2016) considered the nature of family resilience from a conceptual and empirical perspective. Family resilience is especially required in response to stressors and significant transitions, and it was especially needed during the COVID-19 pandemic and is still needed postpandemic. Readers interested in learning more about family resilience will be well-served by reading a new contemporary analysis of family resilience during the pandemic by Prime and colleagues (2023). There is a clear role for mattering in family resilience. Indeed, Prime et al. briefly highlighted the potential role of mattering and caring relationships in family resilience. The discussion earlier in this book on family processes and the development of mattering has implications for building individual resilience in children and family resilience. Children from families distinguished by mattering mutuality are likely being raised in resilient families. If so, their capacity to bounce back and adapt should be strong and sustained.

In this chapter, I revisit our school board project in terms of some of our guiding objectives and conceptual views and the results that emerged. First, however, given that research and theory on mattering in resilience are still in short supply in the published psychological literature, perhaps there is a need to make a strong case to convince future investigators. Next, I list the reasons I feel a greater focus on resilience is imperative. A few reasons are elaborated on. If these reasons fall short for some readers who are still unconvinced, I urge them to reconsider the conclusion reached by Emmy Werner in her seminal work (Werner & Smith, 1982). This is sound advice even for those readers who recognize why research on mattering and resilience is urgently needed.

RESILIENCE AND ADAPTABILITY: SO WHY STUDY MATTERING ANYWAY?

This chapter is an extended analysis of mattering and resilience first introduced in an article in which we argued strongly for emphasizing interpersonal resilience as a specific form of resilience (Flett et al., 2015). A particular emphasis in this initial article was the ability of children and adolescents to bounce back from maltreatment. These themes and observations were then continued in a subsequent chapter (Flett, 2018b), in which it was proposed that a focus on mattering and resilience should be a key part of the foundation of a mentally healthy school filled with resilient and adaptable students. The chapter goes considerably beyond previous work in multiple respects.

There are many valid ways of conceptualizing resilience. Bonanno and Diminich (2013) distinguished between what they referred to as minimal-impact resilience and emergent resilience. *Minimal-impact resilience* involves bouncing back from the experience of acute life events typically involving loss or trauma that are experienced as "isolated stressors in an otherwise normative or noncaustic environment" (Bonanno & Diminich, 2013, p. 380). Bonanno and Diminich noted that this type of situation typically results in focused and proscribed coping efforts to address a unique event. In contrast, *emergent resilience* is required to address chronic stress. The term refers to being resilient when coping with chronic and pervasive life challenges, such as the enduring stress that accompanies such situations as living with poverty, parental mental illness, or natural disasters. These chronic stressful life situations "tend to produce more enduring patterns of variability and tend to lead to more enduring changes in a wide range of psychological and physiological functions" (Bonanno & Diminich, 2013, p. 380). The premise of this chapter is that mattering is a key factor that has a role to play in both minimal-impact and emergent resilience. Just as emergent resilience is matched with long-term ongoing stress, mattering that is deeply ingrained and persists over time is particularly needed to address chronic stress.

Various theorists have emphasized the need to consider resilience from a relational perspective (e.g., Cacioppo et al., 2011). This emphasis on interpersonally based resilience fits well with observations that resilience should be conceptualized as a multidimensional construct (see Luthar et al., 2000). Mattering as a psychosocial construct is central to developing interpersonal resilience. It is difficult to imagine a child developing strong interpersonal resilience without the confidence and sense of efficacy that comes from knowing that you matter to others.

Viewed from a resilience perspective, a focus on mattering qualifies past conclusions. For instance, Kim and Cicchetti (2003) concluded that for maltreated children, self-system processes and personality are more central to resilience outcomes, and relationship factors are less important to their resilience. However, this view of the self-system and affect does not reflect mattering as a potentially powerful psychosocial source of worth (and self-worth if internalized). Mattering ties together the self-system and relationship factors, and the maltreated child who is able to gain and retain a sense of mattering is more resilient in a way that represents an enormous advantage over the maltreated child without a sense of mattering ever being established. The maltreated child with a feeling of mattering should be more resilient and adaptable and also have a self-orientation that includes social self-efficacy and self-esteem. These characteristics are especially likely if mattering was generated, at least partly, by engaging in activities focused on adding value to others.

PATHWAYS FROM MATTERING TO RESILIENCE

There are myriad ways that mattering can contribute to a child's resilience. First, mattering as a feeling can boost resilience through its link with positive affect and other positive feelings. We saw in Chapter 8 that mattering is linked with happiness and positive affect in adolescents. This is important to keep in mind, given longitudinal evidence showing that the experience of positive affect predicts increases in resilience (Gilchrist et al., 2023). The positive affect that results from feelings of mattering should result in an expansion and growth of a positive sense of self and heightened levels of self-confidence, self-efficacy, and enhanced motivation that can boost the capacity to be resilient and adaptable as needed. This contention is speculative, but it is worth revisiting adolescent descriptions of what mattering feels like (see Proulx, 2023). A theme throughout their accounts is how the feeling of mattering elevates and enhances the growth of the self. In one prototypical example, one adolescent remarked,

> When people acknowledge and recognize your efforts by telling you that you did a good or even a great job on something and that you matter, it can be

> incredibly motivating, boosting your confidence and making you believe in yourself even more. (Bellows, 2023)

Young people with a sense of mattering are resilient, partly because they are able to maintain and restore positive affect after experiencing disappointments and upsets. This was established in the research reported by Hamby et al. (2020). They included in their research a measure of restoring positive affect laden with items such as "I can cheer myself up after a bad day." Mattering was substantially correlated with this measure ($r = .47$) in their sample of 440 youth. It is such findings that point to the potential power of mattering.

Mattering also supports resilience because the feeling of mattering carried by young people helps them to maintain a sense of connection to others even when they may be physically quite far away. It is a resource that can help ease adjusting to a transition. It has been noted that caring adults can encourage adolescent girls to pursue opportunities that can lead to having a better life but require them to cope with disconnections (Debold et al., 1999). Physical separation could pose a threat to a sense of connection, but this is less problematic for young people who carry the mattering feeling with them. Mattering is similar to a secure attachment style in providing comfort and strength when isolated.

Mattering may also boost resilience through its association with positive attributes such as endurance, planfulness, positive future outlook, impulse control, and low engagement in risky behavior (Hamby et al., 2020; Somers et al., 2022). It boosts the ability to adjust and bounce back through its link with other attributes such as social self-efficacy and self-esteem.

Another pathway that links mattering with resilience and adaptability is suggested by Rosenberg's cogent and insightful description of how high self-esteem adolescents address the major problem of adolescence—protecting against threats to self-esteem and finding ways to enhance their sense of worth (Moore, 1981). Rosenberg summarized his self-esteem research by stating that high self-esteem adolescents learn to be selective regarding what information they attend to and how they interpret it. According to Rosenberg, they protect themselves through selection introjection, selective causal attribution, and selective social comparison. In short, they limit their exposure to painful feedback and harmful suggestions and are less prone to be hard on themselves. It should similarly be the case that youth with high levels of mattering to others will be selective and use these same tendencies in ways that should foster resilience and adaptability.

Resilience can also be built through what can be absorbed and learned from caring adults who foster feelings of mattering. Bandura (2001) discussed the Werner and Smith (1982) research he first heard about in 1980, summarizing his view on having caring adults as follows:

> A critical factor is the development of a stable social bond to a competent, caring adult. Such caregivers offer emotional support and guidance. They promote meaningful values and standards. They model constructive styles of coping and create opportunities for mastery experiences. (Bandura, 2001, p. 18)

All these attributes can foster resilience in young people who have caring adults. Bandura (2001) also called for an agentic view of young people's resilience. They can select and shape situations and interactions to build their efficacy and capability to rebound from adversity. Agentic resilience is built through being proactive and engaging in actions that result in reward and a growing sense of mastery and capacity to overcome setbacks and challenges. This perspective fits well with the ability of young people to build resilience through engaging in efforts to add value to others.

The hypothesized role of mattering in enhancing resilience through growing and enhancing the self justifies an increased research focus on mattering and resilience. Exhibit 9.1 lists 10 additional reasons there needs to be an emphasis on mattering in resilience research.

The first reason introduces a new theme that has not yet been included in the conversation about how and why anti-mattering is so destructive. We regard experiences that have been classified as anti-mattering as part of the stress experience for young people on top of all their other stressors. Young people with a stable sense of mattering are in the best position to withstand regular exposure to this type of stress. It is considerably worse for the young person with low or no resilience who feels targeted as part of their broader experience of being marginalized and minimized by others.

It is possible to identify many narrative accounts of anti-mattering experiences that induce stress and trauma. Our empirical evidence of anti-mattering as a form of stress comes from new unpublished research with an extended version of the Inventory of Negative Social Interactions (INSI) developed originally by Lakey and colleagues (1994). This 40-item inventory asks respondents to rate the frequency of adversities directed at the self by others. Sample items inquire about how often other people have done such things as "talked down to you," "put you down for what you believe," and "believed a rumor about you." We supplemented the original scale by adding anti-mattering experiences such as "Treated you like you were invisible," "Seemed disinterested in what you had to say," and "Made you feel like you don't matter." Initial work in a university sample of about 300 participants confirmed that scores on these items were robustly correlated with total scores

EXHIBIT 9.1. Reasons to Focus on Mattering in Resilience and Adaptability

1. Adversities and anti-mattering experiences represent part of the stress experience for many young people, so a stable sense of mattering provides an essential buffer.
2. Schlossberg (1981, 1989) noted that much of our stress is due to life transitions. In new and uncertain situations, we naturally feel insignificant and invisible (see Flett & Zangeneh, 2020). But those who feel like they matter know they will be eventually seen and heard, and they are better positioned to manage and work through these feelings.
3. Mattering is powerful. Elliott and colleagues (2005) described mattering "as a powerful motivator that resides deep within the self-concept; it is the beginning of a chain of potency that exerts a profound influence on other dimensions of the self, and ultimately behavior" (p. 235). Mattering is especially powerful in fostering the capacity to adaptively disengage and distance the self from criticisms and various forms of mistreatment.
4. Mattering is highly resonant for most people because they know how it feels, and they understand its potential to lift up young people as well as themselves. Its resonance is one of the many reasons that mattering has enormous knowledge mobilization potential.
5. Mattering is modifiable and can be grown and developed. Feelings of not mattering can be controlled and reduced, if not eliminated.
6. Mattering is often accompanied by feelings of empowerment and personal control that can be self-generated through efforts to add value to others and make a difference.
7. The scope and potential of mattering are broad because mattering is felt and grown across multiple life roles and contexts (e.g., home, school, work, community).
8. The feeling of mattering and engaging with and interacting with others reduces self-focus and is a welcome distraction from worry, rumination, and bouts of self-doubt.
9. Mattering promotes hopeful engagement and proactively addressing problems and challenges instead of avoiding them.
10. Mattering connects us with people and builds attachments that provide us with a sense of comfort and safety that makes us less likely to feel isolated and lonely when we are alone.

on the 40-item INSI. Moreover, total scores on this four-item subscale are substantially correlated ($r = .51$) with levels of anti-mattering.

But what about adolescents when it comes to this type of stress? We began our school board project with pilot work centered on a 47-item stress measure labeled "Student Life Experiences." This survey was created after reviewing stressors listed on other measures such as the Inventory of High School Students' Recent Life Experiences (see Kohn & Milrose, 1993). This measure included one item we added to assess stress in the form of being made to feel like you do not matter. Middle and high school students made four-point ratings (0 to 3) of the extent to which each experience was a part of their lives over the previous month. The four response options were as follows: 0 (*never or not usually part of my life*), 1 (*sometimes part of my life*), 2 (*very much part of my life*), and 3 (*always or almost always part of my life*).

A factor analysis of the 43 items yielded multiple factors, including one factor that contained the item assessing anti-mattering experiences. The items composing this factor formed a "social adversity" factor. These items are shown in Table 9.1.

These items reflect various adverse social experiences faced by our respondents. Collectively, these adverse experiences undermined, at least to some degree, the sense of worth or value of most young people. Several experiences would likely involve public interactions that could lead to feelings of humiliation. The pattern of responses across scale items reflects the fact that being made to feel like you do not matter often co-occurs with cyberbullying and being demeaned online, along with other forms of being bullied. It is also related to being pressured by classmates or friends and the experience of social rejection.

The participants in this study also completed brief two-item measures of mattering and self-esteem and one anti-mattering scale item. The correlations in Table 9.2 reflect how adolescents with low self-esteem and feelings of not mattering to others are more likely to report that stressors are also part of their lives. As expected, being made to feel like you do not matter as a form of stress was correlated strongly with the overall self-reported level of the anti-mattering feeling ($r = .55$). Many additional troubling themes are represented as stressors in Table 9.2. Anti-mattering as a feeling was associated with a perception of having no one to get help from ($r = .43$). Other correlates include feelings of loneliness and not belonging.

Why might anti-mattering add to these feelings? One possibility is having a life marred by having people who do not listen to you. We measured this as a source of stress and found that this stress theme was also associated significantly with self-reported levels of anti-mattering ($r = .35$). However,

TABLE 9.1. Items and Factor Loadings for a Social Adversity Factor

Item	Loading
Not belonging or fitting in at school	.44
Being made to feel bad about yourself online	.72
Being bullied	.71
Being teased	.58
Being pressured by classmates or friends	.41
Being made to feel like you do not matter	.45
Being rejected by somebody	.39
Finding out bad things are being said about you online	.66

TABLE 9.2. Correlations Between Stressors and Mattering, Anti-Mattering, and Self-Esteem

Stressor	Mattering	Anti-mattering	Self-esteem
Being let down by a friend	−.20	.31	−.22
Feeling of not belonging or fitting in at school	−.44	.44	−.39
Being made to feel bad online	−.24	.25	−.18
Feeling lonely or not connected to others	−.32	.44	−.32
Being bullied	−.26	.30	−.22
Being teased	−.21	.36	−.20
Having people who do not listen to you	−.21	.35	−.24
Having to keep feelings inside or hidden	−.32	.53	−.43
Being made to feel like you do not matter	−.37	.55	−.43
Being rejected by somebody	−.20	.36	−.19
Having bad things said about you online	−.23	.30	−.21
Not being as popular as you would like	−.24	.43	−.25
Having no one to get help from	−.25	.43	−.25
Feeling like you have to be perfect	−.21	.50	−.29
Being worried or uncertain about your future	−.13	.30	−.13

Note. *N*s vary but are typically 313 or greater. Correlations that exceed .18 or −.18 are significant at $p < .01$ or greater.

as discussed by Tucker and colleagues (2010), being listened to is central to the feeling of mattering. The feeling of being invisible tends to be predominant in accounts of people who feel like they do not matter to others, but the feeling of not being heard is just as impactful, which, when taken to the extreme, is in the form of the cognition "no one is listening to me." Deep connection means deep listening when people mutually matter to each other.

Adolescents with low levels of mattering are under considerable stress. This conclusion is supported by research. The study by Hill and Madigan (2022) described earlier in this book examined mattering, anti-mattering, perfectionistic tendencies, and academic stress in 350 gifted students from the United Kingdom. Academic stress was measured with three items pertaining to the present school term. Items focused specifically on academic stress related to grades and implications for the future—for example, "I am worrying a great deal about the effect this term will have on my future." Analyses showed there was a small but significant negative association between academic stress and mattering assessed by the General Mattering Scale ($r = -.12$) and a considerably stronger positive association between academic stress and anti-mattering as assessed by the Anti-Mattering Scale ($r = .28$).

THE ROLE OF MATTERING IN ADAPTING TO THE STRESS OF TRANSITIONS

The second theme represented in Table 9.1 involves transitions. Children and adolescents must also contend with the stress inherent in life transitions. The life upheaval and uncertainty make most transitions unpleasant. However, transitions should have less impact on young people who feel relatively secure and know that they matter to significant others. In addition to being a main contributor to research and theory on mattering, Nancy Schlossberg is more broadly known for her work on adapting to transitions. Schlossberg (1989) signaled the relevance of mattering in transitions when she observed,

> My work on transitions—events or nonevents that alter our lives—convinced me that people in transition often feel marginal and that they do not matter. Whether we are entering first grade or college, getting married, or retiring, we are concerned about our new roles. We wonder, will we belong? Will we matter? (p. 1)

Concerns about mattering are less likely to pose a problem for the young person with an internalized and stable sense of mattering to others. The child or adolescent with this resource has the image of caring people to call on in uncertain new situations when they do not have the comfort of being in the physical presence of those people, but they have the sense of worth and confidence that comes from having these people in their lives.

MATTERING AND ADAPTIVE DISENGAGEMENT

Mattering can strengthen the self so that resilience includes a capacity for *adaptive disengagement* (Leitner et al., 2014), the tendency to distance ourselves emotionally or physically. We (Flett et al., 2015) identified adaptive disengagement as a core facet of interpersonal resilience, and this theme is reflected in the interpersonal resilience component of the multidomain resilience inventory described later.

Mattering should be linked with interpersonal resilience and a psychosocial resource in general but should also be associated with less sensitivity to criticism and greater adaptive disengagement so that negativity does not have a lasting impact on the child or adolescent's worth. In terms of developmental experiences, mattering likely emerges in mutually caring relationships with adults and siblings who provide models of how not to let emotions be ruled by the harsh comments and actions of others. The young person without a sense of mattering will, in essence, lack a "deflector shield" and be vulnerable to harsh comments and unfair treatment. Some people naturally minimize the importance of being treated badly, but this capacity is not evident among young people with low interpersonal resilience who are vulnerable to hurt and humiliation.

OTHER CHARACTERISTICS OF MATTERING THAT FOSTER ADAPTABILITY AND RESILIENCE

Resilience and adaptability are most likely to be found among self-aware people with a strong sense of self. Young people with a strong feeling of mattering to others tend to have a sense of empowerment and self-efficacy. They also have a sense of mastery, and if they have internalized mattering so that they matter to themselves, they will have a sense of determination and persistence that reflects their sense of hope, optimism, and value to themselves. My colleagues and I (Flett et al., 2015) observed in a discussion of mattering as a form of interpersonal resilience that internalizing mattering into a sense of mattering to oneself is vital to being resilient and adaptable. Conversely, "People who maintain an identity reflecting the theme, 'I don't matter' will not proactively address stressors and, in all likelihood, will have negligible levels of self-care" (Flett et al., 2015, p. 20).

RESEARCH ON MATTERING IN RESILIENCE AND ADAPTABILITY

The next section is an overview of findings from our research project. Published research on resilience among young people is almost nonexistent. However, the main exception is our first study on mattering among students in China. We (Flett et al., 2014) evaluated feelings of mattering and academic buoyancy in 232 adolescents from advanced and nonadvanced high schools in China. Academic buoyancy and general mattering were modestly associated in the overall sample, but the association was more robust among the students in an advanced high school. Perhaps academic resilience and evaluated mattering contributed to their typical tendency to have a comparatively advanced academic performance.

Our project took a multidomain approach when conceptualizing and assessing resilience. The need and potential benefits of a multidomain approach were introduced in one of our earliest studies of students from China. We (Flett et al., 2014) proposed that there is a need to consider individual differences in resilience not only in terms of general emotional resilience but also in terms of an achievement-based or goal-related form of resilience (i.e., bouncing back from achievement setbacks) and an interpersonal resilience that can be invoked after experiencing challenging interpersonal tests and problematic interpersonal situations.

The 20-item inventory we used in our school board project consisted of a five-item adaptability scale and a 15-item multidomain resilience scale with three factors (i.e., emotional, academic, and interpersonal resilience). The adaptability scale items were adapted from those found in an existing measure of adaptability (see Martin et al., 2012). Creating our resilience subscales was necessary because a brief multidomain self-report measure aligned with our objectives did not exist. Academic resilience items were derived from an established measure of academic buoyancy (see Martin & Marsh, 2008). We generated the emotional resilience subscale items and adapted some previously included in the broad school board survey measure. The five interpersonal resilience items were developed to reflect some of the interpersonal resilience facets outlined in Flett et al. (2015).

Confirmatory factor analyses of the items composing the resilience measure when administered to the middle and high school students in our pilot sample established that the proposed factors exist in a meaningful way as clearly identifiable and meaningful factors, distinguishable despite scores across the four subscales being highly intercorrelated. Items in the 20-item inventory emphasize self-perceptions of the ability to bounce back. There is also an emphasis on effectively managing negative affect related to academic and interpersonal stress. Representative sample items are in Exhibit 9.2.

The results from our school board project support the initial decision to include a primary emphasis on mattering. These results are reported here

EXHIBIT 9.2. Scale Items Reflecting Adaptability and Domains of Resilience

Adaptability

I am able to think through my options to help me in a new situation.

I am able to change how I do things when I have to.

Emotional Resilience

I don't let bad feelings get me down for very long.

When I am feeling sad or angry, I find ways to make myself feel better.

Academic Resilience

I don't less stress at school bother me for too long.

I don't let setbacks and problems at school impact my goals.

Interpersonal Resilience

When other people criticize me, I don't think about it for too long.

If someone treats me badly, I won't let them impact my goals.

in detail for the first time. The measure we developed had 20 items in total. There were four five-item subscales tapping three resilience domains (i.e., academic, interpersonal, and emotional) and perceived adaptability.

The participants in our pilot sample from the school board project were 350 students in Grades 7, 8, or 9. They completed the combined measure of resilience and adaptability. This self-report measure was accompanied by brief two-item measures of self-esteem (i.e., items from the Rosenberg Self-Esteem Scale) and mattering (e.g., "I feel like I matter to other people," "I feel like I am important to other people").

The correlational results from the school board project are depicted in Table 9.3. Significant associations were found except for between mattering and academic resilience in Grade 7. The combined data for the total sample show that the lowest association was between mattering and adaptability. The strongest links were between mattering and emotional and interpersonal resilience.

Further evidence linking mattering with resilience domains was subsequently found in our main study in the school board project, which had two samples—one elementary student sample and one high school student sample. The participants in the first sample were 543 students from six elementary schools. Their mean age was 12.38 years ($SD = 0.66$). The same 20-item multidomain measure was used in this study. Mattering was assessed with two single-item scales that assessed mattering in general (i.e., I feel like I matter to other people) and school mattering (e.g., At this school, I feel like I matter). The correlational results are shown in Table 9.4. The magnitude of the correlations was lower overall than those obtained in the pilot phase. However, once again, mattering in general and mattering in school were associated with higher levels of resilience and adaptability.

Stronger results were obtained from the participants in the high school sample that participated in the school board project. Table 9.4 shows the

TABLE 9.3. Correlations Between Mattering and Measures of Resilience, Adaptability, and Stress

Initial sample (Grade 7–9)	Mattering (Grade 7)	Mattering (Grade 8)	Mattering (Grade 9)	Mattering (total)
Academic resilience	.18	.55**	.45**	.41**
Interpersonal resilience	.41**	.67**	.44**	.47**
Emotional resilience	.53**	.61**	.48**	.50**
Adaptability	.33**	.47**	.40**	.38**

Note. $N = 350$ (initial sample), including 79 students in grade 7, 76 students in Grade 8, and 149 students in Grade 9.
**$p < .01$.

TABLE 9.4. Correlations Between Mattering and Resilience Project Measures in Children

Type of resilience	Mattering (general)	Mattering (school)
Academic resilience	.22**	.25**
Interpersonal resilience	.28**	.24**
Emotional resilience	.27**	.25**
Adaptability	.23**	.25**

Note. $N = 543$ elementary school students.
$^{**}p < .01$.

TABLE 9.5. Correlations With Mattering in High School Students

Type of resilience	Mattering (total)	Mattering (no IEP)	Mattering (IEP)
Academic resilience	.35	.36	.38
Interpersonal resilience	.37	.37	.39
Emotional resilience	.43	.41	.47
Adaptability	.32	.30	.38

Note. Correlations of .21 or greater are significant at $^{**}p < .01$ or greater. $N = 1{,}261$ (total sample), including 904 students without an IEP (Individual Education Plan) and 306 students with an IEP.

results for mattering in general and mattering in school. The results are shown for the total sample, the 904 high school students without an Individual Education Plan (IEP), and the 306 students with an IEP. Typically, an IEP is required for students with specific learning and/or behavioral challenges. Once again, mattering was linked with all resilience domains and adaptability for students with or without an IEP.

These results consistently show that elevated levels of mattering in middle and high school students are associated with resilience and adaptability. Elliott (2009) concluded that having even one person who gives someone special attention to a young person is protective, but "the higher the level of mattering across all possible sources, the more secure the self-concept" (p. 19). One implication of our findings is that mattering is also particularly beneficial when accompanied by a capacity to be adaptable and resilient that cuts across multiple life domains.

MATTERING PROMOTION IN PROGRAMS PROMOTING RESILIENCE AND ADAPTABILITY

Much more research is needed, but resilience programs that explicitly focus on mattering should have a discernible positive impact, especially on those young people with a strong but unmet need to matter to others. Consideration should be given to the messaging that accompanies these programs. When the program is introduced, it is an opportunity to tell students that the initiative reflects the fact that the well-being of students is important and people care about them.

One possibility is to add a focus on mattering to existing programs. Consider, for instance, a prevention program known as the RALLY project (Malti & Noam, 2008). RALLY is an acronym that represents "Responsive Advocacy for Life and Learning in Youth." This program to build resilience is unlike most others in that it is centered on the role of caring and nurturing relationships with a particular emphasis on the teacher's role in fostering the strengths and capabilities of their students. A key element of this program is that students can develop and benefit from people who essentially assume the role of caring mentors. Specific training in showing and communicating mattering could be part of the mentoring experience.

Unfortunately, other researchers have seldom cited this impressive program and the research findings emerging from Malti and Noam's (2008) work. The program is largely unknown and has had limited impact. This is not uncommon among potentially impactful programs due to limited implementation beyond the original project, despite the extensive work and dedication of the researchers leading it.

SUMMARY

In summary, this chapter presented the case for research and theory on mattering and resilience, including the key observation from Emmy Werner that having at least one supportive family member led to greater resilience in children (Werner & Smith, 1982). This chapter reflects an extended view of resilience that includes distinguishing between resilience (i.e., bouncing back) and adaptability (i.e., adjusting to the circumstances) and resilience having distinct domains (i.e., emotional, academic, and interpersonal resilience). Mattering was associated with higher adaptability and greater resilience across the three domains of resilience, suggesting that children and adolescents with a feeling of mattering have broad capabilities to respond to challenges.

Relevant research findings were also summarized to illustrate that feelings of not mattering can be part of the daily stress experiences of young people. However, the good news is that there is considerable evidence from our project and the work of other investigators that supports the reasonable notion that young people who know they matter and that people care about them should have a form of protection that is evident in terms of adaptability and resilience.

I conclude this chapter by discussing this work within the context of the influential resilience work by Ann Masten, whose work is based on the theme that resilience is essentially "ordinary magic" (Masten, 2014, p. 7). In this context, ordinary magic refers to Masten's premise that the capacity to overcome adversity is not rare, and most young people can bounce back and adapt through common processes and everyday experiences. While this is undoubtedly the case, this chapter is based on the premise that mattering has its own magical properties that amount to "extraordinary magic" when it comes to building resilience and adaptability. There is a special and unique role for mattering in developing resilience and adaptability, and we need to tap into its power and potential.

10 SOCIAL MEDIA USE AND THE NEED TO MATTER

The quote "It was the best of times, it was the worst of times" could be an apt description of the social media experiences of youth. Charles Dickens (1859/2003) wrote this line as a classic introduction to his famous novel *A Tale of Two Cities*, but today, it can reflect the social media experiences of young people. It is indeed a tale of two online social worlds in that social media use can have positive impacts when meaningful connections are established; however, there can be equally strong negative impacts and consequences for young people.

This chapter considers mattering and its relevance to social media use by young people. Why focus on social media use? First, accessing and being exposed to social media takes up a substantial proportion of the daily lives of young people. There have been some alarming reports about how much time young people spend on social media in terms of typical daily use. It has been proposed that no more than 2 hours per day is a key guideline (Sampasa-Kanyinga et al., 2019), but actual use is often much higher, up to 3 to 5 hours per day or more, including for adolescents engaged in high-risk behavior (see Vente et al., 2020). Excessive use has been seen as a strong

https://doi.org/10.1037/0000449-011
Mattering as a Core Need in Children and Adolescents: Theoretical, Clinical, and Research Perspectives, by G. L. Flett

contributor to the prevalence and severity of mental health difficulties experienced by adolescents, especially adolescent girls. Numerous studies have confirmed these concerns (see Beeres et al., 2021; Riehm et al., 2019; Vente et al., 2020). Heavy social media use among adolescents has been implicated in more severe distress (see Mougharbel et al., 2023). Social media is part of a combination known as "the triple" among adolescents because it tends to be accompanied at high levels by stress and sleep problems (Daniels et al., 2021).

The level of concern about the extent and impact of social media was high enough for the U.S. Surgeon General, Dr. Vivek Murthy, to issue his "Social Media and Youth Mental Health" advisory (Office of the Surgeon General, 2023). Key themes in this advisory include that as many as one third of young people report that they use social media almost constantly, and social media presents a meaningful risk of harm to youth, though it also provides some benefits.

The advisory from the U.S. Surgeon General coincided with a similar advisory issued earlier in the same month by the American Psychological Association. The "Health Advisory on Social Media Use in Adolescence" (American Psychological Association, 2023) recognized when social media use is positive and negative. The potential for distress was recognized in the emphasis on exposure to cyberhate and the need to safeguard young people who are members of marginalized groups.

More recently, concerns about social media use among adolescents have been examined in a best-selling book titled The Anxious Generation (Haidt, 2024). This book makes the case that excessive social media use is largely responsible for the mental health issues experienced by young people. Haidt (2024) concluded that social media exposure is particularly harmful to girls and is exacting a toll on their mental health. He focused on four specific harms—social deprivation, sleep deprivation, attention fragmentation, and addiction.

Accounts that link social media use among young people with youth suicide stand as clear illustrations of the need to be concerned and proactive. Excessive social media among youth has been linked to suicide ideation and suicidal behavior (see Twenge et al., 2018). It was learned from bereaved parents who contributed to a psychological autopsy analysis of social media use by their children who died by suicide that being shamed and bullied online was implicated in their deaths (see Balt et al., 2023). The negative impacts of social media were highly evident during the U.S. Senate hearings in January 2024 (Fung & Duffy, 2024; U.S. Senate Committee on the Judiciary, 2024). These hearings included emotional accounts from bereaved parents who demanded explanations and apologies from the chief executive officers of the largest social media companies in attendance at these hearings.

The second reason for focusing on social media use is that if the need to matter is as ubiquitous as has been proposed, it should be a relevant need that underscores the social media use of youth in general and certain youth in particular. Accordingly, in this chapter, I propose that the need to matter to others is a key motivator for many young people who heavily access social media. I also consider the vulnerability of the young person with an unmet need to matter who is spending excessive time on social media. If the need to matter applies to everyone, it follows that it is part of the picture for young people obsessively engaged with social media. It is generally acknowledged that low and vulnerable self-worth is linked with excessive social media use among young people, so it follows that a construct like mattering, which captures a key element of social self-worth, should be especially pertinent to the use of social media.

The analysis provided here illustrates how essential it is to expand the mattering construct to include elements such as anti-mattering and the fear of not mattering to others. The feelings and fears of not mattering likely play a key role in engaging with social media and escalating excessive use into an addiction to social media.

One primary concern is that the feeling of mattering for some young people will depend on social media feedback. Research has established that there are measurable individual differences in the tendency for self-worth to depend on social media feedback (see Sabik et al., 2020). Current research has, thus far, considered self-worth dependency in terms of how social media affects worth framed in terms of levels of self-esteem. A representative scale item from the Self-Worth Dependent on Social Media Scale is "My self-esteem depends on how others respond to my social media posts." This scale item could have just as easily read, "Whether I matter depends on how others respond to my social media posts." It can confidently be predicted that a subset of young people will endorse dysfunctional beliefs and attitudes such as "If others don't pay attention to me online, I don't matter." That is, it is certain that many youth based their self-worth online on getting attention and a sense of mattering and importance via online interactions.

Unfortunately, an emphasis on feelings of mattering versus not mattering has not been part of core conversations about social media and excessive smartphone use. This needs to change. The extent of their need to matter must become a key part of any meaningful conversation about adolescents' use of social media. A focus on mattering is, at present, a mostly untraveled route for researchers seeking to arrive at a much greater understanding of young people and their use of social media.

One illustration of the relevance of mattering comes from a close inspection of a measure developed to assess online social media experiences. The positive social experiences subscale of the Online Social Experiences Measure (OSEM; Kent de Grey et al., 2019) is saturated with item content that captures what it feels like to matter via social media. The 20 items in the original subscale include "Members of my online social networks care about me as a person" and "Members of my online social networks show appreciation for what I do." These items fit the definition of mattering, but thus far, the obvious link with mattering has not been noted by researchers in the social media literature.

Unfortunately, in keeping with my earlier claim about the relevance of feelings and fears of not mattering, anti-mattering online is just as relevant, if not more relevant. The 20 items in the OSEM negative social experiences subscale are just as saturated with items tapping anti-mattering and social media. Representative items are "I felt ignored or unimportant because others didn't respond to something I posted online" and "Someone in my online social networks has dismissed my opinion or my beliefs."

The relevance of the need to matter is even more evident when person-centered analyses are provided. Case studies also illustrate the relevance of mattering. Indeed, it is common for young people to get the attention and the sense of being cared about that they crave only online (e.g., D. L. King et al., 2012).

The best rationale for including this chapter is the initial research described later that links mattering with social media use. This research is not extensive, but it represents a bridge to understanding the worlds and experiences of young people. Social media use offers a pathway to support for many young people who feel like they do not matter. However, it can also become highly problematic, especially when young people are engaged in the passive use of social media, which involves frequently viewing social media content but not using it in ways that can build connections and a positive sense of community.

SOCIAL MEDIA USE AND THE NEED TO MATTER

As suggested earlier, given the interpersonal nature of the need to matter to others, it follows that the social media use of many young people is motivated, at least in part, by their unmet need to matter. It has been established in qualitative research with first-year university students that while they seek to belong through in-person interactions, they also seek to belong through social media use (see Berezan et al., 2020; Stebleton et al., 2022). Here, we can be reasonably certain that the need to matter is more directly implicated and that the strong association between feelings of not mattering and loneliness means that many young people have two key unmet psychological needs (i.e., the need to matter and the need for connection), and the use of social media is one route to possibly meeting both. It is certainly a way for one's voice to be heard. Active users of Facebook seeking to belong acknowledge having an impact on other users and realizing, "My opinions matter to other members" (see Berezan et al., 2020, p. 259).

It was mentioned earlier in this book that an excessive need to matter should be found among certain young people with narcissistic tendencies. A dysfunctional need to matter expressed in terms of needy attention seeking seems to be at the heart of how social media combines with narcissism in adolescents who have experienced social rejection. Evidence is accumulating that links the need for attention to social media use among young people. A longitudinal study with two assessment points 1 year apart examined narcissism in 307 Dutch adolescents (see Hawk et al., 2019). This study focused on the key mediators of attention seeking via social media and social media disclosure. Attention seeking was assessed by such items as "I post messages and pictures because I get attention from others" and "I think it is important to get as many 'likes' as possible on my posts." The key finding that emerged from this research is that adolescents characterized jointly by higher levels of trait narcissism and social rejection at Time 1 reported greater attention seeking at Time 2. Attention-seeking needs and tendencies often took the form of inappropriate and excessive self-disclosure online.

The findings of this study closely reflect the behavior and characteristics of an adolescent girl who became known to our family during our daughters' time in high school. We first learned about Susan[1] when we were visited by a distraught mother (a teacher with whom we had become friends) after she inadvertently read a message on her daughter's computer. She learned that one of the girls interacting with her daughter was threatening to attempt suicide. The mother came to us seeking support, partly because educators have a duty to report and intervene when a young person is in peril. To our knowledge, there was no suicide attempt. However, this teacher, now accompanied by one of us, went in person to inform parents they had never met that their daughter was sharing online her intent to attempt suicide. It is my understanding that this adolescent girl received treatment for mental

[1]The details about the individuals in this chapter have been changed to protect their confidentiality.

health issues in subsequent years. She had a substantial profile and social media presence, partly due to excessive social media use and sharing private aspects of her life via social media. Susan developed a distinct penchant for expressing beliefs and opinions that attracted enormous attention and hundreds of online followers. Receiving attention can operate as a form of positive reinforcement. Clearly, at the root of this behavior was a need to be significant, which was apparently not being satisfied at home despite having parents who loved and cared about her.

THE PROS AND CONS OF LOGGING ON FOR THOSE WHO ARE LONGING TO MATTER

The benefits versus costs and consequences of social media use as it relates to the need to matter are considered next. One overarching premise is that the social media experience of young people and associated motives for engaging in social media use should differ depending on the child's history of mattering to others and current feelings of mattering versus not mattering to others. Some evidence indicates that there are individual differences in the extent to which self-worth depends on social media feedback (Sabik et al., 2020). In addition, there are individual differences in social media mindsets: People vary in whether they see themselves as in control of social media versus being controlled by it (A. Y. Lee & Hancock, 2024). Young people with a strong sense of mattering to significant others are relatively immune to having self-worth depend on social media, and they should hold more positive mindsets.

A key focus is to compare young people who are secure in the knowledge that they matter to the people who matter most to them with those who are insecure and do not have a strong sense of mattering to the people they wish would regard them as important. There should be a greater need to connect when young people believe that the key people in their lives do not understand or truly know them. The research described in a subsequent section of this chapter does not consider this key distinction of having a history of mattering versus not mattering to significant others.

In this regard, it can reasonably be extrapolated from the original Rosenberg and McCullough (1981) work that introduced the mattering concept that young people with low perceived mattering to parents are highly prone to excessive use of social media. This core hypothesis has not yet been tested because research has focused on feelings of not mattering in general. Young people who feel unimportant to their parents seek to matter elsewhere through other relationships, which inevitably leads many young people to engage in problematic usage of social media.

Mattering to parents also matters when conflicts inevitably arise. Conflicts between adolescents and their parents, including conflicts related to excessive social media use, are more or less intense depending on preexisting relationships. Mattering to parents among adolescents has been linked with more positive parent–child communication styles and exchanges (see Schmidt et al., 2020). Attempts to monitor and mediate the degree and nature of social media use are better received if the young person knows that these attempts are by someone who truly cares about them, and these feelings are reciprocated. Parents' sense of mattering as parents and parental self-efficacy also come into play in terms of willingness to intervene and being able to positively affect the use of social media.

The Benefits of Social Media Use

Social media is appealing to many because it can provide a sense of connection and community. Ideally, this sense of connection is accompanied by the sense of being valued and cared about in ways that correspond closely to some of the questionnaire items in the OSEM that tap into a positive social experience.

Social media can also provide vital emotional support at key times in a young person's life. There are several examples of young people acknowledging the support they received during challenging times. I have witnessed the support provided to people on X (Twitter) who openly express online the theme "I don't matter to anyone." The caring responses received are heartwarming and can restore a lost sense of faith in others.

Young people can proactively use social media to make a difference and affect key issues in the local community and at national and international levels. My friend and colleague John Morrison, a retired principal, once said that, as a classroom teacher, the project with the greatest positive impact on his students was a campaign launched to heighten awareness and change an issue related to the environment. Numerous accounts of youth activism focused on making a difference are centered on the theme "My voice mattered" and, by extension, "I mattered in a way that shaped my identity and feeling about myself" (e.g., Fullam, 2017; Seo et al., 2014).

Finally, social media can be used to identify opportunities to add value to specific individuals who need it. This becomes immediately evident by surveying various forms of media and seeking out key phrases such as "you matter." Support is frequently provided to people who are struggling and need a reminder that people are rooting for them and that they are not alone, no matter how isolated they feel.

A key emphasis for Haidt (2024) and other authors is that using social media can result in more social connections, but it typically does not address the need for quality social connections. Close and caring relationships are missing in the lives of many young people. Haidt does not mention mattering in his book, but an unmet need to matter signifies that core interpersonal needs are not being met. Clearly, being online does not provide what is ultimately being sought. The benefits of mutually mattering to someone are best experienced in person. Mattering is largely about the quality of relationships and having a bond with people that is a source of comfort and satisfaction.

Potential Costs, Consequences, and Problems of Social Media Use

There are many potential harms of social media use. Although people on X (Twitter) may support people who express that they do not matter, others are chided, and there are an alarming number of messages with the theme "What makes you think you matter? No one cares what you think." The possibility of negative social experiences involving various anti-mattering exchanges has already been mentioned. Vulnerable young people may take it to heart when they are ostracized, excluded, and ignored. It is not rare for these experiences to become amplified and take the form of being cyberbullied in ways that can involve a profound sense of being humiliated or tricked into acting in ways that humiliate oneself.

Robin Kowalski discussed at length the association between feelings of not mattering and being the target of cyberbullying behavior (see Kowalski & Wingate, 2024). Chapter 9 illustrated that stressful experiences of being made to feel you do not matter correlated significantly with reports of being cyberbullied.

Qualitative accounts have focused on how social media use can result in unwanted emotional experiences (e.g., feelings of inferiority, insecurity, hurt, and loneliness) and undesirable behaviors when people become self-critical (see Samari et al., 2022). It is particularly problematic when risky behavior arises out of a need to get the attention of others.

One of the more subtle negative features of social media is that most people, now that we are postpandemic, would endorse the view that positive in-person experiences are preferred; positive online experiences are still relatively superficial. It is not uncommon to acknowledge that even when there are benefits from positive online relationships, people are not always available online or in preferred ways, and being online can simultaneously add to feelings of disconnection. Of course, there are also times when a sweet positive experience turns sour. For example, children and adolescents may become upset when they learn online that their friends attended an event to which they were not invited.

One of the biggest potential drawbacks of social media is how it translates into unwanted social comparisons, and this element is, in all likelihood, considerably more problematic than we realize. It is problematic for any young person to be too invested and engaged in social media use, especially those young people with heightened insecurity and a cognitive preoccupation with social comparison.

SOCIAL COMPARISON AND EXPOSURE TO PEOPLE WITH PERFECT LIVES

There are multiple concerns when it comes to the impact of being constantly exposed online to social comparisons. One danger that has not been discussed thus far goes back to the facets of mattering. It is possible to become so consumed by social comparison that it is reflected in chronically using the mattering element to judge oneself and others and put pressure on oneself. An insecure adolescent can become preoccupied with whether peers are attracting more interest and attention. It is possible to envision a young person with an unmet need to matter who is prone to envy, and, as such, they must get more attention and interest to feel good about themselves. It is also possible that the problem is not the level of attention and interest but that someone else seemingly has a better life and is more special.

Descriptions and accounts of the negative impacts of social media exposure include frequent references to being exposed to social comparisons that can easily make young people feel bad about themselves. It is common for young people to say they had to get away from social media because they just could not stand it anymore and had become increasingly aware that it was affecting their moods and feelings of loneliness. Much research has focused on the impacts of exposure to images of other young people with perfect appearances that must seem unattainable to most. There are also numerous references to being exposed to images of people with perfect lives (see Fox, 2019). Weinstein (2017) documented the feelings of adolescents who were acutely aware of positive-only social media presentations of people who seem to have a perfect life and to be carefree and happy. Of course, because no one is perfect and it is rare to have a perfect life, this invariably highlights the contrast between the ideal life of the person depicted online and the reality of the imperfect lives that most of us lead.

It has now reached the point that research on social media exposure and its impact on adolescents includes "perfect life" as one of the experimental conditions. A recent study by Devos and colleagues (2023) included this condition in research that documents how young people can be made to feel highly discrepant because of how perfect lives compare to theirs. Chronic exposure to perfect life comparisons can result in a chronic need to live up to expectations while being aware that peers and contemporaries are living up to comparisons. Feelings of dejection and demoralization seem reasonable and inevitable, given that there might be a regular dose of unwanted and undesired comparisons.

Devos and colleagues (2023) incorporated the perfect life theme in assessments of how much exposure young people have to positive-only social media portrayals and how it affects them (see Schreurs, Meier, & Vandenbosch, 2023). Their outcome measure assesses exposures to others with ideal appearance (i.e., looks beautiful) and ideal, perfect lives. The items on the scale ask about exposure to people who seem to be having a lot of fun, are happy, and look successful. There is also a social emphasis tapped by items that refer to people online who seemingly have many great friendships and share nice things with the caring people in their lives.

There can be no mistaking how this negatively affects the well-being of young people who are particularly vulnerable. Consider, for instance, the story of Courtney. Courtney is a married 24-year-old graduate student undergoing treatment for anxiety and depression (see Bettmann et al., 2021). She is acutely aware of being pressured to be the perfect wife and realizing, through social media, that she is incapable of having the perfect life that others seem to have. Her excessive use of social media affects her in multiple ways, including reinforcing her negative moods, feelings of shame, and unrealistic expectations.

How does this relate to individual differences in feelings of mattering? The young person who desperately needs to matter and currently feels little sense of mattering is bound to be influenced greatly by constant exposure to crafted images of people who apparently have perfect lives. This is understandable; if someone does have a perfect life, it would mean that this person has achieved the exulted status of being "a somebody" who matters greatly to other people and has people who matter to them. A highly idealized image of the perfect life includes portrayals of people frequently being in the company of several individuals who care about them, treat them as a priority, and spend time with them. Of course, all this is portrayed as happening in person with the full benefits of face-to-face contact.

The other chief concern about frequent social media use goes back to our case example of Courtney and her negative reaction to her constant exposure to other people's perfect lives. Our recent work is focusing increasingly on how people react and respond when they feel they do not matter. The term "anti-mattering reactivity" reflects our sense that when someone treats you as if you do not matter, personal vulnerability or personal strength resides in the reaction to this treatment. Resilient young people channel their inner Taylor Swift and "shake it off," but this is not the case for those who are vulnerable.

The capacity to cope is reflected when someone says, "He made me feel unimportant," which is what a vulnerable young person might say. In contrast, a resilient young person might say, "He tried to make me feel unimportant, but I am not going to let other people rule my emotions." Of course, it is not easy to arrive at this healthy perspective. On the basis of her qualitative study of young people between the ages of 18 and 24, Fox (2019) concluded that, despite being acutely aware of the false reality of perfect life portrayals, her participants were still affected by portrayals that added to their sense of loneliness. It is likely that they also added to concerns about not mattering.

I return to these issues in the final section of this chapter, where I examine what can be done from a prevention perspective. When public warnings and advisories are issued about the dangers of social media exposure, it has reached the point of being "a clear and present danger," and action is urgently needed. First, however, it is important to consider these issues as part of a review and analysis of existing research.

ANTI-MATTERING, FEAR OF NOT MATTERING, AND SOCIAL MEDIA USE

Why should anti-mattering and the fear of not mattering matter when it comes to excessive social media use? And how might a feeling and fear of not mattering contribute to problematic use that escalates into a full-blown addiction?

An unmet need to matter should have a central role, given more general work on needs and social media use. Research has established that social media use among adolescents is linked with a failure to satisfy core needs such as autonomy, competence, and connection (see Zhang et al., 2024).

A recent conceptual model proposed by Parent (2023) considered at length how adolescent social media use could potentially satisfy core psychological needs that make up the self-determination model. The opportunity to connect with others via social media can help address the need to matter and feel valued by others. One clear hypothesis is that there is a need for a sense of personal significance, and as such, the need to matter should be predictive of social media use in ways that go beyond a general need for a sense of belonging or social connection.

The young person with a sense of not mattering to others lacks a core element of social worth during a developmental period. A high level of anti-mattering can be regarded as a salient indicator and cognitive reminder of not meeting social expectations and not faring well compared with peers who seem to matter to others. Children and adolescents who feel unimportant may gravitate toward using social media to connect with others and feel more connected in ways that avoid the potential shame and embarrassment of seeming or being socially inadequate or making a mistake when interacting with peers. It may also be a way to combat or lessen feelings of loneliness. However, there is no substitute for developing caring interactions with others through frequent in-person interactions.

Social media addiction will likely reflect, at least to some extent, the powerful reward value of getting attention when someone shows interest in the young person after they establish an online connection. As noted earlier in this book, according to Rosenberg and McCullough (1981), key elements of mattering include the feeling of mattering and the sense of significance that comes from others paying close attention and seemingly taking a personal interest in us. Online exchanges can provide this interest and attention. Social media use can also be a distraction that helps manage negative emotional states.

The fear of not mattering should be particularly influential in maintaining excessive social media use and creating some resistance to efforts to reduce social media use. A youth who has become addicted to social media and has a fear of not mattering may continue this pattern of behavior partly due to the perception of the negative consequences of not being involved with social media. The abiding concern may be a fear of being overlooked and no longer seen or heard. The feeling of not mattering that existed previously may be associated with painful memories. Indeed, interacting with people online rather than in person may be to protect the self from future adverse reactions and social judgments.

What empirical support is there for these observations? Relevant research is summarized next. This research is limited in scope but clearly links the mattering construct with social media use among young people.

RESEARCH ON MATTERING AND SOCIAL MEDIA USE

One recent analysis suggested that lonely adolescents often turn to social media to satisfy their need to matter and address their loneliness. D. Smith and colleagues (2021) focused primarily on belongingness rather than mattering, concluding that establishing a sense of mattering on social media is vital to gaining a sense of belonging. The need to matter to others is a strong overarching influence that is likely at the root of the social media engagement of young people. This engagement can be double-edged in that it may satisfy the need to matter but at a considerable cost. Indeed, D. Smith et al. cautioned that social media use could be a boon or a bust in that it can either enhance or undermine the social well-being of adolescents, depending on its use and the nature of their experiences.

Empirical work on mattering and the use of social media is still in the infancy stage regarding research development. What research has been conducted thus far, and what does it suggest about a possible link? A study by J. C. Watson and colleagues (2022) was based on data from a nationally representative sample of adolescents in the United States, with a mean age of 17.38. Participants used social media across multiple platforms, with the median being 3.1. The three most popular platforms in this sample were Snapchat, Instagram, and Facebook. The overall amount of social media use was excessive, estimated at 5.5 hours per day, which far exceeds the recommended criteria for acceptable and potentially healthy use of social media. As noted earlier, 2 hours or less is the recommended cutoff. I find it useful to remind myself that the median represents the most common response in the sample, and many young people far exceed 5.5 hours per day.

This study also provided key information about the correlates of individual differences in feelings of mattering among young people. Mattering was assessed with the General Mattering Scale (Marcus & Rosenberg, 1987). The association between lower levels of mattering and problematic social media use was statistically significant but far from robust. There was also a small but significant negative association ($r = -.19$) between feelings of mattering and total hours spent on social media among adolescent girls. However, it was observed in commentary (see Flett, 2022) that even a modest association between low mattering and problematic social media use is potentially troublesome, given the established links between excessive exposure to social media and psychological distress in adolescents.

It is vital to keep the emphasis on people rather than variables. In the J. C. Watson et al. (2022) study, lower levels of mattering and problematic social media use were also linked with anxiety and depression. We must remain cognizant of the fact that many young people who are excessively using social media have chronic and persistent depression or anxiety. Of course, young people who are already suffering and perhaps feel like they do not matter do not need to be made to feel worse by being reminded that others they see online seem to have happy and successful lives and matter to the people around them.

An investigation by Maftei and Diaconu-Gherasim (2023) was the first study of social media use and anti-mattering in middle school students. This study was conducted with 480 Romanian students with a mean age of about 12. They completed the Anti-Mattering Scale (AMS; Flett et al., 2022) and an adapted measure that tapped social media use for social information (e.g., to learn about other people's lives), mood regulation (e.g., to make themselves feel better when down), and conformity reasons (e.g., to be liked by friends). Key additional measures were the six-item Bergen Social Media Addiction Scale (Andreassen et al., 2016) and the 21-item Depression Anxiety Stress Scales (DASS-21; Lovibond & Lovibond, 1995). Total distress scores were reported. Statistical analyses showed that anti-mattering had a significant correlation ($r = .38$) with levels of social media addiction. This is alarming, given how consequential it is to have feelings of not mattering to others (for a review, see Flett, 2022).

Social media use and anti-mattering were found to be primarily due to mood regulation ($r = .36$) and conformity because of a desire to be liked and appeal to peers ($r = .27$). There was also a weaker association between anti-mattering and using social media for social information reasons ($r = .19$). What can be concluded from this study? Early adolescents who feel invisible and unheard seem to turn to social media as a distraction from negative moods and negative arousal states and to gain a sense of connection to peers with whom they hope to develop and maintain an affiliation. The most unique and important finding is the established link between anti-mattering and social media addiction in young people who are at a time in their lives when they are likely struggling with personal identity issues and are highly susceptible to social media.

The analyses also revealed a robust association between anti-mattering and DASS scores ($r = .70$). This finding attests to the profound stress and distress associated with feelings of not mattering in this sample. This finding is the one to point to if anyone needs to be convinced about the emotional impact of feeling like you do not matter, especially if you are someone already dealing with a sense of being marginalized.

In addition, tests by Maftei and Diaconu-Gherasim (2023) of a mediational model supported an association of anti-mattering with social media addiction, which, in turn, was associated with psychological distress. However, this research was cross-sectional, so it was not possible to test other sequences of the various effects and pathways. It remains plausible that a reciprocal relation between anti-mattering and feeling unvalued contributes to subsequent social media use, which can then escalate into addiction; the extreme use of social media, especially in passive forms, can exacerbate the level of anti-mattering among certain adolescents.

Another study on social media addiction and anti-mattering is relevant but was conducted with 450 Italian adults. Silvia Casale and her colleagues (2022) confirmed the presence of a significant positive association between anti-mattering and social media addiction, but the association was weaker ($r = .25$) than that found in the sample of Romanian middle school students (Maftei & Diaconu-Gherasim, 2023). Other results predicting social media addiction showed that anti-mattering, fear of negative evaluation, and fear of intimacy were all significant contributors to a multivariate model. Perhaps the fear of intimacy among those who feel like they do not matter feeds the use of social media to keep people at a distance and avoid negative social judgments because socially anxious people anticipate making mistakes in person.

This study also included a measure of online social support. Casale et al. (2022) found a small but significant association between anti-mattering and the reported availability and provision of online support. This signifies that a significant proportion of adults with elevated anti-mattering apparently endorse the view that they could post a message on Facebook, for example, and get the support they need from people responding to them online.

My colleagues and I have now started a research program investigating the role of feelings and fears of not mattering in excessive social media use. The work is being led in China by I-Hua Chen and has yielded initial results in new unpublished research that strongly support the contention that an unmet need to matter plays a key role in problematic social media use. One new cross-sectional investigation includes over 6,000 adolescents from China. They were administered the AMS, the Fear of Not Mattering Inventory (Chen et al., 2022), and the Bergen Social Media Addiction Scale. They also completed measures of negative emotional states. Anti-mattering was strongly associated with elevated scores on the measure of social media addiction ($r = .38$), thus replicating the recent findings obtained from adolescents in Romania (Maftei & Diaconu-Gherasim, 2023). Notably, the association between the fear of not mattering and social media addiction was more robust ($r = .42$). Evidence was also obtained for a model that tested excessive social media use as a mediator of the link between feelings and fears of not mattering and negative emotional states. The links with facets of the mattering construct are strong enough to suggest that there may indeed be unique roles for an unmet need to matter and a fear of not mattering in the social media addiction of young people and their susceptibility to social influence.

How do these findings fit with claims and evidence that social media is more harmful for girls? The overall evidence regarding links with mattering and anti-mattering provides only limited support for this claim. J. C. Watson et al. (2022) found significantly higher levels of social media addiction and distress among adolescent girls in the United States. There was also a small negative correlation among girls only between levels of mattering and hours spent online. Unfortunately, the research conducted in Romania did not consider sex differences related to anti-mattering among adolescent girls versus boys (Maftei & Diaconu-Gherasim, 2023). Our new study with Chinese adolescents, described earlier in this chapter, found comparable results. Anti-mattering was strongly associated with elevated scores on the measure of social media addiction for adolescent girls ($r = .39$) and adolescent boys ($r = .38$). The association between the fear of not mattering and social media addiction was identical for girls ($r = .44$) and boys ($r = .44$). Thus, it remains an open question whether the role of social media exposure and feelings and fears of not mattering is a bigger problem for girls.

It is worth reflecting on what these fresh findings are telling us. Young people who spend too much time on social media tend to be elevated in feelings and fears of not mattering, and it is clear that, by and large, they are not experiencing the kinds of close and caring relationships they covet. The implications for prevention are discussed next.

WHERE PREVENTION SHOULD BE FOCUSED

As acknowledged earlier, research on mattering and social media use is just beginning, and programmatic research is urgently required. However, there is already enough information to suggest that there are reasons for grave concern, and it is time to do something about it. There are two obvious suggestions, which are clearly articulated in the public advisories that have been issued. First and foremost, social media use must be restricted, especially among children. Second, young people must be trained to heighten their social media literacy. The findings cited here indicate that this social media literacy must focus on how feelings of not mattering are likely, if not inevitable, that this can cause significant pain, and, in some instances, can result in feeling humiliated. Young people stand to benefit from anti-mattering training that heightens the likelihood of responding in proactive, adaptive ways that minimize negative reactivity. Ultimately, students must be encouraged in advance to seek help when they get to a point where self-harm or harming others becomes a consideration.

It is also clear that prevention efforts must be centered actively on social comparison awareness. Young people need to understand and learn to accept that seeing snippets of someone else's life online is no basis on which to judge whose life matters more. This focus certainly needs to emphasize debunking and contextualizing the crafted perfect lives of peers as they are portrayed online.

At the same time, it is just as important to encourage the use of social media as a way of connecting with other people to establish a sense of mutually mattering to each other. It is heartening to hear accounts of young people with physical disabilities who have been able to compensate for physical isolation by connecting with other young people online so that potential feelings of social isolation become feelings of social connection.

SUMMARY

In summary, in this chapter, I proposed that the feeling and fear of not mattering to others is a key contributor to social media use among youth. Initial research supporting this contention was summarized and reviewed. Factors and processes that contribute to the link between feelings of not mattering and social media use were considered, with a particular emphasis on how the fear of not mattering can escalate problematic use into addiction. Social media offers the possibility and promise of developing connections with others that satisfy key unmet needs, but this behavior is fraught with potential costs and consequences and is usually not a healthy alternative to more effective ways of managing negative emotions.

PART IV CLINICAL CONSIDERATIONS

11 MATTERING AND ANTI-MATTERING IN YOUTH ADDICTION AND SUBSTANCE USE

While their psychological well-being typically garners attention when considering how children and adolescents are faring in contemporary society, we should never lose sight of the number of young people who have problems with excessive drinking and other forms of addiction. This chapter examines feelings of mattering versus not mattering in the misuse of substances.

The excessive use of substances is a matter of life or death for many young people. Consider, for instance, an incident involving students from our local middle school. I learned of a close call experienced by two eighth-grade boys who were celebrating the end of the school year. As it turned out, life almost came to an end for these two boys. Each boy drank an entire 26-ounce bottle of alcohol. They were saved from death due to alcohol poisoning by what seems like divine intervention. A caring teacher from their school had a premonition that something was wrong, so he conducted an impromptu search of the school's surroundings. This teacher, seemingly on a mission, found the boys unconscious under some bushes just in the nick of time. I have often reflected on what feeling or sixth sense seemed to compel this heroic teacher to conduct his search.

https://doi.org/10.1037/0000449-012
Mattering as a Core Need in Children and Adolescents: Theoretical, Clinical, and Research Perspectives, by G. L. Flett

Young people may begin to establish a pattern of addiction in adolescence that may ultimately shorten their lives during adulthood. The world was shocked in October 2023 to learn of the death of Matthew Perry at the age of 54. He shared in his exceptionally open autobiography that his problems with addiction began at the age of 14 when he had his first drink and started on the path to alcoholism (see Perry, 2022).

Of course, there are multiple factors, processes, and pathways to excessive substance use among young people. This is beyond dispute and well-documented. But when contemplating possible contributing factors, it is important to consider the potential role of feelings of not mattering to others. This theme is the focus of this chapter.

One key caveat about this topic is that it can apply to children and adolescents representing all socioeconomic levels. When it comes to feelings of not mattering, this is one time when being financially advantaged is not a panacea. Seminal research by Suniya Luthar on adolescents in affluent communities and high-achieving schools showed that being raised in conditions of economic advantage might not be all that advantageous for many young people. Luthar and her colleagues documented the problems experienced by these youths in terms of internalizing symptoms (i.e., anxiety and depression); she also identified communities in which young people had prominent problems with substance abuse (see Luthar & Barkin, 2012; Luthar et al., 2020).

Luthar and Kumar (2018) reviewed and analyzed the existing data and pointed to evidence showing that parental monitoring and supervision are important in limiting adolescent substance use, with some parents becoming highly engaged in containing substance use and abuse (see also Luthar & Goldstein, 2008). They emphasized that children must believe that repercussions implemented by parents for substance use will be nontrivial. Importantly, these researchers noted that a sense of mattering to the parents might primarily be conveyed to adolescents during these difficult interactions. That is, parents are showing they care. It is conceivable that the caring relationship is one of the most fundamental positive influences for young people fortunate enough to have one or more caring people in their lives. Luthar and Kumar (2018) went on to sagely suggest that, for parents who are bewildered by all the messaging of potential risk and protective factors, a focus on how the parents relate to their children is probably the best place to start.

Parents who focus on their relationships with their children should arguably concentrate on how much their children feel like they matter. This emphasis fits well with the emphasis Diana Baumrind placed on reducing the risk of addiction among young people. Her seminal work on parenting styles included an extensive focus on parental styles and adolescent addiction (see Baumrind, 1991; Baumrind & Moselle, 1985). Baumrind (1991) proposed that adolescents are optimally competent when their parents are both demanding and responsive and capable of adjusting the freedom from control in response to their children's developmental level and maturity. The authoritative parenting style combines being demanding and responsive; Baumrind (1991) found evidence in her longitudinal study that supported this approach to reduce levels of substance use in adolescents. Being demanding and responsive comes with opportunities to convey to young people that they matter, are cared about, and are trusted to do the right thing. While Baumrind (1991) did not discuss mattering per se, she did note that adolescent girls who experienced only "good enough" parenting were not getting what they needed. *Good enough parenting* was defined as being only slightly demanding and responsive. These girls had surprisingly low self-esteem. Baumrind concluded that they needed something more from their parents. Specifically, she emphasized that they needed a stronger sense of being special to their parents (i.e., they matter). Baumrind (1993) reiterated this emphasis on needing to feel special as part of a subsequent rejoinder to Sandra Scarr about what children ultimately require in their lives.

Baumrind (1991) also described another type of parent as entirely uninvolved. Not surprisingly, adolescents from these families were characterized by a host of problems, including substance use. The young person with uninvolved parents will almost certainly feel unimportant to the people who are important to them. They will operate according to the perspective that their parents do not care about them and their actions. This conclusion is supported by research evidence that links perceived emotional neglect with low scores on the General Mattering Scale (see Flett, Goldstein, et al., 2016).

There have not been many studies of mattering and substance use among youth, but there is mounting evidence that points to the protective role of meaningful relationships with significant others. For instance, Tracie Afifi and associates (2023) sought to identify protective factors for decreasing nicotine, alcohol, and cannabis use among adolescents with a history of adverse childhood experiences. They analyzed data from about 1,000 adolescents who live in the province of Manitoba in Canada. These adolescents participated in the Well-Being and Experiences Study in 2017 and 2018. It was found that about two in 10 adolescent boys (20.5%) and about three in 10 adolescent girls (29%) had engaged in substance use over the previous 30 days. The protective factors illustrated the potential benefits of family and school influences. The authors concluded that family relationships are important, and positive relationships among parents and their children may reduce substance use. Specifically, the quality of the relationship with the parent was seen as vital. Protective actions included hugging adolescents; telling them, "I love you"; and connecting by having a meal together regularly. These actions are akin to showing and telling these young people they matter and reinforcing this message by spending time with them. Given such findings, it is almost certain that, if it had been included in this investigation, a variable representing mattering to parents would have been a robust predictor of lower substance abuse.

The school- and community-based measures evaluated by Afifi and associates (2023) contain other items that hint at a role for feelings of mattering at school and in the community. Here, the protective factors included feeling close to other students, having a trusted adult available at school, taking part in volunteer activities, feeling involved in the community, and feeling motivated to help and improve the community. The community findings can be seen as evidence that having value and giving value to the community are highly protective.

The summary conclusion to be drawn from this discussion is that children or adolescents who are made to feel special in their families, at school, and in the community have an essential resource needed for protection. This conclusion is in keeping with a key observation from Baumrind and Moselle (1985), who noted that the initial sensation of taking a drug may provide young people with a strong feeling of being special, and for some young people, this might be their first time feeling this way. The experience is powerful for the young person chronically aware of not being special to others and unfamiliar with the sensation and satisfaction of being special. Thus, what is reinforcing here and ends up being craved is the perception and feeling of being uniquely special, prized, and powerful instead of feeling weak, lost, insignificant, and imperfect.

We now consider relevant research evidence specific to individual differences in mattering to others. This theme was the subject of a recent review paper in which we concluded that mattering is a key protective resource, and, as might be expected, feelings and fears of not mattering are associated with considerable risk of substance abuse and other forms of addiction (see Flett, Casale, et al., 2023). The key evidence related to adolescents is summarized next. We (Flett, Casale, et al., 2023) noted that although there have been relatively few investigations thus far, the various lines of inquiry converge to suggest there is clear support for the protective role of mattering and the destructive role of not mattering to others.

RESEARCH ON MATTERING AND SUBSTANCE USE

Research now summarized is limited in scope but consistent. The review begins with information from broad surveys conducted in various states in the United States.

Survey-Based Research Findings

Community surveys have yielded key information. An infographic summary of findings based on survey data from Maine points to the potential protective benefits of feelings of mattering to others. The infographic depicts results from the statewide 2019 survey (Maine Department of Health and Human Services, 2022). Results showed that when asked the single item assessing mattering, 57% of high school students in Maine indicated that they felt like they mattered in the community. This feeling was highly protective in that students with a feeling of mattering were deemed to be 65% less likely to have considered suicide and 57% less likely to have symptoms of depression in the prior year. In addition, within the previous 30 days, they were 24% less likely to have used any substances compared with students who did not have a feeling of mattering in the community.

Community surveys conducted in Anchorage, Alaska, have yielded findings consistent with these results. Assessments over a 7-year span (2007–2013) with almost 5,000 adolescent participants show that a feeling of mattering in the community is clearly protective. Again, some important results have come from simply using a one-item measure of feelings of mattering in the community (see Garcia et al., 2014). Mattering in the community among youth in Alaska was associated with three clear indicators: currently drinking, binge drinking, and marijuana use. The feeling of mattering was associated with an 18.9% lower likelihood of currently drinking, a 16.7% lower likelihood of binge drinking, and a 34.7% lower likelihood of smoking marijuana.

What other empirical evidence is there that mattering has a protective role in potentially limiting substance abuse and related problems? Murphey and colleagues (2004) used the same one-item measure to assess over 2,000 adolescents from Vermont. They compiled a measure of six developmental assets that included the one-item measure of mattering in the community, along with other assets typically mentioned by those who feel like they matter (e.g., having a voice in decisions, volunteering). Murphey et al. reported that higher scores on their combined measure of developmental assets were associated significantly with less alcohol use and binge drinking and less frequent marijuana smoking.

Additional Research Investigations

Elliott (2009) provided the most detailed analyses thus far of feelings of not mattering and self-destructive tendencies among youth. His measures included indices assessing binge drinking and illicit substance use. The measure of illicit substance use was a combined measure that included the use of cocaine, heroin, methamphetamines, steroids, or inhalants. While the total sample of participants was over 2,000, the resulting data involving alcohol and drugs are based on about 1,800 adolescents. In total, 8.5% of the participants engaged in binge drinking, and the overall level of illicit drug use was considerably lower (i.e., just under 3%). Lower levels of parental mattering were associated robustly with both binge drinking and illicit drug use. Moreover, the measure of parental mattering outperformed a measure of self-esteem in terms of the obtained associations.

Other key data come from more recent research conducted with rural youth. Schmidt et al. (2020) assessed 381 middle school youth in Grades 6 to 8 from rural school districts in Michigan. The inclusion of multiple mattering measures is a key aspect of this study. The measures included indices tapping mattering to friends and parents as well as mattering at school and in the community. Detailed results relating to substance use are not reported in the journal article, but these results can be accessed in Schmidt's (2018) doctoral dissertation. The substance use index was a five-item scale from the Monitoring the Future study (Johnston et al., 2011). It assesses the past month's use of cigarettes, chewing tobacco, snuff, or dip; cigars, cigarillos, or little cigars; marijuana; and beer, wine, or liquor. Participants also completed a four-item measure that taps daily self-regulation and willpower. What did the results reveal? Schmidt reported small but significant correlations between greater substance use and lower levels of mattering at school, in the community, and to parents. One especially noteworthy finding was the significant associations between all four mattering indices and the measure of daily self-regulation (r's ranging from .32 to .55). The clear implication that needs to be tested in future longitudinal research is that mattering predicts daily self-regulation, which, in turn, becomes a form of self-control that limits the propensity to engage in substance misuse.

A broad search of the literature yielded other pertinent information. Haddock et al. (2020) evaluated the usefulness of a mentoring program. Correlational analyses of baseline data from 676 adolescents indicated a small yet significant negative association between a substance abuse measure and scores on a six-item scale with items from the Mattering Index (see Elliott et al., 2004). Other results support a possible meditational model linking mattering, depression, and substance abuse, where mattering was associated negatively with depression ($r = -.45$), which, in turn, was linked with substance use ($r = .29$).

Additional key evidence comes from several studies conducted by Edwards and colleagues. Edwards and Neal (2017) reported the findings of research conducted with just under 25,000 youths between the ages of 13 and 19. Community mattering was assessed once again. This initial study found a negligible but statistically significant association between mattering and binge drinking ($r = -.06$, $p < .05$).

However, stronger evidence emerged from a subsequent study by Edwards and colleagues (2021) focused on mattering at school. Their participants were 400 American Indian (AI) and Alaska Native (AN) youth in Grades 7 to 10. The key results for our purposes were based on four items from the 2013 Youth Risk Behavior Survey (Centers for Disease Control and Prevention, 2014), which assessed self-reported levels of school mattering, alcohol use, depressive symptoms, and suicidal ideation. Correlational results established that lower levels of mattering at school were associated with alcohol use ($r = -.17$, $p < .01$), depressive symptoms ($r = -.37$, $p < .01$) and suicide ideation ($r = -.36$, $p < .01$). Lower levels of mattering at school were also associated with being bullied at school, racism-related bullying, and being electronically bullied. As we noted (Flett, Casale, et al., 2023), it is plausible that racism-related bullying contributed to lower feelings of mattering at school, which, in turn, was associated with alcohol use, depression, and suicide ideation.

Another comparative study of different types of victims by Siller et al. (2022) pointed to the potential impacts of the link between feelings of not mattering and binge drinking behavior. This research was conducted with data from 738 middle school students and 1,311 high school students. Evidence was found among both middle and high school students that being a victim of bullying or multiple forms of victimization were linked with lower mattering at school, binge drinking, and depressive moods. There were also some indications that these links were especially evident among Hispanic/Latino students; this fits with the emphasis on the need to consider marginalization and the life experiences of minority students (see Flett, Casale, et al., 2023). Unfortunately, this research did not assess anti-mattering and fears of not mattering to others because the likely role of mattering was probably underestimated.

GAMING ADDICTION AND THE NEED TO MATTER

I close this chapter by noting that Silvia Casale injected an important emphasis on gaming addiction in our recent review paper. We stated in Flett, Casale, et al. (2023) that online games involving multiple participants could address unresolved needs when an adolescent with a high need to matter assumes a role that enables the gamer to feel depended on because they serve an important function. It is easy to envision how the rewarding sense of being and feeling significant could escalate into a problematic level and intensity of gaming behavior.

These themes were considered by the authors of a study that investigated multiple screen addiction, mobile social gaming addiction, and general mattering in almost 600 Turkish university students (see Saritepeci et al., 2022). The researchers reasoned that one byproduct of the social isolation and restrictions in daily social activities experienced by adolescents is to turn to mobile social gaming to achieve a sense of mattering. This study yielded a small but significant association between scores on the General Mattering Scale and excessive gaming behavior. This may represent another research context in which stronger results would have emerged if levels of anti-mattering had also been assessed.

Research on mattering and anti-mattering in various forms of addiction and substance use is still at an early stage, and there are several potentially important and revealing directions for future research that merit consideration. One key consideration is how mattering might moderate or mediate other well-known factors that have reliably predicted key outcomes related to addiction and substance use. A longitudinal study with four phases yielded evidence indicating that peer relatedness mediated the link between affiliation with deviant peers and alcohol use (Van Ryzin & Roseth, 2019). The peer relatedness measure created by Furrer and Skinner (2003) measures mattering to peers, with item content tapping the feeling of being important and special. Van Ryzin and Roseth (2019) emphasized that their results illustrate that positive peer affiliations can be protective against the risk of excessive drinking. Mattering is entirely in keeping with this perspective.

SUMMARY

In summary, this chapter focused on how feelings of not mattering relate to addiction and substance use. It was shown that, with one exception, deficits in mattering are linked with addictive tendencies. There are at least three reasons there should be much more to this story as future research emerges. First, stronger associations should emerge when there is a more complete assessment of the mattering construct, including both mattering and anti-mattering and deficits in mattering to significant others. Second, it is highly likely that feelings of not mattering will have stronger associations when research considers how an excessive unmet need to matter relates to the addictive tendencies of young people experiencing considerable stress and/or trauma. Finally, vital insights are likely to emerge when there is more of a person-focused emphasis; there is a need to examine the subset of people who feel like they do not matter and are engaged in risky behavior.

One obvious point merits being repeated in closing this chapter. The young person with a high degree of internalized anti-mattering will likely have low self-control and no hesitancy to engage in various forms of reckless actions. Behavior expressed by the young people who fit this description likely signifies psychological vulnerabilities related to a core sense of not mattering. When young people who seem to have many things going for them act impulsively and recklessly, it amounts to a silent alarm being triggered. Hopefully, there is someone attuned to what might be going on who is ready, willing, and able to follow the lead of the teacher mentioned earlier who interceded on behalf of the two boys who put themselves in jeopardy.

12 THE NEED TO MATTER IN YOUTH DELINQUENCY, AGGRESSION, AND VIOLENCE

Mattering is the prime mover in a chain reaction involving self-esteem and attitudes toward violence. . . . If you don't matter, it sets up a chain of unfortunate feelings and events that makes it difficult to get along.

—Gregory Elliott, *For Family Violence Among Adolescents, Mattering Matters*

A growing trend in personality psychology is to focus on constructs that can explain people in the world with personality features that render them capable of acting in an extremely antisocial manner toward others. At extreme levels, this involves a capability to do things that destroy or take away other people's lives without a hint of remorse expressed by the perpetrator. This burgeoning area examines the malevolent side of personality under the heading "dark psychology." It was the subject of an edited book by Zeigler-Hill and Marcus (2016) published by the American Psychological Association titled *The Dark Side of Personality*.

The premise of this chapter is that repeated frustrations of the need to matter accumulate in the form of negative tension and arousal and set the

https://doi.org/10.1037/0000449-013
Mattering as a Core Need in Children and Adolescents: Theoretical, Clinical, and Research Perspectives, by G. L. Flett

stage for aggressive and violent acts and a range of socially unacceptable behaviors (e.g., bullying, cyberbullying, crime, vandalism). Frustrations will be in the form of either inconsistent or almost total lack of care and closeness from significant others, blatant emotional and physical mistreatment, or perhaps both. Resentment will build in someone who grows increasingly isolated and alienated as core human needs are frustrated, including the need to matter and connect with others. This resentment may be exacerbated through exposure to people, in person or online, who, through social comparison, seem to have superior lives.

In a recent review article, I stated that it is meaningful to consider that the need to feel important to others can take a dark turn, culminating in a destructive form of "dark mattering." It was proposed that there exists "a type of 'malevolent mattering' characterized by a tendency to engage in acts with the goal of feeling more important and valued, albeit through destructive, oppositional, antisocial, and potentially self-destructive acts" (Flett, 2022, p. 19). If everyone has a need to matter, we must remember that children who are oppositional also need to feel they matter, and problems ensue when this need is repeatedly frustrated in youth with difficult temperaments. By extension, detailed accounts of the externalizing spectrum in children and adolescents (e.g., Tackett & Krueger, 2011) must be modified to include a focus on the core need to feel significant and avoid feeling insignificant. For some, this is satisfied through the feeling of being powerful and in control that accrues through mattering by engaging in behavior intended to dominate and demean others.

A central theme of this chapter is that the feeling of not mattering is at the root of much of the crime, delinquency, violence, and aggressive acts expressed by youth. The essence of this chapter is reflected in the question, "Why treat society like it matters if you feel it has treated you like you don't matter?" A related question is, "Why be kind and caring to the people in your family or your school when you have become convinced you don't matter to them, and they don't seem to care about you or have any understanding of or interest in how you feel?" As suggested, anti-mattering can fuel much antipathy and enmity and set the stage for antisocial acts in various forms.

Malevolent mattering is an apt term because it refers to the propensity to darkly express and channel the unmet need to matter into antisocial, destructive acts. This concept will be explored in terms of its fit with well-known theories of aggression, crime, and delinquency. This chapter summarizes what has been stated thus far and the relevant research that supports the notion that there is a need for programmatic inquiry that considers malevolent mattering.

We begin by revisiting the classic views of Rosenberg and McCullough (1981) and Elliott (2009). Morris Rosenberg and Gregory Elliott introduced the notion that the need to matter plays a role in violence, aggression, delinquency, and crime. It is not coincidental that they also supplied the first relevant data linking feelings of not mattering with antisocial tendencies.

Elliott (2009) also provided a detailed analysis of how feelings of not mattering served as a catalyst for the murderous behavior of Timothy McVeigh and Seung-Hoi Cho. When seeking to understand a specific individual, multiple contributing factors are implicated, but the frustrated need to matter must not be overlooked.

KEY EARLY DEVELOPMENTS: ROSENBERG AND McCULLOUGH (1981)

Rosenberg and McCullough (1981) provided the first indication that feelings of not mattering could play a destructive role in society. Their views were informed by the observations of William James (1890), who noted in a famous passage that, in essence, if no one noticed us and continually "cut us dead" as if we were nonexistent, one would become filled with rage combined with "impotent despair" (p. 294) rooted in seemingly being unworthy of any attention.

Rosenberg and McCullough (1981) focused on failing to matter to parents and suggested that this heightens the need to matter to peers. Some young people will satisfy this need to matter by affiliating with deviant peers who fill the need to connect with others and be seen as important. They observed further that delinquency makes unimportant people feel important. Their account emphasized that delinquent and oppositional behavior elicits strong, angry reactions from a range of people; these angry responses are highly rewarding because young people go from being unable to get other people's attention to becoming the object of their attention and anger. Antisocial tendencies are further rewarded by the appreciation and recognition afforded by delinquent peers who value the contribution to the gang or group effort. In essence, not mattering experienced as a lack of attention escalates the reward value of the attention when it is later received.

Rosenberg and McCullough (1981) suggested that parents who criticize their children for a bad report card are at least showing some interest, and these children have a sense of mattering that is lacking when parents are disinterested and unengaged. Those parents who are not involved have failed to establish boundaries that outline right versus wrong and do not support these boundaries with consequences for inappropriate behavior. This lack of "setting conditions and standards," with an absence of parental monitoring of a child with a propensity to act out, may be a pathway for the child who satisfies an unmet need to matter by engaging in deviant behavior.

Rosenberg and McCullough (1981) supported their observations by citing extensive research evidence. They described results from three studies involving large samples of adolescents, focusing most extensively on the Youth in Transition study conducted by Bachman and colleagues (1967). This research was based on a national study of 2,213 boys in 10th grade from 87 high schools throughout the United States. Rosenberg and McCullough (1981) reported initial results showing that low parental mattering is associated with indices of delinquency, including school delinquency and theft.

Rosenberg (1985) reported additional results linking low parental mattering with antisocial tendencies. These findings were summarized earlier in Chapter 5. Recall that it was shown in Table 5.2 that low parental mattering was associated modestly but significantly with an index of overt aggression and a measure of the impulse to aggress against others. It was also associated with the negative emotions of irritability and resentment, and societal disconnection was shown in terms of the association that anomie had with lower levels of mattering to parents. Rosenberg (1985) labeled the correlates shown in Table 5.2 as reflecting a hostility-embitterment-disenchantment cluster.

Researchers studying violence, aggression, crime, and delinquency have seldom, if ever, cited these important results provided by Rosenberg (1985) or considered what his results signify. Clearly, adolescent boys who feel relatively unimportant in relation to their interactions with their parents seem to have an anger and resentment that fuels an orientation to direct aggression at others and act impulsively without concerns about the consequences. The sense of meaninglessness and alienation signified by the association that low parental mattering has with anomie raises the strong possibility that at least a proportion of the boys with this life orientation will engage in aggression and perhaps violence, as well as other forms of oppositional and extra punitive behavior.

Rosenberg (1985) emphasized that the results from the Youth in Transition study were not attributable to related individual differences in self-esteem. Statistical tests that controlled for levels of self-esteem left these results virtually unchanged. Thus, it was with great confidence that Rosenberg concluded that the adolescent boy without a strong sense of mattering to his parents is hostile, embittered, sour, disenchanted, and depressed. The tendency to also be depressed suggests that many of these adolescent boys have a form of hostile depression and a readiness to respond when someone mistreats them in ways that activate their acute sensitivities and vulnerabilities.

If Rosenberg could comment today on the state of society and the current experiences of youth, as was suggested earlier, it is safe to assume that he would also revisit the vulnerability of youth with low self-esteem and low mattering and discuss the allure and impact of excessive involvement with violent video games. There is now a wealth of evidence evaluating the impact of playing violent video games. Brockmyer (2022) concluded in a contemporary review that exposure to violent video games does indeed increase the risk of desensitization to violence, which, in turn, could increase aggression and reduce prosocial behavior. Some research has indicated that boys higher in trait aggressiveness and lower in empathy are attracted to violent video games, and this is accentuated among boys with lower levels of educational attainment (see Lemmens et al., 2006). The feeling of efficacy that comes from being a proficient player of violent games may help provide the sense of having an impact on others that is otherwise missing in young people who feel that they are not important or worthy of other people's attention.

ADDITIONAL EARLY DEVELOPMENTS: THE VIEWS AND CONTRIBUTIONS OF GREGORY ELLIOTT

Gregory Elliott was the next scholar to consider the darker side of the mattering construct. His work is based on over 2,000 interviews conducted as part of the Youth at Risk study. Elliott summarized findings from this work in journal articles and his book *Family Matters: The Importance of Mattering to Family in Adolescence* (Elliott, 2009). The information in this book has important social connotations. It is a "must read" for researchers studying the role of feelings of not mattering in aggression, delinquency, and violence.

As one example of the revealing findings in his book, Elliott (2009) showed that low parental mattering among adolescents was associated with carrying a weapon such as a knife or gun. He noted that the frequency of carrying a weapon was low overall, but the association between low mattering to parents and carrying a weapon has vital implications for the prevention of violence.

Elliott (2009) also analyzed mattering and proneness to crime and violence from a conceptual perspective. He discussed extant findings with reference to sociological frameworks such as strain theory and control theory and noted how the symbolic interactionism accounts of delinquency are significant in extending the scope and importance of deficits in mattering to others.

Elliott also emphasized the relevance of a model from the psychological field focused on the experience of frustration. The original frustration–aggression hypothesis (see Dollard et al., 1939) and the extended model reflect the basic premise that experiencing frustration will create a propensity to direct aggression against others (see Berkowitz, 1989). Elliott reasoned that it is deeply frustrating to have a sense of not mattering to significant others. It can also be a source of shame and embarrassment.

Blame and hostile attributions need to be considered when seeking to connect a frustrated need to matter with subsequent aggression and violence. At present, there has been no research or theory focused on youth perceptions of who is to blame for feelings of not mattering, but I suggest that many young people made to feel they do not matter have no difficulty blaming others for these feelings. Other-directed blame among angry young people with a frustrated need to matter is a combination that can account for developing a dark form of mattering.

Elliott and colleagues (2011) investigated mattering and violence in the family in a sample of 1,817 adolescents between the ages of 11 and 18. Mattering was assessed with a 15-item measure of mattering to parents. Items were taken from the Mattering Index (Elliott et al., 2004) but were modified to assess mattering to one's family. Eight scale items were worded positively (e.g., People in my family count on me in times of need. My successes are a great source of pride to my family), but seven scale items were worded in an anti-mattering direction (e.g., My family does not seem to notice when I come and go. My family does not care what happens to me). Analyses indicated that low mattering was associated with violence, even after controlling for age, race, socioeconomic status, and family structure. This association was mediated by self-esteem and attitudes toward violence. Surprisingly, it was also found that according to their self-reports, adolescent females and not males were more violent.

Other research by Schenck et al. (2009) yielded a complex set of results centered on the theme that young people need to matter to stepfathers and nonresidential fathers. The key finding for our current purposes is that, particularly in terms of self-reports of mattering and key outcomes, mattering to various types of fathers was associated negatively with an index of externalizing behavior that included delinquency and violence.

As part of his conceptualization, Elliott (2009) astutely observed that the role of mattering in violence is rooted in personal and social identity. Clearly, issues of self and identity are paramount here. This was illustrated in a compelling analysis by Susan Harter (1990). While Harter did not consider the concept of mattering per se, she considered similar themes in her work on contingent parental support. The work by Harter and colleagues (2003) titled "What We Have Learned From Columbine" is particularly relevant to the themes in this chapter. My summary of this work follows.

Harter et al. (2003) showed that suicide and violence ideation were strongly correlated ($r = .55$) among adolescents. These variables were also associated with a host of constructs studied as potential mediators, including perceived competence and social support. Harter et al. also illustrated how these constructs were interconnected and reflected in the thoughts, motives, and actions of 11 adolescent school shooters. The most high-profile perpetrators discussed were Eric Harris and Dylan Klebold, who killed 11 students and one teacher at Columbine in Littleton, Colorado. Harris and Klebold also recorded their thoughts in diaries. This analysis by Harter and associates is emphasized here because it fits well with the findings linking feelings of not mattering with anger, resentment, aggression, and violence and the unique emphasis on externalized blame. However, Harter et al. focused on self-esteem and did not explicitly mention the mattering construct. By and large, the 11 adolescents who became school shooters were portrayed as targets who endured various forms of mistreatment and humiliation before their murderous actions. Collectively, they were neglected and rejected in ways that ought to have fueled hostility and feelings of not mattering to others. When reading life accounts of adolescents who became school shooters, it is almost impossible not to wonder how things could have turned out differently if some key people had entered their lives at just the right times and provided them with the care, consideration, and support they needed to make them feel like they mattered. This theme is evident in a detailed account later in this chapter of a well-known perpetrator.

Harter et al. (2003) also described their experimental research that examined reactions to hypothetical scenarios involving humiliating experiences. One vignette illustrated the type of experience that can easily foster feelings of being devalued and not belonging or mattering to others. The boy in this vignette was named Brian. He was portrayed as the only student in his class who was not invited to a party. In addition, the boy hosting the party insulted Brian by publicly telling him in class that he was a loser, which then elicited demeaning laughter from the other students. When asked how they would react, adolescent participants indicated that they would feel humiliated, distressed, and angry. Moreover, they would direct this anger at other students, but they would also direct it at themselves.

Robin Kowalski and her colleagues have considered at length the factors that seem to contribute to school shootings. Their analysis focused on destructive impulses built up among school shooters following a history of repeated rejection (see Kowalski et al., 2021). Robin Kowalski (2022) reflected on their findings, and in terms of proposed solutions, she stated that the mental health needs of these young people must be urgently addressed. Most notably, she underscored their need to have instilled in them a sense of mattering to others and the community.

An intriguing analysis by Baird and colleagues (2017) proposed that becoming a school shooter is more likely when a boy who already feels unimportant experiences the transition to high school. The pattern involves future school shooters attending elementary school in a relatively small school but then transitioning to a large high school where it is easy to feel anonymous and insignificant and to dehumanize other students. They also emphasize the appeal of national recognition afforded by media accounts of school shooters and its value for young people who crave recognition and significance. This latter emphasis is in keeping with Kruglanksi's quest for a significance model and research that emphasizes how extremism and violence stem from a quest for importance and recognition (see Kruglanski et al., 2013, 2022).

The following case example shows the attraction and appeal of feelings of mattering to a young person with an unmet need to matter. Lee Boyd Malvo was the younger component of the two-person team that became referred to as the DC sniper. The other person, the team leader, was an older adult (John Allen Muhammad), and Malvo was his protégé. They are believed to have killed 17 people in sniper attacks in the Washington, DC, area and along Interstate Highway 95 in Virginia. The attacks took place during 3 weeks in October 2002.

Malvo's story is well-documented, partly because the diary he wrote 2 years after his imprisonment was published (see Malvo & Meoli, 2014). This book was a disquieting read on multiple levels. Malvo suffered extreme physical and psychological abuse from his mother and was abandoned by his father (see Kovaleski, 2003). His mother was described as an exceptionally cruel perfectionist who physically punished Malvo for having an excellent report because he fell short of perfection. She was alleged even to have punished him for his failed suicide attempt when he was 12 years old.

Malvo's mother left him with various people throughout his life while she pursued work opportunities elsewhere. He expressed themes related to feelings of not mattering and not being cared for in his diary and stated in a 2017 interview on Jamaican television that the most important thing parents can give their children is their time; it is what he did not receive. He also alleged that between the ages of 7 and 15, he lived in 21 different places with various people. While moving to these places, he increasingly needed someone to care about him.

Malvo's case seems like a clear example of how a lack of being cared about and a growing sense of not mattering in a young person can combine with a series of adverse early childhood experiences to create a built-up rage. Muhammad is portrayed as sensing Malvo's vulnerability and using it to his advantage by expressing affection for him to recruit Malvo as his partner in the killing spree. Collectively, they seemed to have a relationship marked by mutual mattering that was exceptionally malevolent.

The most revealing thing about Malvo's story is the transformation that occurred when his mother asked her aunt (Aunt Bloom) to take him in. Aunt Bloom could not do so due to health concerns. However, she arranged for Malvo to live with her oldest daughter, Simone, who was starting her teaching career. Malvo documented in his diary that he developed a close bond with Simone, who began their time together by surprising him by asking him what he expected of her rather than vice versa. Simone seemed to understand Malvo. Notably, Simone pledged to always listen to him. She also arranged to have him transferred to her high school, where he stayed with her after school while she completed her teaching duties, and they would then set out together for home. Malvo recounted that they cooked and played board games together, and Simone even changed her plans for further education to honor her commitment to Malvo and his well-being. She was also a role model of giving to students, which Malvo witnessed after school while waiting for her. Not surprisingly, as life was changing for Malvo, he started to turn his life around, at least in the short run. He began to do exceptionally well in school and felt attached to the school.

What changed? Unfortunately, Malvo's positive path hit a roadblock 5 months later when his mother showed up and immediately demanded him back. It was evident to her that he had become close to Simone, so his mother is alleged by Malvo to have beaten him for no good reason other than sheer jealousy. As for feelings of not mattering, Malvo noted that once he was back in his mother's presence and away from the caring and considerate Simone, he was back to thinking, "I'm not even appreciated" (Malvo & Meoli, 2014, p. 70). It seems obvious that Malvo would never have become part of the DC sniper team if he had been able to continue living with Simone and receiving her care and attention.

THE PROTECTIVE ROLE OF MATTERING IN THE COMMUNITY

Love and attention from caregivers is ideally combined with a sense of mattering in the community. The study of community mattering by Murphey et al. (2004) is cited multiple times in this book. This study found, among other things, that higher community mattering scores were associated with less frequent engagement in physical fighting over the prior 12 months in 30,916 Vermont adolescents in Grades 8 to 12. Another team of investigators described results from another sample indicating that feelings of not mattering in the community were associated with a greater likelihood of girls having a history of involvement in mutually violent dating relationships (Chiodo et al., 2012).

Mattering in the community is also associated with less delinquency. Crean (2012) studied 2,611 youths in Grades 6 to 8 recruited from urban schools in upstate New York. A four-item measure of mattering to adults in the community was associated negatively with a multiple-item indicator of delinquent behavior, including carrying a weapon. Community mattering was also associated positively with a composite measure of decision-making skills, suggesting that a feeling of mattering is linked with planning and making quality decisions with an explicit emphasis on "staying away from people who might get me into trouble."

These findings would not be surprising to anyone highly familiar with 4-H programs found in rural communities. An overview paper by Astroth and Haynes (2002) documented extensive evidence that involvement in 4-H is associated with a lower likelihood of antisocial behavior across a range of indicators. For instance, it is linked with a lower likelihood of shoplifting or stealing, riding in a car with someone who has been drinking, or damaging property for the fun of it. Youth in 4-H programs are more likely to assume leadership roles. Mattering has essentially been measured by a six-item subscale that includes feelings of mattering in the community and being made to feel important, useful, listened to, and cared about.

CONTEMPORARY ANALYSES

More recent analyses are in keeping with the conceptual views and empirical results outlined in this chapter. D.-M. Lewis (2017) adopted a case study approach to examine mattering and the failure to matter among adolescent young offenders. She focused on 15 young offenders aged 18 to 21, addressing three issues: (a) the conditions that contribute to the feelings of mattering versus not mattering; (b) how failing to matter translates into impulsive, risky behavior, including antisocial behavior; and (c) how young offenders found ways to get what Lewis refers to as a forced version of mattering to others and society.

What led to feelings of not mattering? Some pointed to the loss of a parent, while others recounted being abandoned by significant others. The role of abandonment fits with evidence linking low mattering with emotional neglect (Flett, Goldstein, et al., 2016) and an early childhood schema reflecting abandonment (see Flett, 2018a). D.-M. Lewis (2017) noted that this lack of mattering is often expressed in aggression and violence, but these same tendencies can be turned inward and directed against the self. This focus often provides the impetus for various forms of self-harm, including suicidal behavior. D.-M. Lewis echoed early concerns from Elliott (2009) about how not mattering to parents often results in a tendency to become socially invisible in ways that exacerbate the sense of isolation and alienation from others. Some participants reported engaging in behavior that forced a sense of mattering, but mostly in terms of negative affiliations.

Baskerville (2020) reported a similar analysis of truant youths from New Zealand. She interviewed 13 adolescents (seven girls and six boys) between the ages of 13 and 18. The focus was on truancy rather than aggression and violence. Truancy is an oppositional behavior that may or may not be accompanied by violence, aggression, or externalizing behavior. Feelings of not mattering were deemed to contribute to truancy.

Fortunately, Baskerville's (2020) work is distinguished by a more optimistic stance. She documented how the experience of peer care and support and engaging in positive experiences could address an unmet need to matter and put the young person on a pathway to more positive life outcomes rather than to antisocial tendencies and related problems. Some of this mattering came in the form of no longer being exposed to negative anti-mattering experiences (e.g., not being bullied or sworn at), but the participants also reported having desired positive interactions. For instance, one male adolescent named James said, "I got attention from them that I wasn't getting from classmates" (p. 842).

Billingham and Irwin-Rogers (2021, 2022) provided an exceptionally detailed analysis of how feelings of not mattering contribute to the propensity of young people to be violent. They referred to the "terrifying abyss of insignificance" and how the feeling of not mattering can amount to a psychological shock that can be highly traumatizing to the young person who feels a sense of mattering to no one. Aggression and violence can be the route to a sense of being important when they are made to feel they are insignificant. Indeed, Billingham and Irwin-Rogers (2021) said such acts can turn someone who felt like a nobody into someone who counts. Billingham and Irwin-Rogers (2021) also summarized various potential sources of feelings of not mattering (i.e., economic, social-technological, political, and cultural), implying that these sources converge to heighten a sense of being unimportant and uncared for in ways that can exacerbate a proneness to engage in aggression and violence. This emphasis on these broad sources reflects the reality that the overall feeling of mattering reflects relational mattering and mattering in the community and society.

Billingham and Irwin-Rogers (2021, 2022) proposed sagely that much can be learned by considering those places where young people feel they matter. A focus is needed on the contexts that promote a sense of mattering and draw in young people who need to feel valued and gravitate to settings where this need is partially met. Of course, as noted by these authors, this can set the stage for also examining what most people would consider negative places and negative affiliations, as is the case with young people who satisfy their need for significance by becoming a member of a gang composed of other young people who engage in various forms of antisocial behavior.

One other study illustrates how mattering at school can be protective. Banyard and colleagues (2020) described research with a sample of 2,232 adolescents assessed on a battery of self-report measures, including a single-item self-assessment of mattering at school. Various indices of antisocial tendencies were also included. Small but significant associations were found between lower mattering at school and elevated in-person harassment, online harassment, and sexual violence. School mattering was unrelated to racial or school bullying.

NOT MATTERING IN SOCIETY

Collectively, the evidence represents strong support for the need to matter at home, at school, and in the community. Our new project with adolescents from France is also relevant (Virat et al., 2024). Recall that this project assessed mattering in society, in keeping with Fromm's (1941) seminal observations about how events in society can make people feel small. Fromm was reacting to the chaotic world situation in Europe during World War II. He added the important observation that when the world makes people feel small, insignificant, and powerless, the key is how they react. Do people who are feeling small and insignificant react in an adaptive manner, or do they succumb and react in a maladaptive manner?

Our correlational findings suggest that too many youths are ready to respond in a less-than-optimal way. The sample of 428 adolescent participants reported their perceived societal mattering and previous delinquency, delinquent intentions, peer delinquency, and attitudes toward the justice system.

Our analyses showed that lower levels of societal mattering were associated with reports of previous delinquent behavior and current delinquent intentions. Moreover, low societal mattering was linked strongly with negative attitudes toward the justice system ($r = -.42$). This finding suggests that feeling insignificant in society is linked with a somewhat caustic view of the justice system, perhaps colored by feelings of unfairness tinged with cynicism due to past experiences that have made young people feel unimportant. Linear regression analyses showed that societal mattering predicted delinquent intentions, controlling for past delinquency. Moreover, mediation tests established that peer delinquency and attitudes toward the justice system partly mediated this association.

Our results align with Rosenberg and McCullough's (1981) conclusions that a frustrated need to matter and affiliation with deviant peers can set the stage for behavior with clear societal consequences. Overall, converging lines of evidence suggest that Rosenberg and McCullough were astute when they suggested, "For the adolescent, mattering matters profoundly" (p. 180). They then concluded that mattering is important for society and is "a significant source of social cohesion" (p. 180). Conversely, prolonged upheaval is tied to an epidemic of young people feeling societally irrelevant. The inevitable conclusion is that for too long, too many people have paid the price for society's failure to promote mattering among all children and adolescents.

SUMMARY

The evidence cited in this chapter showed that some of the young people who have a frustrated need to matter express themselves by engaging in socially unacceptable acts. The unmet need to matter, combined with anger and frustration, can be expressed in various antisocial forms. This chapter began by considering the initial evidence from researchers who initiated and sustained the mattering field in its earliest days. The cases of school shooters and Lee Malvo demonstrated how a feeling of not mattering and not being cared about can fuel extremely antisocial and destructive acts.

This behavior seems to reflect acting without concern for the long-term consequences. It is likely that some youth who feel they do not matter also perceive that they have nothing to lose because they simply cannot envision a positive future. However, as work by Oyserman and Markus (1990) has shown, interventions that build a positive possible self are highly effective; the evidence summarized in this chapter suggests that they will be even more effective if a sense of worth through mattering is also developed.

13 MATTERING AND DEPRESSION IN YOUTH

After watching the classic movie *The Breakfast Club*, it may seem as if writer, director, and producer John Hughes (1985) had a window into the thoughts and feelings of all teenagers. Feelings of not mattering are represented in this timeless movie about five high school students who spend their Saturday in detention at their school. The character Allison Reynolds (also known as "the basket case") is the epitome of the dark mood resulting from not mattering to parents. She is dressed in black and wears excessive dark eye makeup that adds to her dark aura. Allison remains silent throughout most of the movie and often hides under her coat. Viewers eventually learn that Allison has a difficult home life because her parents invariably ignore her. How bad is it? Allison reveals that she is only pretending she has Saturday detention because she simply has nothing better to do. She represents students who feel invisible and unimportant due to a sense of not mattering to the key people in her life.

This chapter considers research that illustrates the association between feelings of not mattering and depression among children and adolescents. Factors and processes that can play a role in this association are also examined. The focus on this topic seems essential, given the indications that the

https://doi.org/10.1037/0000449-014
Mattering as a Core Need in Children and Adolescents: Theoretical, Clinical, and Research Perspectives, by G. L. Flett

already high prevalence of depression among young people is becoming an even bigger problem. The Youth Risk Behavior Survey from the Centers for Disease Control and Prevention released in February 2023 indicated that mental health problems among high school students in the United States continue to escalate (CDC, 2023). This research was conducted on a nationally representative sample of over 17,000 adolescents. The survey results for 2021 found that 42% of high school students reported that they felt sad or hopeless for at least 2 weeks, to the extent that they could not engage in their usual activities. This represents a substantial increase over the 28% found in 2011. It was broadly reported in the media that the 2021 results were especially alarming among adolescent girls, with approximately 57% (i.e., almost three out of five) indicating that they had experienced depressive symptoms in 2021. In short, adolescent girls like Allison now represent the norm.

The CDC (2023) report also documented significant increases in the portion of high school students with suicide ideation, a suicide plan, and a suicide attempt. Overall, 22% of students reported suicide ideation, while 18% reported a suicide plan and 10% reported an actual suicide attempt. Suicide and feelings of not mattering are examined in the subsequent chapter and a companion article (see Flett, 2024a).

The CDC (2023) report also noted that three key questions were added to the 2021 survey. One item assessed perceived levels of school connectedness. Overall, as might be expected, elevated school connectedness proved to be highly protective, but comparatively lower levels of school connectedness were found among female high school students, students of color, LGBTQ+ students, and students who had any same-sex partners.

There are multiple ways that feelings of not mattering could result in feelings of depression among young people; most pathways and processes should apply to some degree to people of any age. Feelings of not mattering are likely implicated in the initial vulnerability to depression but also the persistence of depression. What are the likely routes to depression that are rooted in feelings of not mattering? Next, four contributing factors representing pathways to becoming depressed are identified. The factors and processes reflect numerous case accounts that include the personal revelations of depressed children and adolescents, as well as insights arising from relevant research investigations.

PATHWAYS AND PROCESSES

The pathways and processes identified in this section primarily share a focus on either some aspect of the self or a process involving self-evaluation. These routes to depression remind us that depression is a failure to achieve a desired self and instead to have a highly negative self (see Beck, 1967).

The Pain of Shame and Having an Undesirable Self That Matters to No One

The first proposed route to depression is when the feeling of not mattering to others becomes an intense source of shame and pain. Shame is a self-conscious emotion. Guilt is another negative emotion that is considered a self-conscious emotion. Pride is a positive emotion that also reflects a self-conscious state (see Tangney, 2002). Self-conscious emotions such as shame and guilt are relevant to feelings of not mattering, given that shame and guilt have been characterized by Muris and Meesters (2014) as emotions that stem from the self being seen through the eyes of others. They involve the perception of being negatively regarded by others, as is the case with feelings of not mattering to others.

Charles Darwin (1872) and Helen Block Lewis (1971) proposed and documented that shame involves feeling small and diminished. The link between shame and feeling small has been confirmed in subsequent research (see Tangney et al., 1996). The young person who feels unimportant, and this is accompanied by a strong sense of shame, will almost certainly feel small and diminished. Perhaps this young person will feel small and weary and need that bridge over troubled water sung about so eloquently by Simon and Garfunkel. This complex and painful emotional state is clearly at variance with the need to matter because feelings of shame and not mattering will result in not wanting attention and scrutiny. Shame is experienced when a young person feels as if their undesirable, worthless self is exposed and potentially on display for everyone to see, so there is intense public self-consciousness. It means being highly discrepant from the positive self that garners interest and the positive attention of others.

The joint experience of feelings of shame and not mattering represents a pathway to depression due to having a highly negative sense of self that is centered on a feeling of being small. Unfortunately, young people perceive that others see them in this manner. This negative state becomes amplified if it is seen as likely to persist in the future.

Depression is particularly likely when this state is accompanied by an interpersonal form of overgeneralization (see Beck, 1967) that results in a harsh internal dialogue and negative thoughts about mattering to no one and perceiving that no one cares. Overgeneralization adds to a sense that nothing about the self is of worth to other people. This overgeneralized view then becomes difficult to refute if the young person is lonely, isolated, and unlikely to encounter someone who does care. Indeed, shame tends to be accompanied at a phenomenological level by a strong sense of isolation (Tangney et al., 1996; Wicker et al., 1983).

My colleagues at the University of British Columbia have created a new measure of automatic self-recriminations that underscores the close link between feelings of not mattering and negative cognitions about the self. This measure has a subscale designed to tap the internal dialogue involved in not mattering to others (see Hewitt et al., 2024). Item content taps themes of not mattering to anyone and thinking no one cares. Again, there is an emphasis on the entire self not being worthy of the interest, care, and attention of others.

Feelings of Not Mattering and the Behavioral Model of Depression

A modified version of Lewinsohn's (1974) behavioral model of depression represents another route to depression that could relate to feelings of not mattering. The essence of this model is that depression is likely when someone is socially avoidant and interacts infrequently with other people. This low activity level results in a low frequency of pleasurable events such that the person prone to depression experiences a low rate of response-contingent positive reinforcement. Young people who feel unimportant, isolated, and lonely will miss out on positive exchanges that strengthen a positive sense of self. Importantly, through the lack of positive engagement with others, they also lose out on opportunities to add value and give value to others. This emphasis is vital because it uses Prilleltensky's (2020) emphasis on adding value to others but now couches it in terms of the vulnerability that accrues when this is not part of the young person's life.

Importantly, the same processes can operate in recovery. There are numerous case accounts of young people who bounced back from depression and dysphoria by gaining a better view of themselves and their capabilities by making a difference in the lives of other people. This other-directed activity provides them with a sense of meaning, purpose, and possibility. Given that volunteering should add to feelings of mattering, it is not at all surprising that extensive research has documented a link between volunteering and recovery from depression among adolescents (see Ballard et al., 2021). Another route is participating in group therapy and experiencing the lift that comes from supporting fellow group members and making a positive difference in their lives.

Depression, Feelings of Not Mattering, and Social Comparison

The third pathway to depression is centered on social comparison. According to Festinger's (1954) seminal theory, social comparison is a process of self-evaluation and information seeking that occurs when individuals are uncertain about the adequacy of their performances or the correctness of their opinions. When people are concerned or uncertain about their characteristics and their performance, they use available information about other people as a guide for self-evaluation.

Children and adolescents who are uncertain about themselves, especially in terms of lacking a feeling of mattering to others, are highly attuned to social comparison information. Their insecurities and ways of appraising their relative standing in their social worlds result in extensive exposure to social comparisons and a cognitive preoccupation with social comparisons. As suggested in the previous discussion of social media use in Chapter 10, depression is likely when vulnerable young people conclude that they do not matter as much as other young people, and this has occurred because of some defect or deficit in the self.

The most problematic negative comparison for vulnerable adolescents is for them to conclude that their peers are comparatively more popular and more socially integrated. As noted earlier, what has become particularly destructive about social comparison is the ease with which it is now possible to use social media to move beyond comparisons of performance on tests at school and make negative comparisons that contrast how the adolescent's life compares with the lives of friends and peers.

Some new work in our laboratory is focusing on how negative social comparison feedback can have a sustained negative impact. We have identified meaningful individual differences in the tendency to ruminate and be cognitively preoccupied with social comparison outcomes (see Flett, Nepon, et al., 2024). When this tendency exists among young people who feel unimportant, it can serve as a potent reminder that they do not matter as much as friends and peers seem to matter.

The Role of Anti-Mattering Reactivity in Depression

The fourth pathway implicates individual differences in anti-mattering reactivity. The concept of anti-mattering reactivity is uniquely introduced in this book. Cognitive, emotional, and behavioral reactions to feelings of not mattering can be adaptive, neutral, or maladaptive. Depression is exacerbated and prolonged when negative tendencies such as poor emotional regulation and ruminative brooding triggered by events result in feeling unimportant and insignificant. Ruminative brooding likely includes a mattering-specific type centered on the theme, "Why don't I matter as much as I should or as much as they seem to matter?" More generally, avoidance-oriented and emotion-oriented coping after encountering anti-mattering stressors and related problems should have a strong negative impact on vulnerable young people who begin to feel depressed and demoralized.

A paucity of positive forms of anti-mattering reactivity is also implicated for those young people prone to depression. It is vital that young people learn to respond to adversity that arouses feelings of not mattering by being self-compassionate, self-forgiving, and nurturing of themselves. The negative internal dialogue involving harsh thoughts about the self due to a sense of not mattering needs to be supplanted with positive automatic thoughts and comfort directed at the self. Self-acceptance and an orientation toward self-care can provide a shield that stops a young person from internalizing anti-mattering experiences.

It is also sometimes the case that parents are engaged in behavior that is not registering as positively as it should be by depressed young people who are used to feeling unimportant to others. Therapists and counselors can help the vulnerable young person cognitively reframe the actions of others. For instance, in one case example of an adolescent girl named Juana who had diabetes, what was seen by Juana as intrusive nagging and maternal overcontrol was recast as her mother taking a sincere interest in her daughter and supporting her to engage in diabetes self-management and self-care (see Cumba-Avilés, 2017).

There are several other plausible pathways; ideally, these factors and processes will be identified and evaluated in future research programs. The existing research evidence that links feelings of not mattering with depression is summarized next. This research is mostly cross-sectional but does include some longitudinal research.

PUBLISHED STUDIES OF FEELINGS OF NOT MATTERING IN DEPRESSION

The association between mattering and depression is the most studied topic in the research literature on the psychology of mattering. The tendency for adolescents who are comparatively low in mattering to have elevated symptoms of depression was a central element in the original Rosenberg and McCullough (1981) article.

The findings from relevant published studies are described next. Collectively, these investigations show that the association between depression and lower levels of mattering is consistently evident. While the focus here is on research examining feelings of not mattering and depression in children and adolescents, many other studies conducted with adults have confirmed this association with depression. Indeed, one of the earliest studies of mattering by Taylor and Turner (2001) showed in a longitudinal study of adults in the community that lower levels of mattering assessed by the General Mattering Scale (Marcus & Rosenberg, 1987) predicted subsequent depression.

Given that feelings of mattering are protective and consistently predict lower levels of depression, readers might wonder why there is not more research into mattering and depression in young people. I have asked myself this question many times. On a related note, why has the promotion of mattering not been broadly implemented as a way of reducing the number of young people prone to depression? Rosenberg and McCullough (1981) provided enough convincing evidence over 40 years ago to make this happen. Unfortunately, just like those young people who hide their depression, this key research finding has flown under the radar, and, as a result, it has not received the attention it warrants.

Cross-Sectional Research

Rosenberg and McCullough (1981) described the results from large samples of adolescents. These studies were hampered by the use of rudimentary measures of mattering to parents, and the measures differed across the four samples. Nevertheless, the results showed consistently that mattering to parents is protective in that it is linked with lower levels of depression. Most importantly, Rosenberg and McCullough (1981) established that mattering was predictive of depression, even after statistically taking into account the association that low self-esteem had with low parental mattering and depression. This research was the first of many studies indicating that the feeling of not mattering is a specific and unique source of vulnerability to depression.

A study by Mueller (2009) on protective factors and barriers to depression is relevant due to the inclusion of a measure described as tapping "parent–family connection," but the measure of mattering to parents is similar to the mattering described by Rosenberg and McCullough (1981). Adolescent participants were from the National Longitudinal Study of Adolescent Health. Results were reported for a subsample of 754 gifted and 748 nongifted adolescents. The six items in the parent–family connection measure included an item tapping interest (i.e., How much do you feel that your family pays attention to you?) along with measures tapping feeling understood and cared about by parents. The scale item assessing family and parent interest had the highest factor loading in the parent–family connection subscale. Mueller found that higher scores on this scale were associated with less depression in both subsamples, and it predicted depression after statistically taking into account other predictors (e.g., a negative self-concept and school belongingness). Thus, mattering in the parent–family context was associated uniquely with less depression in gifted and nongifted adolescents.

Dixon and colleagues (2009) assessed mattering, depression, and anxiety in 177 participants (125 girls and 52 boys) from public middle schools in the southwest United States. Mattering was measured with a modified version of the General Mattering Scale. Among girls, mattering to others was related negatively to anxiety ($r = -.42$, $p < .01$) and depression ($r = -.27$, $p < .01$). Similarly, for boys, mattering to others was related negatively to anxiety ($r = -.39$, $p < .01$) and depression ($r = -.37$, $p < .01$).

The next section describes extensive evidence linking low mattering with depression in four studies conducted with children and adolescents from China. This research was made possible because of the affiliations developed over the years by my colleague and former postdoctoral student Chang Su, who was a teacher in China for many years.

Mattering and Depression in Chinese Children and Adolescents

The first study by Flett, Su, et al. (2016) evaluated 218 Grade 4 children from China. This study had a more explicit emphasis on correlates of depression and included positive protective factors (i.e., mattering, self-esteem, and unconditional self-acceptance) and negative orientations involving risk and vulnerability (i.e., dependency and self-criticism). As expected, mattering was linked significantly with lower levels of depression. Moreover, the results of a regression analysis showed that significant unique variance was predicted by elevated dependency and lower levels of mattering, self-esteem, and unconditional self-acceptance. Two key implications can be derived: First, mattering is not redundant with self-esteem. Both are implicated in experiencing less depression. Second, young people benefit from being accepted as themselves, but this acceptance should not be conditional on meeting expectations placed on them by other people or themselves. This finding accords with the emphasis that Carl Rogers (1961) placed on unconditional self-worth.

More recently, Flett, Su, Nepon, Ma, and Guo (2023) evaluated mattering in 172 early adolescents in Grades 7 and 8. This research compared mattering and self-esteem in terms of their ability to predict unique variance in various measures. This study included measures of mattering, self-esteem, depression, anxiety, loneliness, positive affect, negative affect, and shame. The results showed that both mattering and self-esteem were associated with higher levels of positive affect and lower levels of negative affect, depression, loneliness, and shame. However, mattering and self-esteem were unrelated to anxiety in the study scores. Surprisingly, when self-esteem and mattering were pitted against each other as predictors in a regression analysis, in this singular instance, self-esteem but not mattering was predictive of less depression. The predictive superiority of self-esteem contrasts with most findings in the published literature, especially those reported by Rosenberg and McCullough (1981).

It was still the case, however, that mattering was a significant unique predictor when it came to the other indices in this study. The results showed that both mattering and self-esteem were significant predictors of positive affect, shame, and loneliness. The uniqueness of mattering in being associated specifically with less shame and less loneliness is probably a reflection of the fact that mattering, loneliness, and shame share a psychosocial emphasis.

Next, we consider the results from 232 Chinese high school students from advanced and nonadvanced high schools. These participants completed an extensive battery of measures, producing different sets of results that were reported in Flett et al. (2014) and, more recently, in Flett, Su, Nepon, Ma, and Guo (2023). The first article described the results when we focused on self-report measures of mattering, academic buoyancy, shame, social anxiety, and depression. This initial investigation found that mattering was associated significantly with lower depression. It was also linked positively with academic buoyancy and lower levels of shame and social anxiety. The findings were comparable for high school students from advanced and nonadvanced high schools.

Further analyses focused on other measures included in the same sample. Our sample of 242 high school students completed the General Mattering Scale, the Educational Stress Scale (Sun et al., 2011), and measures of school burnout, loss of face, and depression. Participants also completed the Involuntary Subordination Questionnaire (ISQ; Sturman, 2011) and its four subscales assessing submissiveness, defeat, entrapment, and social comparison. The correlations are reproduced in Table 13.1. The significant associations with each ISQ subscale represent unique findings in the mattering field, so certain results are discussed in some detail next.

The results indicated that mattering was negatively correlated with student burnout and depression. Mattering was also associated negatively with pressure. As can be seen in Table 13.1, mattering was also linked negatively with total involuntary subordination and all four subscales. It was also negatively associated with depression and burnout. It is evident from Table 13.1 that defeat and entrapment were exceptionally robust correlates of levels of depression. It is quite likely that if we had tested it, support

TABLE 13.1. Correlations Between Mattering and Measures of Burnout, Pressure, Facets of Involuntary Subordination, and Depression

Variable correlates	Mattering (general)
Burnout	−.29**
Pressure	−.23**
Loss of face	−.14
Defeat	−.30**
Entrapment	−.38**
Social comparison	−.46**
Submissiveness	−.29**
Depression	−.37**

Note. $N = 242$ high school students. Data from Flett, Su, Nepon, Ma, and Guo (2023).
**$p < .01$.

would have been obtained for a model that links feelings of low mattering with depression via the mediators that reflect feeling defeated and feeling trapped.

The association between feelings of not mattering and feelings of defeat reflects a view of being overpowered by life and having a low status in the world. Someone who agrees with these items might feel like one of life's losers rather than one of the winners. This perspective on life is troubling, given the age of our participants. Many of our participants were likely affected by feelings of defeat in not meeting their achievement expectations and goals. While mattering is largely psychosocial, feeling defeated in the achievement realm undermines feelings of mattering for young people who feel that they must achieve at a remarkable level to be unique and special in the eyes of others.

Parenthetically, the broader pattern of correlations with the data from this sample indicated that feelings of being defeated were strongly linked with elevated levels of academic pressure (r = .50). Perhaps the pressure felt extended to views and beliefs centered on the theme of a pressure to be important through achievements.

The association between feelings of not mattering and feeling trapped has internal and external elements. Some ISQ items reflect being trapped by outside forces (e.g., I feel trapped by other people), but others tap being internally trapped (e.g., I would like to escape my thoughts and feelings. I want to get away from myself). The sense of being trapped by others is understandable when the feeling of being insignificant is due to mistreatment by others. Feeling internally trapped can signal a deep sense of internal disquiet and awareness of a self and identity that is undesirable. The desire to escape thoughts and feelings has additional significance, given the link between suicidal thoughts and feelings of not mattering to others, discussed in the next chapter.

The negative correlation between mattering and social comparison needs to be replicated, but it clearly suggests that adolescents with low levels of perceived mattering do not compare themselves favorably with others. This finding takes on added importance when considered within the context of the acknowledged exposure to social comparison information that is part of the excessive use of social media.

Given the obtained intercorrelations among the variables in this study, once again, it was deemed important to evaluate mattering in terms of whether it could predict unique variance in depression scores. The results of a regression analysis showed that mattering predicted a significant 5% of unique variance in depression levels beyond the variance attributable to the loss of face, student burnout, and pressure. Related analyses found that mattering also predicted unique variance in levels of defeat and entrapment beyond the variance accounted for by the loss of face, student burnout, and educational stress.

Additional Research

In research outside our lab, Haddock et al. (2020) reported results that fit with the themes in this chapter. Their sample of 676 high school students completed the six-item mattering measure derived from the Mattering Index (see Elliott et al., 2005), along with measures of depression, anxiety, and trait anger. Parents provided a report of their child's internalizing behaviors based on items from the Child Behavior Checklist (Achenbach, 1991). The correlational results shown in Table 2 of the Haddock et al. (2020) article confirmed that mattering was associated negatively with depression ($r = -.42$) and anxiety ($r = -.50$). There was a negligible association with trait anger ($r = -.08$). Mattering was also associated negatively with parental reports of internalizing symptoms ($r = -.29$).

Higher levels of depression have also been linked with feelings of not mattering in the community. When mattering in the community is assessed, it is typically measured in terms of the degree of agreement or disagreement with an item phrased as "In my town or community, I feel like I matter," to which respondents must indicate their degree of agreement. Edwards and Neal (2017) established that feelings of not mattering in the community were associated significantly with depression in almost 25,000 high school students from New Hampshire. Analyses showed that feelings of not mattering in the community predicted depression and poorer academic performance beyond the variance accounted for by physical and sexual dating victimization and demographic characteristics.

Longitudinal Research

Do individual differences in mattering predict vulnerability to depression over time in longitudinal research with children and adolescents? At present, only a few published articles have examined mattering and depression in young people from a longitudinal perspective.

Marshall and Tilton-Weaver (2019) reported the results from a two-wave study with children in Grades 6 to 9. The mean age of participants at the beginning of the study was 12.23 years. The Time 2 assessments were 1 year later. Participants completed Marshall's (2001) mattering scale and measures of depression and problem behavior at both times. The mattering inventory provides separate subscale measures of mattering to mother, father, and friends. Mattering to mother and father assessed at Time 1 was associated significantly with depression at Time 1 and Time 2. However, tests found no cross-lagged associations. Mattering to friends was not associated significantly with depression at either time in terms of correlations. Marshall and Tilton-Weaver concluded that viewed from a temporal perspective, mattering may be less protective of adolescent well-being than would be expected on the basis of cross-sectional research. This conclusion seems premature because other relevant variables, such as life stress, were not assessed. Moreover, including the Anti-Mattering Scale (Flett et al., 2022) at both times might have revealed a different pattern.

Waterman and colleagues (2021) also evaluated mattering and depression two times; in this instance, mattering was assessed in terms of mattering at school. Waterman et al. found a significant negative association between mattering at school and depression when they were both assessed concurrently at Time 1 ($r = -.31$) and Time 2 ($r = -.27$). In addition, mattering at school at Time 1 was also associated with depression at Time 2 ($r = -.25$). Unfortunately, because it was not the primary focus of this investigation, the ability of mattering at school to predict changes in levels of depression over time beyond Time 1 levels was not evaluated.

ASSOCIATED PERSONALITY VULNERABILITIES AND IMPLICATIONS FOR TREATMENT

One key theme yet to be introduced is that feelings of not mattering are associated with other personality vulnerabilities implicated in depression among children and adolescents. These associated vulnerabilities suggest the need to address various vulnerabilities when feelings of not mattering are implicated in depression. Some depressed young people are highly perfectionistic. The trait dimension known as socially prescribed perfectionism (i.e., perfectionism demanded by others and society) is linked with feelings of not mattering (e.g., Flett et al., 2012; Mohammed et al., 2023). The combination of this form of perfectionism and the pressure it involves for an adolescent who feels unimportant to others will likely be linked with considerable pain and shame.

Anti-mattering has also been linked to self-criticism and dependency (see Flett et al., 2022). Self-criticism is an introjective personality orientation that emphasizes achieving personal goals, being highly competitive, and being exceptionally hard on oneself when failing and falling short of expectations (see Blatt & Zuroff, 2002). Dependency is an anaclitic personality orientation involving a preoccupation with other people and an intense need to keep them in close proximity. The type of depression associated with this orientation is experienced and expressed in feelings of helplessness and weakness (see Blatt, 1974). The young person with a feeling of not mattering who also has these other personality features has a strong sense of inferiority, guilt, shame, and helplessness combined with a sense of insignificance and perhaps invisibility.

Collectively, these personality features have in common a highly negative sense of self and an insecure attachment style. Interventions must focus on strengthening the sense of self not only by reducing the negative but also by boosting the positive through a focus on learning self-compassion and developing a pattern of self-reward rather than self-punishment. However, this emphasis is not enough, given the insecure attachment style and what it represents in terms of early experiences that link the self with others. Some success has been reported in treating depression in adolescents with interpersonal psychotherapy (see Gunlicks-Stoessel et al., 2019); a version that emphasizes feelings of not mattering should prove to be effective.

There are many pathways to depression, and several vulnerabilities can be involved. When it comes to mattering, what is most important to convey to clinicians and counselors? The answer is simple yet has paramount importance: For some young people who experience extreme and persistent depression, the feeling of not mattering is their core vulnerability. If reworded for cognitive behavior therapists, this is akin to saying that "not mattering" in these young people is their core schema. This aspect of self and identity is sustained, so feelings of depression will likely persist rather than be episodic.

I realized this while reviewing the individual questionnaire packages of the high school students who participated in the school board project (summarized in Chapter 2 of this volume). I examined the responses of every participant and eventually came across the responses of an adolescent boy with an exceptionally high score on the depression measure. I scanned his other questionnaire responses, and at first I was perplexed and could not fathom why he was so depressed. His scores on other measures tapping self-regulation and mindfulness were not distinct or problematic. The key was revealed when I reached the brief measure of mattering. This high school student responded to the scale item "I feel like I matter" by circling the "strongly disagree" option not once, not twice, but five times! He also spontaneously wrote on his questionnaire, "and I am very sure of this." Two things immediately became apparent to me. First, it is useful to measure how certain someone is about whether they matter. Second, I realized that any clinical attempt to address this boy's depression would fail if his unmet need to matter was not the central focus of intervention. Moreover, it would be essential to understand how and why he felt this way. This example underscores that, for some young people, their sense of who they are is built on feeling entirely insignificant and being highly aware of their unimportance.

I close this chapter on a more hopeful note by returning to the plight of Allison Reynolds and reminding readers of the rest of her story in *The Breakfast Club*. She was transformed by the end of her day in Saturday detention. She emerged from the school smiling, engaged, and eager to move forward. This change occurred because she was noticed and cared about by her fellow members of the Breakfast Club, and she had begun a budding relationship with Andrew Clark, played by Emilio Estevez. Her transformation illustrates how bleak feelings in young people can be alleviated when they get the attention and interest they need and deserve. Clearly, even a little bit of positive personal attention can go a long way. There is incredible power in getting the young person to accept that someone sees them and that they are worthy of the attention.

Therapists and counselors should reflect on how this is especially needed when the feeling of not mattering is the core problem and perhaps "I do not matter to other people" has become the core schema of a depressed adolescent, as was illustrated. But it is likely that the power of learning that you matter to your counselor or therapist is strong enough to lead to improvements in mood and ways of viewing the self for those depressed children and adolescents who are depressed for other reasons and who do not have a deficit in mattering as their main issue. The experience of a positive therapeutic relationship can play a vital role in adding a sense of mattering to the self and identity of young people (for a discussion, see Flett, 2018a).

If we stayed with Allison Reynolds a bit longer, we would see our fictional Allison returning to a home environment where she is never noticed. A key part of intervention for children and adolescents like Allison is to get them to accept the lack of parental attention and help them realize that it is about parental characteristics and issues and not because these children and adolescents are defective and not worth it. This is a classic situation that calls for social self-compassion (see Rose & Kocovski, 2021). When people are treated badly by others, there is a natural tendency to be self-critical and view the mistreatment as due to something about the self. This happens because the situation becomes more controllable by figuring out the problem with oneself and then fixing it. But this does not work. Instead, the key is to be kind and compassionate with oneself in the ways that Kristin Neff has eloquently described (see Neff & McGehee, 2010). Another route is to find people outside the home and develop mutual mattering to give both people the attention they need.

It was necessary to conclude with this theme because one thing that does not get enough attention is that many young people are depressed because they constantly are faced with negative realities. A key in assessing and treating these young people is to establish whether they have a social environment that is not rewarding and may be a constant source of punishment in their lives. It is particularly sad if young people are treated in ways that make anti-mattering feelings veridical. In such instances, developing a warm alliance with a caring therapist and other people in the social network is imperative.

SUMMARY

This chapter sought to align the mattering construct with current indications that depression is becoming more prevalent among children and adolescents. The chapter began by identifying pathways and processes that link feelings of not mattering with depression among young people. Key themes that were highlighted included the role of shame, the development of a highly undesirable self, and the destructiveness inherent in having a social comparison orientation and making frequent negative comparisons with others. One unique focus is that a key element is a negative form of anti-mattering reactivity. That is, distress will be potentiated, maintained, and exacerbated by maladaptive response tendencies activated by experiences that heighten the sense of not mattering to others. Research was also summarized that showed consistently that feelings of not mattering are linked with depression in children and adolescents. The original research by Rosenberg and McCullough (1981) showed in four large samples of adolescents that depression is linked with feelings of not mattering to parents. Some implications for treatment were considered. Ideally, it will be recognized that certain young people have the feeling of not mattering as their core vulnerability or core schema, and it is a great barrier to treatment success and recovery if clinical and counseling interventions fail to address this central aspect of self and identity and how it contributes to dysfunctional forms of reactivity.

14 SUICIDE IN YOUTH AND THE PAIN OF FEELING UNIMPORTANT

The acclaimed suicidologist Edwin Shneidman (2005) wrote a brief note at the age of 86 that cogently summarized what he had learned about suicide. His conclusion was based on a lifetime of work that included analyzing autopsy information and suicide notes. Shneidman stated:

> Each case of suicide has its unique constellation of factors including, at its center, the vital role of idiosyncratically defined psychological pain, which itself is pushed by a pattern of thwarted psychological needs that is specific for that particular person. (p. 2)

Almost 2 decades later, Shneidman's insights are exceptionally relevant to the focus of this chapter on mattering and suicidality in children and adolescents. Young people have considerable risk to the extent that they have a need to matter, which is extremely important to them but is unmet. The risk is amplified if a young person is also experiencing psychological pain (i.e., psychache), including the pain of not mattering. It is possible, if not likely, that the feelings of not mattering add to this psychological pain. A sense of being unimportant may be reflected in thoughts such as "No one would miss me" and "No one cares." The impact should be even greater if mattering is

https://doi.org/10.1037/0000449-015
Mattering as a Core Need in Children and Adolescents: Theoretical, Clinical, and Research Perspectives, by G. L. Flett

seen as unattainable such that there is hopelessness about ever mattering to other people.

The themes outlined are revisited in various sections of this chapter. I regard this chapter as one of the most important chapters in this book, given the risks for certain young people and the broad failure thus far in applied settings to strongly emphasize the need to matter and feelings of not mattering in assessment, treatment, and prevention. This is perplexing, given the broad emphasis in schools and other contexts on the theme "you matter" as a vital component of suicide prevention efforts.

The need for urgent solutions is evident according to what is known at present. There is a discernible increase in the prevalence of youth suicide in certain countries, including Brazil, the United Kingdom, and the United States (see Bertuccio et al., 2024). An alarming trend is the increasing prevalence of suicides among youth of color and LGBTQ+ youth (see Hatchel et al., 2019; Meza et al., 2022; Sheftall et al., 2022). Feelings of not mattering almost certainly contribute to some degree; recent surveys have indicated that LGBTQ+ youth have comparatively low reported levels of feelings of mattering in the community. For instance, as mentioned in Chapter 4, survey data from Texas in 2021 indicated that, overall, a sense of mattering in the community was found in 43.1% of the respondents, but this number fell to 26.9% percent among youth designated as gay, lesbian, or bisexual. These statistics grow in importance when considered within the context of evidence that links youth suicidality and feelings of not mattering in the community.

It is important to go beyond statistics and prevalence rates to consider what it is like for the adolescent who lacks a sense of mattering and feels suicidal. The psychological pain that precipitates a suicide attempt is almost certain to be amplified among young people who lack a positive and stable sense of identity and have concluded that they are not valued by others. This was underscored by an adolescent boy who participated in a study of the phenomenology of adolescent suicide (see Baloyo, 2021). Andrew, who was 19 years old, felt that no one cared for him and that he was not valuable. He wondered to himself whether anyone would even cry for him if he died by suicide. How did Andrew get to this point in his young life? Tragically, starting from a young age, Andrew was abandoned by his mother again and again. He was typically left in the care of his grandmother. Ultimately, his aunt took on the caregiver role, but she eventually grew neglectful and quite distant. It seems clear in this instance that maternal abandonment and subsequent events triggered the suicide attempt. When it comes to the lives some young people have endured, it seems reasonable to conclude that, for some young people, the sense of not being valued and not mattering amounts to being psychologically abandoned.

There is no doubt that for some vulnerable youth, the realization that they are not important and not cared about is highly traumatic and intensively experienced in terms of associated cognitions, emotions, and destructive urges. When interpersonal trauma is seen as a contributor, anti-mattering experiences may play a contributing role. The case of Andrew illustrates how the feeling of not mattering can become linked, seemingly inextricably, with the experience of suicide ideation. Here, I refer specifically to Andrew wondering whether anyone would even cry for him if he were no longer alive.

Similar themes were expressed by a 17-year-old Latino adolescent who was assessed as part of research on stress, depression, and suicide ideation among Latino adolescents (see Hovey & King, 1996). He shared, "Rejection from those I love hurts. I feel as if I don't matter. I think my future will worsen each day a bit more. . . . Life for me is not worth anything now, nor will it ever be" (p. 1189). The risk level was amplified because this feeling of not mattering was combined with a strong sense of hopelessness. A key clinical consideration when assessing feelings of not mattering and suicidality in adolescents is whether the hopelessness extends to a sense of never having the possibility of mattering to others and one's community.

Another troubling case that made its way into the news also merits mention. We learned in 2014 of the suicide of Brandon Larsen (Chicklas, 2014). Brandon had been bullied relentlessly at school. It is easy to envision that a child or adolescent who is the target of bullying would find it humiliating and also arouse feelings of not mattering to others. This seemed to apply to Brandon. One of the two letters he wrote before his death included an explicit focus on his feeling of not mattering, along with a reference to no one liking him and wondering why he was still here. He went on to relate that he was shoved into a locker by bullies who were tormenting him and felt invisible because the teacher across the hall seemed not to care about what had happened. In this instance, according to Brandon, the bullying extended to his tormentors advising Brandon a week earlier that he should take his own life.

Another case recounted by D.-M. Lewis (2017) emphasized the role of losing a previous sense of mattering to a significant loved one. A youth named Sebastian became suicidal after his mother died and he lost her as a source of mattering. His sister was sent to live with other relatives while his father ignored Sebastian and instead spent considerable time with a female neighbor and her children. Ultimately, Sebastian's father developed a relationship with his neighbor and ended up having a child with her. For

Sebastian, this amounted to a loss of mattering compounded by abandonment and rejection from a parent who was capable of giving attention to another child but not him.

These themes were also evident in a case account of a youth named David (see D.-M. Lewis, 2017). David had a mother who had to be hospitalized due to mental illness and a father who was unresponsive to his needs. David experienced a sense of being abandoned and considerable chaos in his family life. He responded by engaging in criminal behavior. Eventually, David was incarcerated and attempted suicide while in custody. D.-M. Lewis (2017) observed that such young people seem barraged with constant reminders of how they have failed to matter to others.

Why emphasize the theme "youth as failures"? This characterization captures the tendency of so many young people to believe that their feelings of insignificance and not mattering reflect them as people. This theme was highlighted in the previous chapter on feelings of not mattering and depression, and it fits with the discussion in Chapter 1 on how feelings of not mattering are incorporated as a form of self-evaluation. It is far too common for young people to reach the erroneous conclusion that there must be something wrong with them; they conclude they are defective or deficient in ways that cause other people to turn away from them. These young people may feel invisible because they are invisible to most people. Similarly, when these young people feel unheard by others, it is easy for them to surmise that they are not worth being listened to in the first place. This generalized sense of being invisible and unheard by everyone can be countered effectively by seeing a clinician, counselor, or social worker who repeatedly makes these young people feel both seen and heard through listening intently to them. This practice and other key approaches are documented in an article that reviews the link between feelings of not mattering and suicidality and outlines important ways to interact with vulnerable young people (see Flett, 2024a).

The internalization of the feeling of not mattering merits a unique way of being described and understood. The sage observations of Ralph Ellison are helpful in this regard. Ellison is, of course, known for writing the timeless classic *Invisible Man* (1952). He used the term unvisible to refer to internalizing being treated as invisible. If you feel *invisible* and feel it stems from you, you become unvisible. By extension, the term *unsignificant* should be introduced to connote when someone attributes apparent social insignificance to something about the self.

When it comes to the link between suicide and feelings of not mattering, there is a conceptual void in terms of explanations for how and why feelings of not mattering come to play a role in suicide. Mattering is linked with vulnerability because of exceptionally low levels of mattering and high levels of anti-mattering assessed by measures such as the General Mattering Scale (Marcus & Rosenberg, 1987) and Anti-Mattering Scale (Flett et al., 2022). Moreover, mattering can also play a role if the vulnerable person experiences a sudden loss of mattering due to changing life circumstances and ways of viewing the self. Some experiences can be traumatic and involve a loss of self, such as the death of a significant other. However, adolescents experience relationship breakups or bullying, which combine heartache with a loss of importance, especially if there is no discernible way to restore previous status. This loss is made worse if it is publicly known and can add to feelings of shame, humiliation, unwanted attention, and being scrutinized.

FEELINGS OF NOT MATTERING AND MULTIPLE PATHWAYS TO SUICIDE

Some ways that feelings of not mattering can result in the risk of suicide and experience of suicide ideation and plans are considered next. However, it is important to first focus on feelings of not mattering and suicidality in context. Feelings of not mattering are not always implicated when someone is lost to suicide; Shneidman's (2005) emphasis on individual experiences must be kept in mind. It is not uncommon to read accounts of a young person who was overwhelmed by profound and unrelenting psychological pain despite being surrounded by people who cared and provided messages of mattering. In such instances, various questions come to mind. Why was that degree of mattering to others not enough reason for living? Did the person not internalize the mattering feedback given to them by others? Some people might know they matter yet be incapable of feeling it. And what can we do to help surviving family members know they are not to blame?

Second, it is important to be realistic about how some young people respond to messages such as "you matter." There is a natural tendency for young people with a highly negative self-concept to discount positive themes and messages because these messages are entirely at odds with their highly negative view of themself and how they expect to be seen and evaluated by others. Some young people may see "you matter" as merely an empty slogan that does not map onto their life realities (Flett, 2024a). This means that convincing a young person that they matter may require an extensive process to get them to eventually realize that "here, at last, is someone who truly understands me and cares about me." I realized this after reading one online response from an adult who had been suicidal for decades. This person said,

"And don't tell me I matter. I know I don't matter and likely never will matter." The young person who is certain of not mattering to others will require prolonged and convincing evidence that they do and that someone does care. Time is an ally in one sense because it becomes increasingly difficult to deny that someone cares when that person spends considerable time with the person in jeopardy.

Feelings of not mattering may have no role in potentiating or exacerbating suicidal tendencies until later in the process. As suggested earlier, feelings of not mattering can stem from significant others not noticing or failing to say or do anything. Another scenario occurs when the young person tells their parents about their suicidal tendencies, and the parents surprisingly react with anger. Imagine the additional hurt and sense of not mattering when a young person takes the brave step of sharing internal thoughts and urges and, instead of getting a caring response, feels like an inconvenience or a burden to their parents. It can make a world of difference when care is shown by inquiring with concern and asking tough questions but then following that by truly listening and trying to understand the young person.

There are three key elements related to mattering that are implicated in the experience of suicidal thoughts and actions (Flett, 2024b). First, feelings of not mattering are strongly linked to loneliness and the failure to establish social and emotional connections with others. We should be especially concerned about the level of risk for the young person who lacks a sense of mattering to others and has a strong sense of isolation and alienation. Why does this matter? The acclaimed suicidologist Ronald Maris (1985) analyzed adolescent suicides and concluded that social isolation is a substantial risk factor, especially if accompanied by a failure to adapt socially. More generally, loneliness is regarded as a factor that heightens suicide risk (see Page et al., 2006). Of course, our research indicates that loneliness and being socially isolated typically co-occur with feelings of not mattering (see Chapter 5, this volume).

Second, feelings of not mattering are also tied closely to feelings of helplessness and hopelessness, but there are some unique distinctions (Flett, 2024b). In this instance, hopelessness is general but also a specific form of social hopelessness. There is a conviction that negative social outcomes will be experienced in the future, and there is nothing that the adolescent can do to stop them from happening. But especially important is the specific cognitive set that comes with perceiving there is no hope of mattering to others (e.g., I will never matter to the people who matter to me, and there is little or nothing I can do about this).

Finally, there is a strong link between the psychological pain described by Shneidman (1984) and feelings of not mattering (Flett, 2024b), which

I first discussed and elaborated on in 2018 (Flett, 2018a). However, it is now proposed that when psychological pain is at extreme levels and is highly cognitively salient, the psychache experienced has an element specific to feelings of not mattering. Some people are particularly at risk when they experience pain in the form of an unbearable state of feeling unimportant and socially insignificant. This may extend to believing, "No one cares about my pain, and I won't be missed." When someone has reached the point that suicide is an option because life has become too much to bear, this decision is likely based partly on the pain and shame that comes from not mattering to specific others or the community.

Key Insights From Qualitative Research

A qualitative study often cited for its focus on adolescent suicidality and perfectionism also has implications for the association between feelings of not mattering and suicidal tendencies. Stephens (1987) analyzed the experiences of adolescent experiences of women who went on to attempt suicide in adulthood. This study of 50 adult women who attempted suicide found that most participants described their adolescence as abjectly unhappy and marked by their parents not wanting to care for them and not loving them. Their accounts leave little doubt that they did not feel valued and felt that they did not matter to their parents. Rather than describing this as not mattering, Stephens (1987) characterized it as a "lack of self-esteem and feelings of insecurity in relationships" (p. 111). The participants described themselves as adolescent girls who felt isolated from family and friends in general, and, as a result, several left home for a life on the streets.

This study is known for identifying two types of suicidal adolescent girls. One group was characterized as "humble pie adolescents," who desperately seek approval and try to be perfect while suppressing their dysphoria and resentment. These adolescents had more instances of multiple suicide attempts as adult women. The participants in the second group were labeled "cheap thrills adolescents" due to their propensity to engage in impulsive and reckless behavior and various forms of "acting out." Stephens (1987) described these young women as striking out aggressively at an interpersonal environment that had denied them a sense of worth and significance. These females were more likely to come from working-class homes.

Anti-mattering is a highly salient orientation when young people feel ignored, dismissed, and as if they are invisible and their concerns do not warrant attention (for a discussion, see Flett, 2024a). If anti-mattering is a factor that contributes to suicide ideation among younger people, it should emerge as a theme in well-done qualitative studies, especially given evidence that anti-mattering is a highly salient theme among people making online posts to suicide forums (see Deas et al., 2023). The relevance of anti-mattering was clear in a recent qualitative study that examined risk and protective factors for suicide among adolescents from Guyana (see Arora et al., 2020). Interviews were conducted with 40 adolescents and 17 adult stakeholders. This work was situated in Guyana because this small South American country is the world leader in youth suicide. Arora et al. (2020) identified five risk factor categories. The clearest example of anti-mattering was related to the academic pressure risk factor. One adolescent attributed a peer's death by suicide to the behavior of a teacher who was described as overusing her authority in ways that made young people feel "small and insecure. Your word doesn't matter and whatever she says is final" (p. 623). Anti-mattering was particularly evident in the adolescents' descriptions of parents who provided little emotional support. This could mean ignoring youth needs, but it sometimes included punishing or invalidating youths who expressed negative emotions. One youth recounted how another youth expressed feelings of suicidality to a family member who did not take it seriously until the suicidal youth was deceased. Unfortunately, this is a frequent theme.

The positive factors identified in this research included having adults around who were attuned to changes in behavior and sensitively inquired and expressed concern. Emotional support was especially appreciated if it came from people described as "non-judgmental, trustworthy, and who took the initiative to approach adolescents who appeared to be in distress" (Arora et al., 2020, p. 625). A related investigation of barriers to mental health help-seeking emphasized the preventive benefits of having adults who listen and show their care and interest by trying to frame their responses in language that suicidal Guyanese youth tend to use (see Arora & Persaud, 2020).

Bostik and Everall (2006) interviewed 50 Canadian adolescents and emerging adults who had all attempted suicide between the ages of 13 and 19. The sense of not being able to communicate openly with parents represented a broader problem of feeling disconnected from their parents. Many participants felt a lack of emotional connection with their parents, and this was interpreted as a lack of care and interest by their parents. These perceptions were then internalized into self-views reflecting the theme of having limited self-worth and value.

Importantly, Bostik and Everall (2007) also sought to identify solutions and strategies to help adolescents heal following a suicide attempt. Numerous participants mentioned it was vital to establish a caring relationship with an individual who made them feel valued and recognized. Bostik and Everall emphasized the need for adolescents to have someone who would miss them if they were gone. This provided a sense of self-assurance that enabled the adolescent to discuss personal matters, be authentic, and no longer hide behind a mask. Hope was also deemed essential.

An article on teachers who had worked with students who returned to their classrooms after the student had attempted suicide serves as a reminder of the important roles played by teachers in the recovery process. Buchanan and Harris (2014) noted that their students clearly mattered to these teachers. While it may seem taxing to learn and implement specific techniques, the natural expression of mattering and caring is in keeping with the natural tendencies of educators who embrace the role of caring adults.

Empirical Research on Mattering and Suicide

Currently, no research has examined the relationship between suicidality and anti-mattering in adolescents, but the existing research provides clear support for the proposed association. The first set of studies measured mattering as a general overall score, typically using a version of the Mattering Index by Elliott et al. (2004). Important supplementary results found in Elliott's (2009) book on mattering in the family are also described. The next research summarized is a contemporary study by Edwards et al. (2021) based on a self-report measure assessing mattering at school. The final section provides an overview of several studies illustrating how a broad single-item measure of mattering in the community was related to suicidality. Other details can be found in Flett (2024a).

General Mattering and Suicide

Elliott and colleagues (2005) examined mattering and suicidality in a large sample of 2,004 adolescents. This is the most extensive analysis, given the supplementary information found in Elliott (2009). Mattering was assessed with 36 items (18 items tapping mattering to friends, and 18 items tapping mattering to parents) derived from the Mattering Index (see Elliott et al., 2004). Suicidality was measured with two items framed in terms of the prior 12 months (i.e., "Did you ever seriously consider attempting suicide?" and "Did you ever seriously consider attempting some action you hoped would cause your death by someone else?"). Adolescents were also assessed in terms of levels of self-esteem. Elliott et al. (2005) reported via an odds-ratio analysis that there was a strong negative association between mattering and suicide ideation. Detailed analyses indicated this was a robust association because as mattering scores fell below the mean, there were sharp elevations in suicide ideation levels. Elliott et al. (2005) also reported that self-esteem was a mediator of the tendency for lower mattering to be associated with suicide ideation.

A recent project used the standard Mattering Index by Elliott et al. (2005). The results from this project have been reported thus far in a master's thesis (Bryan, 2022) and a conference presentation (see M. Smith et al., 2022). M. Smith et al. (2022) characterized the study as a test of "The Model of Girls' Resilience." It included data from 10- to 14-year-olds. Comparisons of mattering, self-esteem, problem-focused coping, and stress showed that mattering was more relevant for understanding suicide ideation in girls than in boys. Mattering and stress were the two strongest correlates of suicide ideation. M. Smith et al. reported that adolescent girls with lower mattering scores were 1.5 times more likely to report acute ideation and 2.5 times more likely to report chronic suicide ideation.

We now return briefly to the original work from Elliott et al. (2005). Elliott (2009) reported some important supplementary analyses of the data that go well past their original findings (Elliott et al., 2005). These results go beyond suicide ideation to include a focus on suicide plans and reports of attempted suicide.

The overall number of adolescents who reported suicide plans was low when they were asked whether they had formulated a plan within the previous 12 months. This necessitated the use of refined statistical techniques, but much was learned. It was established that risk increases considerably even among adolescents with mattering scores only slightly lower than the mean. However, this pattern also can be seen as encouraging from a prevention perspective. How so? These analyses also promote the message that even small increases in mattering to one's family reduce the risk of self-destructive behavior, and the greater the increase, the lower the risk.

The findings for suicide plans also took into account self-esteem and depression. Elliott (2009) found evidence that, even though the overall probability was low, levels of mattering to the family distinguished between participants who did or did not plan to commit suicide. Elliott characterized this as a powerful change in probabilities for those with lower mattering to their families. The results changed substantially when self-esteem and depression were entered as factors. The overall results led Elliott to conclude that "mattering to family raises a person's self-esteem, and self-esteem, both directly and in conjunction with its relationship to depression, lowers the likelihood of planning a suicide" (p. 149).

The same analysis was conducted on the measure of actual suicide. The results indicated that mattering to family had a direct association with reported suicide attempts. This association was attenuated somewhat when self-esteem was included; however, it was still the case that deficits in mattering to one's family contributed to the prediction of reports of suicide attempts in adolescents between the ages of 11 and 13.

Of course, Elliott (2009) also made the key observation that this analysis focused on whether the participants reported an unsuccessful suicide attempt. It is possible that the role of feelings of not mattering was underrepresented here for one obvious sad reason: Some adolescents may already have been lost to suicide.

Mattering at School

Edwards et al. (2021) reported the results of a new survey of 400 youth in Grades 7 to 10. They completed a one-item measure of mattering at school. The main purpose was to document the scope and correlates of victimization among American Indian (AI) and Alaska Native (AN) youth over the previous 6 months. Types of victimization under investigation included sexual assault, dating violence, bullying, sharing of nude photos, sexual harassment, homophobic teasing, and racism. Four items from the 2013 Youth Risk Behavior Surveillance System (Centers for Disease Control and Prevention, 2014) were also included to assess various indicators of youth adjustment: past 6-month depressive symptoms, suicidal ideation, alcohol use, and school mattering (a youth's sense of belonging to school). Mattering was linked negatively with suicide ideation ($r = -.36$). Edwards et al. also found that mattering at school was associated negatively with other predictors, including alcohol use, being electronically bullied, and having forced sex.

A new longitudinal investigation further attests to the protection mattering provides at school. Waterman and associates (2024) conducted a study with 2,539 middle and high school students assessed five times over 3 years. This methodological approach meant that differences between participants and within-person changes could be studied. At a broad level, it was established that suicidality in the prior 6 months was significantly elevated among female adolescents, older adolescents, Hispanic/Latino adolescents, non-White adolescents, and sexual minority adolescents. Within-person analyses showed that within-person increases in cumulative peer victimization were associated with within-person increases in depression and suicidality, but increases were attenuated as a function of school mattering: Higher school mattering seemingly reduced the impact of peer victimization.

Mattering in the Community

Mattering in the community is clearly protective. An impressive study by Murphey et al. (2004) has been referred to in various chapters of this book.

Murphey et al. evaluated the responses of 30,000 adolescents from Vermont who completed an expanded version of the Youth Risk Behavior Survey (Lamonda, 2001). One item tapped perceived mattering in the community (i.e., "young person is valued in the community"). Participants were assessed on five other youth assets in addition to community mattering (e.g., grades in school, parents talking about school, participation in youth programs, community volunteering, students helping to decide what goes on in school). The key outcome variable was a self-report indicator of planning or not having planned suicide. Analyses showed that community mattering was not only beneficial but also the most protective factor when all six youth assets were considered.

Brinkman and colleagues (2021) described a follow-up study in Vermont focused on mattering in the community. The data were from the 2015 Youth Risk Behavior Surveillance Survey. Data were obtained from public middle schoolers ($N = 13{,}648$). Mattering was assessed by a one-item measure (i.e., "Do you agree or disagree that in your community you feel like you matter to people?"). Other measures included questions about food insecurity, breakfast consumption, suicidal ideation, hopelessness, and physical activity. Participants were also asked whether they mattered and whether they had at least one caring teacher in the school who they could talk with if they had a problem. Suicide ideation and hopelessness were assessed as binary variables (i.e., yes or no). Mattering was found to be associated with both hopelessness and suicide ideation. The association between food insecurity and suicide ideation was reduced substantially after controlling for mattering in the community. This reflects the fact that youth who did not feel they mattered in their community reported substantially greater food insecurity. Inequities may underscore low levels of feelings of mattering in the community. Lower suicide ideation was also reported by youth who said they had at least one teacher who they could speak with if they had a problem.

Two recent studies also attest to the protective role of mattering in the community. Semprevivo (2023) reported results from her investigation of data from the 2019 Nashville Youth Risk Behavioral Surveillance System. This sample had 1,407 youth, including 303 LGBTQ youth in Grades 9 to 12. This study examined mattering in the community and found that only 47% of participants felt they mattered in the community. Analyses established that mattering to the community was associated with lower odds of having depression and suicidality. Collectively, 28% of students reported considering, planning, or attempting suicide at some point during the previous 12 months. Notably, mattering was a unique protective factor in predicting suicidality, especially among bullied youth.

Similarly, Harder and colleagues (2023) reported results from the 2019 Vermont survey. The sample consisted of 13,998 middle school students and 18,613 high school students. About three out of five students at either school level indicated they felt they mattered. Measures included the same item tapping community mattering and an item inquiring about the presence of suicide plans and suicide attempts over the previous 12 months. Analyses confirmed that mattering in the community was linked with a substantially reduced likelihood of having a suicide plan. One of the clearest indicators of why community mattering is important was that three out of four students with a suicide plan reported that they did not feel a sense of mattering in the community.

The extensive use of demographic information is a distinguishing strength of this study. It was found, in general, that students with minority identities were significantly more likely to make a suicide plan and attempt suicide. Community mattering, when it was present, was highly protective for heterosexual and LGB students but only slightly more protective for heterosexual students. The odds of a suicide plan were 77% lower for heterosexual students and 58% lower for LGB students. The only group in which community mattering was not beneficial in terms of suicide attempts was transgender students. One of the most troubling findings reported by Harder et al. (2023) is that only about one in three students designated as LGBTQ indicated they felt they mattered in the community.

MATTERING AS A PROTECTIVE RESOURCE

I would be remiss if I failed to mention that there is also a wealth of data from Maine, where mattering in the community is regarded as a key metric. An infographic based on the 2019 data from the Maine Integrated Youth Survey illustrates the protective impact of the feeling of mattering in the community (see Maine Department of Health and Human Services, 2022). This pictorial display focused on data from the 2019 sample of over 55,000 high school participants. Importantly, this work focused on mattering as a protective resource rather than solely on the vulnerability inherent in feelings of not mattering in the community.

What did survey results from Maine reveal in terms of mental health? Once again, a feeling of mattering in the community was protective. Other significant differences were found in terms of depressive symptoms in the past year (20% vs. 47%), having considered suicide in the past year (9% vs. 26%), and any current substance use (32% vs. 42%).

Several protective factors differed by mattering status, with the high-mattering group adolescents more likely to have other protective factors. These results are summarized in Table 14.1. These results are useful in suggesting the factors that may underscore and contribute to a feeling of mattering in general and in the community.

Mattering has been assessed for many years in surveys conducted in Texas. It is a topic I have discussed recently as part of a series provided by the Texas School Safety Center. Data from Texas also accord with the conclusion that mattering is a protective resource. The key measure of interest was once again the single self-report item that assesses perceptions of mattering in the community; again, it was the case that asking just one item yielded valuable information. Olcoń and colleagues (2017) reported results from 2,560 high school students who took the 2013 Texas Youth Risk Behavior Survey. Suicide was measured in terms of one item tapping suicide ideation and another tapping the presence or absence of a suicide plan. Statistical analyses suggested that community mattering lowered the odds of suicide ideation by about 34%, and it lowered the odds of a suicide attempt by 20%. Of course, these results have implications beyond statistics—young lives are in the balance.

Chino and Fullerton-Gleason (2006) considered the responses of 690 American Aboriginal adolescents who completed the 1998–1999 Youth Risk Behavior Survey. All participants lived on a reservation in New Mexico. The key variable was an index of the presence or absence of a past or current suicide attempt. Sadly, about one in four youths (24.2%) indicated they had attempted suicide, and one in 10 indicated attempting suicide at least twice. The suicide attempt variable was scored as dichotomous (i.e., the reported presence or absence of a prior attempt). A composite of three items tapped mattering in the community and related variables (i.e., feeling important to people in the community and having caring neighbors). Youth reports indicated that not having attempted suicide was associated with all

TABLE 14.1. Associated Resources for High Versus Low Community Mattering Groups

Protective factor	% Agreement
Parents help me succeed	84% versus 68%
Caring and supportive teacher	88% versus 71%
Family love and support	88% versus 72%
Support from other adults	63% versus 35%
Grades were mostly A's and B's	85% versus 72%

Note. Data from Maine Department of Health and Human Services (2022).

three protective variables. These results point to protective mechanisms that can become key targets in the quest to reduce suicide risk.

Extensive data from Alaska also linked mattering in the community with less suicidality (see Heath et al., 2015; Sidmore, 2015). Mattering can also reduce risk among young people who experienced early adverse events. Results reported for Rochester, New York, indicated that when the focus was on students who reported two or more adverse childhood experiences, mattering in the community was associated with a lower likelihood of considering suicide (see Rochester Regional Health, 2018; Scharf, 2018).

The most recent relevant findings are summarized in two related articles (see Berny et al., 2024; Berny & Tanner-Smith, 2024). This research once again shows that an index that includes an emphasis on community mattering is associated negatively with having a prior suicide attempt. What is most noteworthy about this research is that the participants were 294 adolescents from Minnesota, Wisconsin, and Texas who had received formal substance abuse treatment or were enrolled in a recovery high school. Clearly, mattering can prove beneficial when adolescents are characterized by risk factors, such as addictive tendencies or psychological vulnerabilities such as feeling like a burden (see Barnett et al., 2020).

One overarching concern is that feelings of not mattering can come into play at the system level. This issue is discussed next and was also considered at length in Flett (2024a).

SUICIDE AND SYSTEMIC FEELINGS OF NOT MATTERING

A key factor is the extent to which treatment services and the mental health system as a whole can make a person with suicidal thoughts give up hope of ever being treated, seen, or viewed as someone who matters. The degree to which available services leave clients feeling they matter versus unvalued and insignificant can be a vital criterion for program evaluation and service delivery. This conclusion follows from the results of a revealing study conducted with 52 parents who lost their children to suicide. This research is now briefly summarized.

A qualitative study was conducted in Sweden by Werbart Törnblom and colleagues (2015) to gain some unique insights into the factors contributing to youth suicide. A total of 78 interviews were conducted with parents; the focus was on 52 youths (19 females and 33 males) who took their own lives. The full range of what was revealed is beyond the scope of this chapter. However, suffice it to say that enough factors were identified to permit the researchers to build a comprehensive model of the processes implicated in youth suicide.

How do feelings of not mattering come into play? Unfortunately, many parents provided reports of an unresponsive system or mental health professional who was in a position to help and convey "you matter" to the vulnerable adolescent but instead did the opposite in the view of the parents. The bereaved parents recounted story after story of professionals who failed to understand and often failed to listen to the client or family members. One parent described professionals as the following: "They were unavailable, inattentive, did not ask the right questions, did not listen to the parent's story or to the girl's pain" (p. 1107). It is easy for a young person to feel even more insignificant when the facade is dropped and an attempt is made to reach out, but the potential helper minimizes the young person's pain. This analysis suggested that girls were more likely than boys to have the experience of no one listening to them, even after a previous potentially lethal suicide attempt. This emphasis on professionals not listening and taking responsibility was incorporated as a central element of the model representing steps toward suicide in a prototypical case.

Unfortunately, it is far too easy to identify case examples of young people who almost certainly got the message that they do not matter when it comes to the system. In my previous book, I highlighted the story of a boy from Ontario, Canada, who also received the message from the mental health system that he did not matter despite having the right to timely and effective treatment (see Flett, 2018a). We learned in 2015 the story of Matthew Leaton, an 18-year-old adolescent. Matthew was hospitalized 15 times in 2 years because of suicidal thoughts, along with extreme anxiety and depression. Matthew's situation was urgent, yet he endured a 9-month wait for treatment. How do we know this led to feelings of not mattering? Matthew described his experience as follows: "I started to feel like I'm not important; I don't matter. I felt like people don't care" (see Armstrong, 2015, para. 6). How many other young people who endure their time on the waiting list reach the same conclusion as Matthew? This is just one of many reasons mental health services for young people need to be dramatically improved and expanded with a sense of urgency.

Matthew's experiences and feelings are reflected in the feedback that youth in the Northwest Territories provided to a standing committee tasked with providing youth suicide prevention recommendations (Northwest Territories Standing Committee on Social Development, 2023). When youth voices are heard, they often reflect themes that can stem from their need to matter. For example, in this instance, a key theme when youths expressed their views was that "they want to feel sincerely cared about" (p. 5). This desire was affirmed by a staff member who noted, "One act of kindness will make a huge difference in someone's life" (p. 5).

Another key committee recommendation emphasized the need for much more extensive and responsive care after a young person has attempted suicide. This was summarized aptly by one youth who told the committee in Yellowknife, "Once we reach out for help, something needs to happen" (Northwest Territories Standing Committee on Social Development, 2023, p. 3). The report noted that many youths indicated that nothing happened and there was no mental health support. Regrettably, the overall summary recommendations from the committee did not mention mattering promotion; sadly, this is usually the case. The issues outlined here are not specific to the Northwest Territories and should not be interpreted as centering them out. It was important that they listened to youth voices.

PRACTICAL ISSUES AND IMPLICATIONS FOR RESPONSIVE ASSESSMENT AND TREATMENT

I conclude this chapter by briefly considering some of the many issues and suggestions that follow from the themes and information recounted here. Additional suggestions are in the final chapter. First, it should be clear by now that mattering and anti-mattering need to be not only incorporated but also featured in clinical assessments of suicide risk and contributing factors to levels of suicidality. The measures commonly used in research are quick and easy to administer, and enough psychometric information is available to support their use and derive norms. However, this psychometric information is unnecessary because anyone with even a bit of training can scan the questionnaire responses and see that the child or adolescent has agreed with items that suggest the presence of feelings of not mattering to others.

Broad surveys of youth that seek to establish the prevalence and predictors of suicidality should routinely add self-report items that tap mattering versus not mattering. The results of these surveys can play a vital role in establishing whether prevention effects are yielding improvements. Levels of mattering can and should be prioritized as a key metric.

Another useful alternative is administering scales that tap into reasons for living and examine whether a young person endorses these reasons. Reasons that align with protecting a sense of mattering include family members caring about what happens, friends caring about what happens, and family taking time to listen. A strong case can be made for adding items to existing measures that more directly tap into the feeling of mattering (e.g., People make me feel like I matter. People would miss me if I were no longer around. I know I can make a difference in the lives of other people).

The feeling of not mattering should also be a focus of treatment, with mattering as a theme that should be seen as a key aspect of the therapeutic alliance between the client and therapist. The young person with a sense of mattering to no one will no longer be able to cling to this feeling and perspective when consistently exposed to a caring and compassionate therapist who is there to ensure that the young person will be seen, heard, cared for, and cared about.

Because there is a distinct possibility that Matthew's experience, described earlier, is the norm rather than the exception, one initial theme in the treatment process for all children and adolescents, if not deemed inappropriate, could involve an inquiry into how the delay in receiving treatment can arouse natural feelings of not mattering and wondering why there is not more urgency and importance attached to the young person's well-being. Here, it must be underscored that even if feelings of not mattering have not played a role in the onset of mental health challenges, they can still be implicated when feelings of not mattering have been generated by how the system has treated a child or adolescent.

Young people who enter treatment with a high degree of anti-mattering will be alert to any signs and indications that fit their broad view of not mattering to anyone, and this lens will be used in how the therapist's behavior is perceived and received. Less than full attention will be noted, and feelings of not mattering will be maintained. The young person who lacks a sense of mattering will be especially attuned to any indication that they are not getting the full and personalized attention they need from a clinician or counselor who has a long list of other young people they need to see on any given day. It is even the case, as noted by one young person, that too much emphasis on a hopeful future can make it seem to some young people that their current problems do not matter and, by extension, they do not matter in the present (see Courtwright et al., 2023).

These observations reflect instances when the young person has come into contact with someone representing the helping profession. Unfortunately, it is safe to presume that most young people who feel like they do not matter will avoid seeking the help they need. A focus on mattering should be included in most, if not all, prevention programs.

A recent evaluation of school-based prevention programs addressing suicidal thoughts and behaviors concluded that these programs have a discernible but small positive effect (Gijzen et al., 2022). The specific recommendations acknowledged a need for more research on programs that target known risk factors, and, by extension, it is evident we need more programs that target specific risk factors. Feelings of not mattering should be seen as one of the most important risk factors to target.

When this type of program is offered as a school-based initiative, it presents an opportunity for key messaging focused on students being aware of how such a program stands as an illustration of how they matter and how their needs have been prioritized. The reasons for the prevention efforts should be communicated to children and adolescents and then reiterated in ways that radiate genuine care and concern. The messages sent should be unmistakable in conveying that every young person matters and that something is being done about their well-being. The opportunity for students to have a voice and the chance to take on a leadership role in these essential initiatives will also heighten the salience of mattering and establish connections between staff and students, who will be seen as working together on a shared mission.

SUMMARY

This chapter provides one of the clearest indications of how mattering can be highly protective for young people when it is present but can involve exceptional risk and vulnerability when absent. Existing research on mattering and suicidality in adolescents was summarized to show that the feeling of mattering to others is associated negatively with suicide ideation, acts, and plans, but feelings of not mattering are associated with considerable psychological pain and heightened risk of suicide. The focus in this chapter on variable-centered research was balanced through the inclusion of case excerpts that illustrated that the feeling of not mattering is central to the vulnerability of suicidal youths. Relevant qualitative research was also cited.

This chapter concluded with a discussion of how the mental health system plays a key role. Young people needing intervention require prompt and effective responses and solutions that counter their sense of not mattering to others. It is far too easy for young people experiencing suicidal thoughts and urges to conclude that a lengthy wait for treatment is just one more indication that they do not matter to others or that others matter more than they do. Collectively, the observations and conclusions in this chapter reflect the need to focus on mattering and prioritize addressing and preventing suicide among young people.

PART V PUTTING MATTERING INTO ACTION IN KEY CONTEXTS

15 GROWING UP WITH THE FEELING OF MATTERING

Summary and Suggestions

This final chapter is designed to be both a brief overview and a summary of topics addressed throughout this book, as well as a statement of what children and adolescents need to grow up feeling and knowing they matter. Every child deserves to grow up knowing they matter, which is entirely in keeping with calls for the universal recognition of each child's right to matter. I noted in Chapter 3 that in my previous work (Flett, 2018a, 2024a) and the work of others (see Ghaye et al., 2021), there is an emphasis on the right of every child to matter. Hopefully, readers of this book will agree that a sense of mattering must be added as one of the fundamental rights included by the United Nations, along with the 54 rights identified during the United Nations Convention on the Rights of the Child (1989).

The goal from the outset of this book was to examine mattering in childhood and adolescence in an unprecedented way in terms of the scope of topics considered and the depth of analysis. The 14 chapters that precede this final chapter address a vast array of themes, including central themes, such as the assessment of mattering in young people and developmental contributors and considerations. The book begins with initial chapters that

https://doi.org/10.1037/0000449-016
Mattering as a Core Need in Children and Adolescents: Theoretical, Clinical, and Research Perspectives, by G. L. Flett

present the case for why mattering is an essential feeling and a core need. The picture emerges that the mattering construct is complex, and mattering is an essential element of positive youth development. Moreover, as emphasized at the end of Chapter 1, the feeling of mattering is used by young people as a form of self-evaluation and self-assessment that is central to self and identity.

The urgency of this book's focus is perhaps most evident in Chapter 4, where it is demonstrated that far too many young people have a feeling of not mattering. The initial evidence indicates that when mattering in general is the focus, at least 30% of adolescents either feel like they do not matter or are uncertain about whether they matter. When it comes to mattering in the community, it is almost fifty-fifty whether youths feel they matter in their communities. The statistics combine to suggest that far too many young people are experiencing psychological pain.

Chapter 5 extended this analysis through an extensive discussion of young people who feel like they do not matter. This chapter listed 10 keys to understanding these young people and what life means for them. The goal of this chapter was to understand these children and adolescents in terms of how feelings of not mattering are experienced and expressed and consider associated factors and processes. It is also my attempt "to go beyond the numbers" and shift the focus to considering what it is like to be a child or adolescent who lacks a feeling of mattering to others.

The chapters composing the next main section of this book focus on positive youth development and associated outcomes described in Chapter 3. It is important to remember the power of mattering as a positive force in recognizing its niche in positive psychology. Chapter 8 summarized research on the links that mattering has with happiness and flourishing, and the subsequent chapter (i.e., Chapter 9) presented evidence of the role of mattering in resilience and adaptability. Importantly, resilience was considered across multiple domains, and it was shown that consistent initial evidence links higher levels of mattering with emotional resilience, academic resilience, and interpersonal resilience. The key takeaway from this chapter is the statement from Emmy Werner, who emphasized the resilience and change possible when children or adolescents encounter someone who lets them know they matter.

It is evident throughout this book that just as it is the case that mattering is double-edged for older people, it is also the case with young people. It was shown across multiple chapters in the second half of this book that mattering is adaptive, but feelings of not mattering are exceptionally problematic. Adolescents who feel like they do not matter are prone to addictive tendencies and acting out in various antisocial ways, but they often have internalizing problems involving anxiety, depression, and suicidal thoughts and acts. The numerous costs and consequences of feelings of not mattering are especially disconcerting when the focus shifts to the unacceptable proportion of young people who report that they do not matter to others.

Chapter 10 is a unique chapter that may grow in relevance over time. This chapter makes it clear that mattering is highly relevant to the concerns about problematic social media among youth. Excessive use of social media and its destructive impact among young people are themes that have led to recent public advisories and much scrutiny by policymakers and researchers. In Chapter 10, the significance of the need to matter and its role in susceptibility to social media addiction was discussed at length. Moreover, initial data were summarized that indicate a link between social media addiction and feelings and fears of not mattering among adolescents. Most people would likely not be surprised by the contention and evidence indicating that an unmet need to matter is implicated in problematic social media use, but this topic has thus far not been a central element in discussions of contributing processes and factors.

If an unmet need to matter is so problematic, it is incumbent on us to do what we can to instill a sense of mattering in as many young people as possible. But how do we go about it? The next section can be regarded as a list of "dos and don'ts" that can help us get closer to instilling a sense of mattering in every young person. I have gone so far as to brazenly come up with a list of 10 commandments I would invoke if I could. They are framed as commandments rather than suggestions to underscore how imperative it is to promote mattering among young people.

HOW SHOULD CHILDREN BE TREATED TO BUILD THEIR SENSE OF MATTERING?

Every child should grow up with a strong feeling and secure knowledge of mattering to others, but how can this be achieved? My list of 10 mattering commandments reflects what is most essential in achieving this goal. This list has been informed greatly by the insights and observations of sage observers of children. Here, I am referring to a wide range of influential scholars, including such contributors as John Bowlby, Erik Erikson, Urie Bronfenbrenner, David Elkind, Stella Chess, Herbert Birch, and, of course, Morris Rosenberg. But I am also referring to exceptional parents and educators I have had the pleasure to witness in action and learn from.

Many of the 10 musts represented in Exhibit 15.1 are derived from discussions and analyses of themes found earlier in this book. I next briefly

EXHIBIT 15.1. Growing Up Mattering: The 10 Mattering Commandments

1. All children must have at least a modicum of mattering.
2. Mattering experiences must outweigh and outnumber anti-mattering experiences.
3. The child's need to matter must not become subordinate to the needs of the adults and caregivers in their lives.
4. Children and adolescents must have sustained parental presence to feel like they matter.
5. Affective support and mattering must be experienced and felt throughout childhood, adolescence, and beyond.
6. Mattering must be internalized as a value by identifying with and internalizing the value of being valued and cared for by others modeled by caring adults.
7. Parents and other caring adults must show concern for who the child is as a person, not what the child does or can do.
8. The individuality of each child must be honored and appreciated.
9. Efforts to show children they matter must not be shrouded in controlling behavior.
10. Children and adolescents must be shown and taught adaptive responses and effective ways to respond when they have been made to feel unvalued or devalued.

discuss each commandment to provide some context that can help explain why they have been included and why they were selected from a list that was considerably longer at one point.

The first commandment, "All children must have a modicum of mattering," reflects several considerations. Of course, the emphasis is on all children because, regardless of their circumstances, including family circumstances, all young people need to feel they matter, at least to some extent. There are no exceptions. Some children may have an outsized need to matter, but all children have some need to matter. Thus, this need is found among foster children, for instance, and among children with disabilities. This need exists in children from around the globe, and I sincerely hope that research on mattering in children and adolescents will become more of a global enterprise in the future.

The emphasis on "a modicum of mattering" is a nod to the reality of the situations that too many young people experience. We know from extensive research that some children come from horrible family situations, including having homes dominated by parental afflictions that may involve mental health problems and addiction. These children especially need an opportunity to gain a sense of mattering at school in terms of what can be supplied by peers and education, and they will need to develop a sense of mattering in the community, perhaps as a result of time spent with caring adults. Of course, when it comes to family, the transformative role of other caregivers, such as grandparents, also can be enormous.

The second commandment and its emphasis on mattering experiences outweighing anti-mattering experiences was included to signal that even when young people characteristically feel a sense of mattering, they will have anti-mattering experiences. Life involves a series of challenges and transitions that inevitably can cause someone with feelings of mattering to wonder whether they have become someone who does not matter. This tendency was described eloquently by Schlossberg (1989) as part of her work on mattering during transitions. It is possible that for certain hypersensitive young people, anti-mattering experiences are more intense and have more impact than mattering experiences. These children and adolescents may require a much greater ratio of mattering experiences to anti-mattering experiences to feel good about themselves.

The third point reflects the common-sense notion that children greatly benefit when parents place the needs of their children ahead of their own. Rosenberg and McCullough (1981) alluded briefly to circumstances that do not follow this pattern when they cited Horney's (1950) analysis of parents who are egocentric and narcissistic. I have heard some alarming accounts of narcissistic parents failing to address the needs of their children because they have become envious of the talents of these children and the attention they get. Of course, the link between feelings of not mattering and reports of experiencing child neglect (e.g., Flett, Goldstein, et al., 2016) is an indicator of what can happen when family members have not prioritized the needs of children.

One caveat is that some parents and educators become selfless to the point of neglecting themselves. If children matter to you, it is important to demonstrate self-care and encourage them to advocate for themselves when needed.

The fourth and fifth commandments share an explicit reference to both children and adolescents because it is important to emphasize that adolescents also need to matter no matter how much they seem to push parents and other caregivers away. They need the continuing presence and affection of those who matter to them. A key observation made by Rosenberg (1985) is that peers may become desirable to adolescents because friends and peers can provide the sense of mattering that has not been received at home. Another sage observation worth remembering is, "From the viewpoint of the adolescent, mattering matters profoundly" (Rosenberg & McCullough, 1981, p. 180).

The sixth commandment was raised in Chapter 7 on development and reflects the reality that mattering will benefit a young person throughout life if they have internalized and come to value the need for people to matter. The process of internalization is much more likely to occur following frequent exposure to a parent or caring adult who embodies the value of mattering and provides illustrations of treating other people in ways that send the message that they do indeed matter. Of course, it is widely recognized that warm, responsive, and caring models are especially likely to be imitated and have their values taken on and embraced by children in their lives.

The seventh "must do" reflects that mattering is about the person, and as discussed earlier, it should not be conditional or contingent on achievements or having a certain skill. Young people need to be valued as people; interest in them needs to supplement interest in what they do. We need to avoid the conditional mattering or marginalized mattering that Roderick Carey identified in his important work (see Carey, 2020; Carey et al., 2022). This type of mattering results in attention and interest because of what a child or adolescent can do (e.g., the star athlete), with perhaps little to no emphasis on who they are as people and what they need at a personal level. One effective reminder of this is the title of the classic book by Chess and colleagues (1965): *Your Child Is a Person*.

The emphasis on individuality as the eighth must do is partly an acknowledgment of the heterogeneity and individuality among children. Mattering is about being valued as a unique individual. I discussed at length in my previous book on mattering that we need to feel we matter as unique individuals (see Flett, 2018a). Perhaps the best way to frame this is to invite the reader to reflect on the sense of being a uniquely prized person when they have been made to feel special. I apologize to readers who find it difficult to recall having this feeling.

The ninth commandment about the feeling of mattering arising when there is freedom from control stems from the extensive body of research mentioned in Chapter 7, showing that children and adolescents thrive when they experience autonomy support (see Ryan et al., 2015). Children and adolescents thrive when they are in charge of their learning and development while still gaining support and guidance from parents and caregivers when needed. Autonomy support translates into expressing belief in the child or adolescent and their capacity to address problems and challenges as they arise.

The tenth and final commandment in Exhibit 15.1 reflects earlier observations about the need to learn adaptive ways of responding after encountering situations and circumstances I identified as "anti-mattering experiences." Such experiences are inevitable, and some young people will handle them much better than others. The realities here fit with the fact that everyone will be alone many times, but this does not necessarily mean that loneliness will result. If it does, the capability to adapt to loneliness varies considerably among people of various ages. Training and education focused on being mindful of anti-mattering experiences and not internalizing them seem essential. There is also merit in open discussions of mattering versus feeling unvalued or devalued. These discussions can normalize feelings and experiences so that young people do not feel alone and realize they have much in common with other children and adolescents.

Children and adolescents who are interacted with according to these 10 musts are bound to benefit greatly in myriad ways. When I reflect on the power of mattering and the most important protective elements, I keep coming back to mattering making young people less susceptible to social influence by building a strong sense of self, including a sense of worth and mastery. The other main element of mattering is its power to instill a sense of hope and optimism, partly because people are uplifted by it, especially when their sense of mattering is rooted in giving value to others and finding meaningful ways to make a difference in the lives of others.

THE HOPE INHERENT IN MATTERING: CAN IT MAKE A DIFFERENCE?

I close this final section with a few questions. First, do you know what meliorism is? Are you a meliorist? *Meliorism* is essentially having faith that progress in the world is real, and as this progress occurs, the world eventually becomes a better place, typically through the efforts of others. The most remarkable developmental psychologists I have had the pleasure of knowing are meliorists. Their work has been fueled by the belief that the world can become a better place, and they have a role in contributing new knowledge about what our young people need to improve the human condition and the lives of children, adolescents, and their families. They are on a mission and firmly believe it can and will be accomplished.

I consider myself a meliorist because I believe that the world will become a better place. I have needed to remind myself of this often in recent years as events have unfolded in ways that make it seem like we are engaged in a global game of "one step forward, two steps back." When I reflect on myself, I find it impossible not to wonder at times when meliorism starts to transform into naive optimism.

It is natural at this stage in my life to think about the state of the world and where we are headed. I am writing this final chapter at a time when

I have become a grandfather of two precious granddaughters. They are now 18 and 15 months old. What will the world be like for them throughout their lives? I cannot abide the notion that it will not get better for them and their families despite predictions about looming threats, including climate change.

Much of my faith in a better future for the world and its children stems from those times when I have seen advances in psychology put into practice in ways that have made a meaningful difference in people's lives. The psychologists I have known who are infused with hope and optimism are driven by a passion for advancing knowledge that matters. It is not about ego for them. It is about doing work that matters and being assured that they have made a difference in people's lives.

My faith is also due to the power and potential of mattering. Imagine the world we could, would, and should have if everyone became wholeheartedly invested in giving young people a sense of being important. The caveat is that this sense of importance must be focused on children as individuals, as discussed earlier, such that they remain grounded and do not become narcissistic and ego involved.

Throughout this book, I have tried to make a strong and convincing case for promoting mattering among our children by showing how it benefits rather than harms them when they feel like they do not matter to others. The feeling of mattering is a gateway to physical health, mental health, happiness, meaningful achievements, and, most importantly, an engaged and engaging life. Moreover, the journey to get there will not leave the achievers in a diminished and depleted state marked by mental and physical exhaustion.

The final musings in this book are best directed at the children and the adolescents of the world with their futures before them. I often think about the big picture and the messages I want to share with my granddaughters. It is difficult to maintain the view that the world will become a better place when we encounter adults in key roles who show through their actions or inaction that they devalue rather than value children. It is also difficult to sustain hope when, far too often, the broader systems in play seem to be acting like neglectful parents who have seemingly lost sight of the fact that children matter and need to be cared for and about. It is easy to become cynical and demoralized about the lack of urgency when adults say and do things that suggest they do not value current children and future generations. The inaction in dealing with the climate crisis can make these themes and associated thoughts and feelings salient among young people. The varying approaches to the COVID-19 pandemic also made such thoughts and feelings exceptionally salient among young people.

One school board I have worked with places great importance on students building resilience and realizing their potential by becoming strong self-advocates. This approach was mentioned earlier and merits being reiterated. There are times when we need to hear our voices speaking up for ourselves. Advocating for oneself can be effective and is a source of self-support that can be used to enhance a sense of efficacy and mattering. Ideally, settings and programs invested in positive youth development will include encouragement and the opportunity to learn specific strategies that can be used for self-advocacy. It should be the case that being mindful of the need to advocate for oneself will be a key contributor to developing a self-care orientation.

Everyone needs to matter, and everyone has their own story. When I envision an ideal world, it is a place where every child matters. When they are old enough, I hope to have the opportunity to tell my grandchildren that they have the most important part in their own story and in writing the story of their lives. I will tell them it is especially important for them to use their voices when other people seem not to be listening and do not seem to realize how much they need to hear the voices of young people.

I began this book with the story of 10-year-old Mary, my mother, and how she one day returned home to find her family was not there. Do you remember? Everyone and everything was gone. It is already evident that my young granddaughters both love to hear stories and love books. I am looking forward to the day when I can tell them about the day their great-grandmother was 10 years old and came home from school to find that her family seemed to have disappeared. What did Mary do? What did she say? I will especially enjoy telling them why their great-grandmother Mary knew with certainty that everything would be okay and that she went on to have a good life. What was the secret to her success? Mary made sure to have fun, and whenever she could, she made sure to show other people how much they mattered to her and how much she cared about them.

References

ABC News. (2015, February 23). *When no one showed up to autistic boy's birthday party, strangers saved the day*. https://abcnews.go.com/Health/showed-autistic-boys-birthday-party-strangers-saved-day/story?id=29166772

Abramson, L. Y., & Sackheim, H. A. (1977). A paradox in depression: Uncontrollability and self-blame. *Psychological Bulletin, 84*(5), 838–851. https://doi.org/10.1037/0033-2909.84.5.838

Achenbach, T. M. (1991). *Manual for the Child Behavior Checklist: 4–18 and 1991 Profile*. University of Vermont, Department of Psychiatry.

Adams, G. R., & Marshall, S. K. (1996). A developmental social psychology of identity: Understanding the person-in-context. *Journal of Adolescence, 19*(5), 429–442. https://doi.org/10.1006/jado.1996.0041

Afifi, T. O., Taillieu, T., Salmon, S., Stewart-Tufescu, A., Struck, S., Fortier, J., MacMillan, H. L., Sareen, J., Tonmyr, L., & Katz, L. Y. (2023). Protective factors for decreasing nicotine, alcohol, and cannabis use among adolescents with a history of adverse childhood experiences (ACEs). *International Journal of Mental Health and Addiction, 21*, 2255–2273. https://doi.org/10.1007/s11469-021-00720-x

Ainsworth, M. D. S. (1982). Attachment: Retrospect and prospect. In C. M. Parkes & J. Stevenson-Hinde (Eds.), *The place of attachment in human behavior* (pp. 3–30). Basic Books.

American Psychological Association. (2023, May). *Health advisory on social media use in adolescence*. https://www.apa.org/topics/social-media-internet/health-advisory-adolescent-social-media-use

Andreassen, C. S., Billieux, J., Griffiths, M. D., Kuss, D. J., Demetrovics, Z., Mazzoni, E., & Pallesen, S. (2016). The relationship between addictive use of social media and video games and symptoms of psychiatric disorders: A large-scale cross-sectional study. *Psychology of Addictive Behaviors, 30*(2), 252–262. https://doi.org/10.1037/adb0000160

Armstrong, L. (2015, May 5). Ontario youth wait a year or more for mental health care: Report. *Toronto Star*. https://www.thestar.com/life/health_wellness/2015/05/05/ontario-youth-wait-a-year-or-more-for-mental-health-care-report.html

Arora, P. G., & Persaud, S. (2020). Suicide among Guyanese youth: Barriers to mental health help-seeking and recommendations for suicide prevention. *International Journal of School & Educational Psychology*, *8*(Suppl. 1), 133–145. https://doi.org/10.1080/21683603.2019.1578313

Arora, P. G., Persaud, S., & Parr, K. (2020). Risk and protective factors for suicide among Guyanese youth: Youth and stakeholder perspectives. *International Journal of Psychology*, *55*(4), 618–628. https://doi.org/10.1002/ijop.12625

Asher, S. R., & Wheeler, V. A. (1985). Children's loneliness: A comparison of rejected and neglected peer status. *Journal of Consulting and Clinical Psychology*, *53*(4), 500–505. https://doi.org/10.1037/0022-006X.53.4.500

Astroth, K. A., & Haynes, G. W. (2002). More than cows and cooking: Newest research shows the impact of 4-H. *Journal of Extension*, *40*, 1–10.

Atkey, S. K., Goldberg, J. O., & Flett, G. L. (2024). *Mattering, anti-mattering, and self-stigma for seeking help in adolescents* [Manuscript in preparation]. Department of Psychology, York University.

Babore, A., Trumello, C., Candelori, C., Paciello, M., & Cerniglia, L. (2016, June 27). Depressive symptoms, self-esteem and perceived parent–child relationship in early adolescence. *Frontiers in Psychology*, *7*, Article 982. https://doi.org/10.3389/fpsyg.2016.00982

Bachman, J. G., Kahn, R. L., Mednick, M. T., Davidson, T. N., & Johnston, L. D. (1967). *Youth in transition: Vol. I. Blueprint for a longitudinal study of adolescent boys*. The Institute for Social Research, University of Michigan.

Baird, A. A., Roellke, E. V., & Zeifman, D. M. (2017). Alone and adrift: The association between mass school shootings, school size, and student support. *The Social Science Journal*, *54*(3), 261–270. https://doi.org/10.1016/j.soscij.2017.01.009

Ballard, P. J., Daniel, S. S., Anderson, G., Nicolotti, L., Caballero Quinones, E., Lee, M., & Koehler, A. N. (2021, May 4). Incorporating volunteering into treatment for depression among adolescents: Developmental and clinical considerations. *Frontiers in Psychology*, *12*, Article 642910. https://doi.org/10.3389/fpsyg.2021.642910

Baloyo, R. A. (2021). Phenomenology of adolescent suicide attempt: A basis for program design with a transcendence focus. *Journal of Advance Research in Social Science and Humanities*, *7*(10), 21–132. https://doi.org/10.53555/nnssh.v7i10.1059

Balt, E., Mérelle, S., Robinson, J., Popma, A., Creemers, D., van den Brand, I., van Bergen, D., Rasing, S., Mulder, W., & Gilissen, R. (2023). Social media use of adolescents who died by suicide: Lessons from a psychological autopsy study. *Child and Adolescent Psychiatry and Mental Health*, *17*(1), Article 48. https://doi.org/10.1186/s13034-023-00597-9

Bandura, A. (1986). *Social foundations of thought and action: A social cognitive theory*. Prentice-Hall.

Bandura, A. (2001). The changing face of psychology at the dawning of a globalization era. *Canadian Psychology/Psychologie canadienne, 42*(1), 12–24. https://doi.org/10.1037/h0086876

Banyard, V., Edwards, K., Jones, L., & Mitchell, K. (2020). Poly-strengths and peer violence perpetration: What strengths can add to risk factor analyses. *Journal of Youth and Adolescence, 49*(3), 735–746. https://doi.org/10.1007/s10964-020-01197-y

Barnett, J. D., Schmidt, T. C., Trainor, B., & Wexler, L. (2020). A pilot evaluation of culture camps to increase Alaska Native youth wellness. *Health Promotion Practice, 21*(3), 363–371. https://doi.org/10.1177/1524839918824078

Baskerville, D. (2020). Mattering; changing the narrative in secondary schools for youth who truant. *Journal of Youth Studies, 24*(6), 834–849. https://doi.org/10.1080/13676261.2020.1772962

Baumrind, D. (1991). The influence of parenting style on adolescent competence and substance use. *The Journal of Early Adolescence, 11*(1), 56–95. https://doi.org/10.1177/0272431691111004

Baumrind, D. (1993). The average expectable environment is not good enough: A response to Scarr. *Child Development, 64*(5), 1299–1317. https://doi.org/10.2307/1131536

Baumrind, D., & Moselle, K. A. (1985). A developmental perspective on adolescent drug abuse. In J. Brook, L. D. J. Lettieri, D. W. Brook, & B. Stimmel (Eds.), *Alcohol and substance abuse in adolescence* (pp. 41–67). Haworth.

Bean, C., Harlow, M., & Kendellen, K. (2017). Strategies for fostering basic psychological needs support in high quality youth leadership programs. *Evaluation and Program Planning, 61*, 76–85. https://doi.org/10.1016/j.evalprogplan.2016.12.003

Bean, C., Shaikh, M., & Forneris, T. (2020). Coaching strategies used to deliver quality youth sport programming. *International Sport Coaching Journal, 7*(1), 39–51. https://doi.org/10.1123/iscj.2018-0044

Beck, A. T. (1967). *Depression: Clinical, experimental, and theoretical aspects*. Harper & Row.

Beeres, D. T., Andersson, F., Vossen, H. G. M., & Galanti, M. R. (2021). Social media and mental health among early adolescents in Sweden: A longitudinal study with 2-year follow-up (KUPOL study). *Journal of Adolescent Health, 68*(5), 953–960. https://doi.org/10.1016/j.jadohealth.2020.07.042

Bell, R. Q. (1968). A reinterpretation of the direction of effects in studies of socialization. *Psychological Review, 75*(2), 81–95. https://doi.org/10.1037/h0025583

Bellows, E. (2023, November 6). When people acknowledge and recognize your efforts by telling you that you did a good or even a great job [Comment on the article "When have you felt you mattered?"]. *The New York Times*. https://www.nytimes.com/2023/11/03/learning/when-have-you-felt-that-you-mattered.html#commentsContainer

Bender, K., Schau, N., Begun, S., Haffejee, B., Barman-Adhikari, A., & Hathaway, J. (2015). Electronic case management with homeless youth. *Evaluation and Program Planning, 50*, 36–42. https://doi.org/10.1016/j.evalprogplan.2015.02.002

Beneus, L. (2023, November 3). Hearing that someone actually thinks you matter and have a purpose is one of the best feelings to ever exist [Comment on the article "When have you felt you mattered?"]. *The New York Times*. https://www.nytimes.com/2023/11/03/learning/when-have-you-felt-that-you-mattered.html#commentsContainer

Berezan, O., Krishen, A. S., Agarwal, S., & Kachroo, P. (2020). Exploring loneliness and social networking: Recipes for hedonic well-being on Facebook. *Journal of Business Research, 115*, 258–265. https://doi.org/10.1016/j.busres.2019.11.009

Berkowitz, L. (1989). Frustration-aggression hypothesis: Examination and reformulation. *Psychological Bulletin, 106*(1), 59–73. https://doi.org/10.1037/0033-2909.106.1.59

Bernard, M. E., Vernon, A., Terjesen, M., & Kurasaki, R. (2013). Self-acceptance in the education and counseling of young people. In M. E. Bernard (Ed.), *The strength of self-acceptance: Theory, practice and research* (pp. 155–192). Springer. https://doi.org/10.1007/978-1-4614-6806-6_10

Berny, L. M., Mojekwu, F., Nichols, L. M., & Tanner-Smith, E. E. (2024). Investigating the interplay between mental health conditions and social connectedness on suicide risk: Findings from a clinical sample of adolescents. *Child Psychiatry and Human Development*. Advance online publication. https://doi.org/10.1007/s10578-023-01659-x

Berny, L. M., & Tanner-Smith, E. E. (2024). Interpersonal violence and suicide risk: Examining buffering effects of school and community connectedness. *Children and Youth Services Review, 157*, Article 107405. https://doi.org/10.1016/j.childyouth.2023.107405

Bertuccio, P., Amerio, A., Grande, E., La Vechhia, C., Costanza, A., Aguglia, A., Berardelli, I., Serafini, G., Amore, M., Pompili, M., & Odone, A. (2024). Global trends in youth suicide from 1990 to 2020: An analysis of data from the WHO mortality database. *eClinicalMedicine, 70*, Article 102506. https://doi.org/10.1016/j.eclinm.2024.102506

Besser, A., Flett, G. L., Nepon, T., & Zeigler-Hill, V. (2022). Personality, cognition, and adaptability to the COVID-19 pandemic: Associations with loneliness, distress, and positive and negative mood states. *International Journal of Mental Health and Addiction, 20*, 971–995. https://doi.org/10.1007/s11469-020-00421-x

Bettmann, J. E., Anstadt, G., Casselman, B., & Ganesh, K. (2021). Young adult depression and anxiety linked to social media use: Assessment and treatment. *Clinical Social Work Journal, 49*(3), 368–379. https://doi.org/10.1007/s10615-020-00752-1

Billingham, L., & Irwin-Rogers, K. (2021). The terrifying abyss of insignificance: Marginalisation, mattering, and violence between young people. *Oñati Socio-Legal Series, 11*(5), 1222–1249. https://doi.org/10.35295/osls.iisl/0000-0000-0000-1178

Billingham, L., & Irwin-Rogers, K. (2022). *Against youth violence: A social harm perspective*. Bristol University Press.

Blatt, S. J. (1974). Levels of object representation in anaclitic and introjective depression. *The Psychoanalytic Study of the Child, 29*(1), 107–157. https://doi.org/10.1080/00797308.1974.11822616

Blatt, S. J., & Zuroff, D. C. (2002). Perfectionism in the therapeutic process. In G. L. Flett & P. L. Hewitt (Eds.), *Perfectionism: Theory, research, and treatment* (pp. 393–406). American Psychological Association. https://doi.org/10.1037/10458-016

Block, J. H., & Block, J. (1980). *The California Child Q Set*. Consulting Psychologists Press. (Original work published 1969)

Bonanno, G. A., & Diminich, E. D. (2013). Annual research review: Positive adjustment to adversity—Trajectories of minimal-impact resilience and emergent resilience. *Journal of Child Psychology and Psychiatry, 54*(4), 378–401. https://doi.org/10.1111/jcpp.12021

Bonell, C., Hinds, K., Dickson, K., Thomas, J., Fletcher, A., Murphy, S., Melendez-Torres, G. J., Bonell, C., & Campbell, R. (2015). What is positive youth development and how might it reduce substance use and violence? A systematic review and synthesis of theoretical literature. *BMC Public Health, 16*, Article 135. https://doi.org/10.1186/s12889-016-2817-3

Bornstein, M. H. (2013). Mother–infant attunement. In M. Legerstee, D. W. Haley, & M. H. Bornstein (Eds.), *The infant mind: Origins of the social brain* (pp. 248–265). Guilford Press.

Bostik, K. E., & Everall, R. D. (2006). In my mind I was alone: Suicidal adolescents' perceptions of attachment relationships. *International Journal for the Advancement of Counselling, 28*(3), 269–287. https://doi.org/10.1007/s10447-006-9013-6

Bostik, K. E., & Everall, R. D. (2007). Healing from suicide: Adolescent perceptions of attachment relationships. *British Journal of Guidance & Counselling, 35*(1), 79–96. https://doi.org/10.1080/03069880601106815

Bowlby, J. (1980). *Attachment and loss: Vol. 3. Sadness and depression*. Basic Books.

Brinkman, J., Garnett, B., Kolodinsky, J., Wang, W., & Pope, L. (2021). Intra- and interpersonal factors buffer the relationship between food insecurity and mental well-being among middle schoolers. *The Journal of School Health, 91*(2), 102–110. https://doi.org/10.1111/josh.12982

Brockmyer, J. F. (2022). Desensitization and violent video games: Mechanisms and evidence. *Child and Adolescent Psychiatric Clinics of North America, 31*(1), 121–132. https://doi.org/10.1016/j.chc.2021.06.005

Bronfenbrenner, U. (1977). Toward an experimental ecology of human development. *American Psychologist, 32*(7), 513–531. https://doi.org/10.1037/0003-066X.32.7.513

Bronfenbrenner, U. (1990). Who cares for children? *Research & Clinical Center for Child Development, 12*, 27–40.

Bronfenbrenner, U. (2005). *Making human beings human: Bioecological perspectives on human development*. Sage.

Bronfenbrenner, U., & Morris, P. A. (2006). The bioecological model of human development. In W. Damon & R. M. Lerner (Eds.), *The handbook of child psychology: Vol. 1. Theoretical models of human development* (6th ed., pp. 793–828). Wiley.

Bronfenbrenner, U., & Ricciuti, H. N. (1960). The appraisal of personality characteristics in children. In P. H. Mussen (Ed.), *Handbook of research methods in child development* (pp. 770–817). Wiley.

Brunswik, E. (1955). Representative design and probabilistic theory in a functional psychology. *Psychological Review, 62*(3), 193–217. https://doi.org/10.1037/h0047470

Bryan, J. L. (2022). *The theory of mattering: Implications for adolescent depression and suicidal ideation* [Unpublished master's thesis]. Boise State University.

Bryce, C. I., & Fraser, A. M. (2022). Students' perceptions, educational challenges and hope during the COVID-19 pandemic. *Child: Care, Health and Development, 48*(6), 1081–1093. https://doi.org/10.1111/cch.13036

Buchanan, K., & Harris, G. E. (2014). Teachers' experiences of working with students who have attempted suicide and returned to the classroom. *Canadian Journal of Education, 37*(2), 1–28.

Burisch, M. (1984). You don't always get what you pay for: Measuring depression with short and simple versus long and sophisticated scales. *Journal of Research in Personality, 18*(1), 81–98. https://doi.org/10.1016/0092-6566(84)90040-0

Cacioppo, J. T., Reis, H. T., & Zautra, A. J. (2011). Social resilience: The value of social fitness with an application to the military. *American Psychologist, 66*(1), 43–51. https://doi.org/10.1037/a0021419

Caetano, B., Branquinho, M., Canavarro, M. C., & Fonseca, A. (2022). Mattering and depressive symptoms in Portuguese postpartum women: The indirect effect of loneliness. *International Journal of Environmental Research and Public Health, 19*(18), Article 11671. https://doi.org/10.3390/ijerph191811671

Cao, C.-H., Flett, G. L., Chen, I.-H., Jiang, X.-Y., Zhao, L., & Zheng, W.-M. (2024). *The associations between three mattering measures with exhaustion, loneliness, self-esteem, and hope across different educational levels: Insights from primary, middle, high school, and university students* [Manuscript submitted for publication]. School of Foreign Languages, Shandong Women's University.

Carey, R. L. (2019). Imagining the comprehensive mattering of Black boys and young men in society and schools: Toward a new approach. *Harvard Educational Review, 89*(3), 370–396. https://doi.org/10.17763/1943-5045-89.3.370

Carey, R. L. (2020). Making Black boys and young men matter: Radical relationships, future-oriented imaginaries and other evolving insights for educational research and practice. *International Journal of Qualitative Studies in Education, 33*(7), 729–744. https://doi.org/10.1080/09518398.2020.1753255

Carey, R. L., Polanco, C., & Blackman, H. (2022). Black adolescent boys' perceived school mattering: From marginalization and selective love to radically affirming relationships. *Journal of Research on Adolescence, 32*(1), 151–169. https://doi.org/10.1111/jora.12706

Casale, S., Akbari, M., Bocci Benucci, S., Seydavi, M., & Fioravanti, G. (2022). Interpersonally-based fears and problematic social networking site use: The moderating role of online social support. *International Journal of Mental Health and Addiction, 22*, 995–1007. https://doi.org/10.1007/s11469-022-00908-9

Casale, S., & Flett, G. L. (2020). Interpersonally-based fears during the COVID-19 pandemic: Reflections on the fear of missing out and the fear of not mattering constructs. *Clinical Neuropsychiatry, 17*(2), 88–93. https://doi.org/10.36131/CN20200211

Casale, S., & Flett, G. L. (2023). Interpersonally-based fears and feelings during the COVID-19 pandemic revisited: Research findings and further reflections on fear of missing out and feelings of not mattering. *Clinical Neuropsychiatry, 20*(4), 351–357. https://doi.org/10.36131/cnfioritieditore20230415

Centers for Disease Control and Prevention. (2014). *Youth risk behavior surveillance—United States, 2013*. https://www.cdc.gov/mmwr/preview/mmwrhtml/ss6304a1.htm

Centers for Disease Control and Prevention. (2023). *Youth Risk Behavior Survey: Data summary and trends report*. U.S. Department of Health and Human Services. https://www.cdc.gov/healthyyouth/data/yrbs/pdf/yrbs_data-summary-trends_report2023_508.pdf

Chandler, M. (1994). Adolescent suicide and the loss of personal continuity. In D. Cicchetti & S. L. Toth (Eds.), *Disorders and dysfunctions of the self* (pp. 371–390). University of Rochester Press.

Chen, I-H., Flett, G. L., & Gamble, J. H. (2022). Translation and validation of a Chinese version of the Fear of Not Mattering Inventory and related instruments in the context of COVID-19. *Journal of Concurrent Disorders*. https://doi.org/10.54127/JATS9300

Chess, S., Thomas, A., & Birch, H. G. (1965). *Your child is a person: A psychological approach to childhood without guilt*. Viking Press.

Chicklas, D. (2014, October 16). "It needs to be talked about every day": Teen takes his life after loved ones say he was bullied. *Fox 17*. https://www.fox17online.com/2014/10/16/it-needs-to-be-talked-about-every-day-teen-takes-his-life-after-loved-ones-say-he-was-bullied

Chino, M., & Fullerton-Gleason, L. (2006). Understanding suicide attempts among American Indian adolescents in New Mexico: Modifiable factors related to risk and resiliency. *Ethnicity & Disease, 16*(2), 435–442.

Chiodo, D., Crooks, C. V., Wolfe, D. A., McIsaac, C., Hughes, R., & Jaffe, P. G. (2012). Longitudinal prediction and concurrent functioning of adolescent girls demonstrating various profiles of dating violence and victimization. *Prevention Science, 13*(4), 350–359. https://doi.org/10.1007/s11121-011-0236-3

Cho, E. (2023, November 3). Yes, you get this kind of feeling, a bubbly warm feeling that you get when someone says you matter but you matter, and you don't matter are the same as alone and lonely [Comment on the article "When have you felt you mattered?"]. *The New York Times*. https://www.nytimes.com/2023/11/03/learning/when-have-you-felt-that-you-mattered.html#commentsContainer

Clarke, T. (2023). Do scores "define" us? Adolescents' experiences of wellbeing as "welldoing" at school in England. *Review of Education, 11*(1), Article e3393. https://doi.org/10.1002/rev3.3393

Clay, D., Coates, E., Tran, Q., & Phares, V. (2017). Fathers' and mothers' emotional accessibility and youth's developmental outcomes. *The American Journal of Family Therapy, 45*(2), 111–122. https://doi.org/10.1080/01926187.2017.1303651

Conroy, D. E., Willow, J. P., & Metzler, J. N. (2002). Multidimensional fear of failure measurement: The Performance Failure Appraisal Inventory. *Journal of Applied Sport Psychology, 14*(2), 76–90. https://doi.org/10.1080/10413200252907752

Cooley, C. (1912). *Human nature and social order*. Scribner.

Cornwall, G. (2023, September 27). Want to believe in yourself? 'Mattering' is key. *The New York Times*. https://www.nytimes.com/2023/09/27/well/mind/mental-health-mattering-self-esteem.html

Courtwright, S. E., Jones, J., Barton, A., Peterson, K., Eigen, K., Feuerstein, J., Pawa, A., Pawa, A., Northridge, J., & Pall, H. (2023). Including voices of adolescents with chronic conditions in the redesign of children's mental health systems: Implications for resource allocation. *Journal of Pediatric Health Care, 37*(4), 381–390. https://doi.org/10.1016/j.pedhc.2023.01.004

Crean, H. F. (2012). Youth activity involvement, neighborhood adult support, individual decision making skills, and early adolescent delinquent behaviors: Testing a conceptual model. *Journal of Applied Developmental Psychology, 33*(4), 175–188. https://doi.org/10.1016/j.appdev.2012.04.003

Criscuolo, M., Marchetto, C., Buzzonetti, A., Castiglioni, M. C., Cereser, L., Salvo, P., & Zanna, V. (2023). Parental emotional availability and family functioning in adolescent anorexia nervosa subtypes. *International Journal of Environmental Research and Public Health, 20*(1), 68. https://doi.org/10.3390/ijerph20010068

Cronbach, L. J. (1951). Coefficient alpha and the internal structure of tests. *Psychometrika, 16*(3), 297–334. https://doi.org/10.1007/BF02310555

Croteau, J. (2016). *How Orange Shirt Day honouring residential school survivors came to be*. Global News. https://globalnews.ca/news/2975949/how-orange-shirt-day-honouring-residential-school-survivors-came-to-be/

Crowne, D. P., & Marlowe, D. (1960). A new scale of social desirability independent of psychopathology. *Journal of Consulting Psychology*, *24*(4), 349–354. https://doi.org/10.1037/h0047358

Cumba-Avilés, E. (2017). Cognitive-behavioral group therapy for Latino youth with type 1 diabetes and depression: A case study. *Clinical Case Studies*, *16*(1), 58–75. https://doi.org/10.1177/1534650116668270

Daley, A., Phipps, S., & Branscombe, N. R. (2018). The social complexities of disability: Discrimination, belonging and life satisfaction among Canadian youth. *SSM - Population Health*, *5*, 55–63. https://doi.org/10.1016/j.ssmph.2018.05.003

Damon, W., & Hart, D. (1982). The development of self-understanding from infancy through adolescence. *Child Development*, *53*(4), 841–864. https://doi.org/10.2307/1129122

Daniels, M., Sharma, M., & Batra, K. (2021). Social media, stress, and sleep deprivation: A triple "S" among adolescents. *Journal of Health and Social Sciences*, *6*(2), 159–166.

Darbyshire, P., Muir-Cochrane, E., Fereday, J., Jureidini, J., & Drummond, A. (2006). Engagement with health and social care services: Perceptions of homeless young people with mental health problems. *Health & Social Care in the Community*, *14*(6), 553–562. https://doi.org/10.1111/j.1365-2524.2006.00643.x

Darwin, C. (1872). *The expression of emotion in men and animals*. John Murray. https://doi.org/10.1037/10001-000

Deas, N., Kowalski, R., Finnell, S., Radovic, E., Carroll, H., Robbins, C., Cook, A., Hurley, K., Cote, N., Evans, K., Lorenzo, I., Kiser, K., Mochizuki, G., Mock, M., & Brewer, L. (2023). I just want to matter: Examining the role of anti-mattering in online suicide support communities using natural language processing. *Computers in Human Behavior*, *139*, Article 107499. https://doi.org/10.1016/j.chb.2022.107499

Deater-Deckard, K., & Petrill, S. A. (2004). Parent–child dyadic mutuality and child behavior problems: An investigation of gene–environment processes. *Journal of Child Psychology and Psychiatry*, *45*(6), 1171–1179. https://doi.org/10.1111/j.1469-7610.2004.00309.x

Debold, E., Brown, L. M., Weseen, S., & Brookins, G. K. (1999). Cultivating hardiness zones for adolescent girls: A reconceptualization of resilience in relationships with caring adults. In N. G. Johnson, M. C. Roberts, & J. Worell (Eds.), *Beyond appearance: A new look at adolescent girls* (pp. 181–204). American Psychological Association. https://doi.org/10.1037/10325-007

DeForge, B. R., & Barclay, D. M., III. (1997). The internal reliability of a General Mattering Scale in homeless men. *Psychological Reports*, *80*(2), 429–430. https://doi.org/10.2466/pr0.1997.80.2.429

De Rossi, P. (2010). *Unbearable lightness: A story of loss and gain*. Simon & Schuster.

Derryberry, D., & Rothbart, M. K. (1997). Reactive and effortful processes in the organization of temperament. *Development and Psychopathology*, *9*(4), 633–652. https://doi.org/10.1017/S0954579497001375

Devos, S., Schreurs, L., Eggermont, S., & Vandenbosch, L. (2023). Go big or go home: Examining the longitudinal relations between exposure to successful portrayals on social media and adolescents' feelings of discrepancy. *New Media & Society*. Advance online publication. https://doi.org/10.1177/14614448231188935

Dickens, C. (2003). *A tale of two cities*. Penguin. (Original work published 1859)

Dixon, A. L., Scheidegger, C., & McWhirter, J. J. (2009). The adolescent mattering experience: Gender variations in perceived mattering, anxiety, and depression. *Journal of Counseling & Development*, *87*(3), 302–310. https://doi.org/10.1002/j.1556-6678.2009.tb00111.x

Dixson, D. D., & Scalcucci, S. G. (2021). Psychosocial perceptions and executive functioning: Hope and school belonging predict students' executive functioning. *Psychology in the Schools*, *58*(5), 853–872. https://doi.org/10.1002/pits.22475

Docherty, N. (Writer & Director), & MacIntyre, L. (Writer). (1994, April 12). The trouble with Evan (Season 1994, Episode 20). In K. Crichton (Executive Producer), *The fifth estate*. Canadian Broadcasting Corporation.

Dollard, J., Miller, N., Doob, L., Mowrer, O., & Sears, R. (1939). *Frustration and aggression*. Yale University Press. https://doi.org/10.1037/10022-000

Dvorak, P. (2023, December 6). The adults who rejected a grant won by LGBTQ students failed again. *The Washington Post*. https://www.washingtonpost.com/dc-md-va/2023/12/06/lynchburg-school-board-lgbtq/

Dweck, C. S. (2017). The journey to children's mindsets—And beyond. *Child Development Perspectives*, *11*(2), 139–144. https://doi.org/10.1111/cdep.12225

Ebesutani, C., Regan, J., Smith, A., Reise, S., Higa-McMillan, C., & Chorpita, B. F. (2012). The 10-item Positive and Negative Affect Schedule for Children, child and parent shortened versions: Application of item response theory for more efficient assessment. *Journal of Psychopathology and Behavioral Assessment*, *34*(2), 191–203. https://doi.org/10.1007/s10862-011-9273-2

Eccles, J. S., & Gootman, J. A. (2002). *Community programs to promote youth development*. National Academies Press.

Edwards, K. M., Banyard, V. L., Charge, L. L., Kollar, L. M. M., & Fortson, B. (2021). Experiences and correlates of violence among American Indian and Alaska Native youth: A brief report. *Journal of Interpersonal Violence*, *36*(23–24), 11808–11821. https://doi.org/10.1177/0886260520983273

Edwards, K. M., & Neal, A. M. (2017). School and community characteristics related to dating violence victimization among high school youth. *Psychology of Violence*, *7*(2), 203–212. https://doi.org/10.1037/vio0000065

Elder, G. H., Jr., & Conger, R. D. (2000). *Children of the land: Adversity and success in rural America*. The University of Chicago Press. https://doi.org/10.7208/chicago/9780226224978.001.0001

Elkind, D. (1988). *The hurried child: Growing up too fast too soon* (Rev. ed.). Addison-Wesley.

Elliott, G. C. (1982). Self-esteem and self-presentation among the young as a function of age and gender. *Journal of Youth and Adolescence, 11*(2), 135–153. https://doi.org/10.1007/BF01834709

Elliott, G. C. (2009). *Family matters: The importance of mattering to family in adolescence*. Wiley-Blackwell. https://doi.org/10.1002/9781444305784

Elliott, G. C., Colangelo, M. F., & Gelles, R. J. (2005). Mattering and suicide ideation: Establishing and elaborating a relationship. *Social Psychology Quarterly, 68*(3), 223–238. https://doi.org/10.1177/019027250506800303

Elliott, G. C., Cunningham, S. M., Colangelo, M., & Gelles, R. J. (2011). Perceived mattering to the family and physical violence within the family by adolescents. *Journal of Family Issues, 32*(8), 1007–1029. https://doi.org/10.1177/0192513X11398932

Elliott, G. C., Kao, S., & Grant, A. (2004). Mattering: Empirical validation of a social-psychological concept. *Self and Identity, 3*(4), 339–354. https://doi.org/10.1080/13576500444000119

Ellison, R. (1952). *Invisible man*. Random House.

Erikson, E. H. (1950). *Childhood and society*. Norton.

Erikson, E. H. (1968). *Identity, youth, and crisis*. Norton.

Etherson, M. E., Smith, M. M., Hill, A. P., & Flett, G. L. (2022). Feelings of not mattering and depressive symptoms from a temporal perspective: A comparison of the cross-lagged panel model and random-intercept cross-lagged panel model. *Journal of Psychoeducational Assessment, 40*(1), 60–76. https://doi.org/10.1177/07342829211049686

Fantinelli, S., Esposito, C., Carlucci, L., Limone, P., & Sulla, F. (2023). The influence of individual and contextual factors on the vocational choices of adolescents and their impact on well-being. *Behavioral Sciences, 13*(3), Article 233. https://doi.org/10.3390/bs13030233

Festinger, L. (1954). A theory of social comparison processes. *Human Relations, 7*(2), 117–140. https://doi.org/10.1177/001872675400700202

Flett, G. L. (2018a). *The psychology of mattering: Understanding the human need to be significant*. Academic Press.

Flett, G. L. (2018b). Resilience to interpersonal stress: Why mattering matters when building the foundation of mentally healthy schools. In A. Leschied, D. H. Saklofske, & G. L. Flett (Eds.), *The handbook of school-based mental health promotion: An evidence informed framework for implementation* (pp. 383–410). Springer. https://doi.org/10.1007/978-3-319-89842-1_20

Flett, G. L. (2019). Mattering, anxiety, and fear of failure in children and adolescents. *Perspectives on Early Childhood Psychology and Education, 4*, 277–293.

Flett, G. L. (2022). An introduction, review, and conceptual analysis of mattering as an essential construct and an essential way of life. *Journal of Psychoeducational Assessment, 40*(1), 3–36. https://doi.org/10.1177/07342829211057640

Flett, G. L. (2024a). Mattering matters in youth suicidality: Implications for implementing in practice. *Child Protection and Practice*, *2*, Article 100041. https://doi.org/10.1016/j.chipro.2024.100041

Flett, G. L. (2024b). Toward a mattering-centered model of suicide risk and prevention: Review and recommendations. In M. Zangeneh (Ed.), *Essentials in health and mental health: Unlocking the keys to wellness* (pp. 57–76). Springer. https://doi.org/10.1007/978-3-031-56192-4_4

Flett, G. L., Burdo, R., & Nepon, T. (2021). Mattering, insecure attachment, rumination, and self-criticism in distress among university students. *International Journal of Mental Health and Addiction*, *19*(4), 1300–1313. https://doi.org/10.1007/s11469-020-00225-z

Flett, G. L., Casale, S., Stoakes, A., Nepon, T., & Su, C. (2023). Mattering, substance use, and addictive behaviors: Review, analysis, and implications for treatment and prevention. *Journal of Ethnicity in Substance Abuse*, 1–34. https://doi.org/10.1080/15332640.2023.2218283

Flett, G. L., Flett, A. L., & Wekerle, C. (2015). A conceptual analysis of interpersonal resilience as a key resilience domain: Understanding the ability to overcome child sexual abuse and other adverse interpersonal contexts. *International Journal of Child and Youth Resilience*, *3*, 4–33.

Flett, G. L., Gaetz, S., & Fisher, R. (2024). *Mattering promotion as social innovation: The role of feeling valued by others and having value to others in the prevention of youth homelessness* [Manuscript submitted for publication]. Department of Psychology, York University.

Flett, G. L., Galfi-Pechenkov, I., Molnar, D. S., Hewitt, P. L., & Goldstein, A. L. (2012). Perfectionism, mattering, and depression: A mediational analysis. *Personality and Individual Differences*, *52*(7), 828–832. https://doi.org/10.1016/j.paid.2011.12.041

Flett, G. L., Goldstein, A. L., Pechenkov, I. G., Nepon, T., & Wekerle, C. (2016). Antecedents, correlates, and consequences of feeling like you don't matter: Associations with maltreatment, loneliness, social anxiety, and the five-factor model. *Personality and Individual Differences*, *92*, 52–56. https://doi.org/10.1016/j.paid.2015.12.014

Flett, G. L., & Heisel, M. J. (2021). Aging and feeling valued versus expendable during the COVID-19 pandemic and beyond: A review and commentary of why mattering is fundamental to the health and well-being of older adults. *International Journal of Mental Health and Addiction*, *19*(6), 2443–2469. https://doi.org/10.1007/s11469-020-00339-4

Flett, G. L., & Hewitt, P. L. (2013). Disguised distress in children and adolescents "flying under the radar": Why psychological problems are underestimated and how schools must respond. *Canadian Journal of School Psychology*, *28*(1), 12–27. https://doi.org/10.1177/0829573512468845

Flett, G. L., & Hewitt, P. L. (2022). *Perfectionism in childhood and adolescence: A developmental analysis*. American Psychological Association. https://doi.org/10.1037/0000289-000

Flett, G. L., & Hewitt, P. L. (2023). Reflections on the costs of rigid perfectionism and perfectionistic reactivity: The core significance of the failure to adapt in sports and in life. In A. P. Hill (Ed.), *The psychology of perfectionism in sport, dance, and exercise* (2nd ed., pp. 399–420). Routledge. https://doi.org/10.4324/9781003288015-20

Flett, G. L., Hewitt, P. L., Nepon, T., & Zaki-Azat, J. N. (2018). Children and adolescents "flying under the radar": Understanding, assessing, and addressing hidden distress among students. In A. W. Leschied, D. H. Saklofske, & G. L. Flett (Eds.), *Handbook of school-based mental health promotion: An evidence-informed framework for implementation* (pp. 357–381). Springer. https://doi.org/10.1007/978-3-319-89842-1_19

Flett, G. L., Hewitt, P. L., Oliver, J. M., & Macdonald, S. (2002). Perfectionism in children and their parents: A developmental analysis. In G. L. Flett & P. L. Hewitt (Eds.), *Perfectionism: Theory, research, and treatment* (pp. 89–132). American Psychological Association. https://doi.org/10.1037/10458-004

Flett, G. L., & Nepon, T. (2024). When adding one questionnaire item makes a difference: Representing the theme of feeling cared about in the Expanded General Mattering Scale (The GMS-6). *Journal of Psychoeducational Assessment*. Advance online publication. https://doi.org/10.1177/07342829241255232

Flett, G. L., Nepon, T., Goldberg, J. O., Rose, A. L., Atkey, S. K., & Zaki-Azat, J. (2022). The Anti-Mattering Scale: Development, psychometric properties, and associations with well-being and distress measures in adolescents and emerging adults. *Journal of Psychoeducational Assessment*, *40*(1), 37–59. https://doi.org/10.1177/07342829211050544

Flett, G. L., Nepon, T., Hewitt, P. L., Su, C., Yacyshyn, C., Moore, K., & Lahijanian, A. (2024). The Social Comparison Rumination Scale: Development, psychometric properties, and associations with perfectionism, narcissism, burnout, and distress. *Journal of Psychoeducational Assessment*, *42*(6), 685–704. https://doi.org/10.1177/07342829241238300

Flett, G. L., Su, C., Ma, L., & Guo, L. (2014). Academic buoyancy and mattering as resilience factors in Chinese adolescents: An analysis of shame, social anxiety, and psychological distress. *International Journal of Child and Adolescent Resilience*, *2*(1), 37–45.

Flett, G. L., Su, C., Ma, L., & Guo, L. (2016). Mattering as a unique resilience factor in Chinese children: A comparative analysis of predictors of depression. *International Journal of Child and Adolescent Resilience*, *4*(1), 91–102. https://www.ijcar-rirea.ca/index.php/ijcar-rirea/article/view/205

Flett, G. L., Su, C., Nepon, T., Ma, L., & Guo, L. R. (2023). The General Mattering Scale: Mattering versus self-esteem in predicting distress and psychosocial adjustment among early adolescents from China. *Journal of Concurrent Disorders*. https://doi.org/10.54127/UXUO9895

Flett, G. L., Su, C., Nepon, T., Sturman, E. D., Ma, L., & Guo, L. R. (2023). Mattering, stress, and burnout in feelings of distress, defeat, and engagement among Chinese high school students. *Journal of Concurrent Disorders*. https://doi.org/10.54127/CNKA2584

Flett, G. L., & Zangeneh, M. (2020). Mattering as a vital support for people during the COVID-19 pandemic: The benefits of feeling and knowing that someone cares during times of crisis. *Journal of Concurrent Disorders*, *2*(1), 106–123. https://doi.org/10.54127/ALMC5515

Foley, K.-R., Blackmore, A. M., Girdler, S., O'Donnell, M., Glauert, R., Llewellyn, G., & Leonard, H. (2012). To feel belonged: The voices of children and youth with disabilities on the meaning of wellbeing. *Child Indicators Research*, *5*(2), 375–391. https://doi.org/10.1007/s12187-011-9134-2

Fox, B. (2019). Loneliness and social media: A qualitative investigation of young people's motivations for use, and perceptions of social networking sites. In B. Fox (Ed.), *Emotions and loneliness in a networked society* (pp. 309–331). Palgrave Macmillan. https://doi.org/10.1007/978-3-030-24882-6_16

France, M. K., & Finney, S. J. (2010). Conceptualization and utilization of university mattering: A construct validity study. *Measurement and Evaluation in Counseling and Development*, *43*(1), 48–65. https://doi.org/10.1177/0748175610362369

Fraser-Thomas, J. L., Côté, J., & Deakin, J. (2005). Youth sport programs: An avenue to foster positive youth development. *Physical Education and Sport Pedagogy*, *10*(1), 19–40. https://doi.org/10.1080/1740898042000334890

Fraser-Thomas, J., Côté, J., & MacDonald, D. J. (2010). Community size in youth sport settings: Examining developmental assets and sport withdrawal. *PHEnex Journal/Revue phénEPS*, *2*(2).

Freeman, H. (2023, April 1). Anorexia nearly killed me. *The Sunday Times*. https://www.thetimes.com/uk/healthcare/article/anorexia-nearly-killed-me-by-hadley-freeman-fstvtq06q

Freudenberger, H. J., & Richelson, G. (1980). *Burnout: How to beat the high cost of success*. Bantam Books.

Fromm, E. (1941). *Escape from freedom*. Norton.

Fuligni, A. J. (2019). The need to contribute during adolescence. *Perspectives on Psychological Science*, *14*(3), 331–343. https://doi.org/10.1177/1745691618805437

Fuligni, A. J., Smola, X. A., & Al Salek, S. (2022). Feeling needed and useful during the transition to young adulthood. *Journal of Research on Adolescence*, *32*(3), 1259–1266. https://doi.org/10.1111/jora.12680

Fullam, J. (2017). Becoming a youth activist in the internet age: A case study on social media activism and identity development. *International Journal of Qualitative Studies in Education*, *30*(4), 406–422. https://doi.org/10.1080/09518398.2016.1250176

Funamoto, A., & Rinaldi, C. M. (2015). Measuring parent–child mutuality: A review of current observational coding systems. *Infant Mental Health Journal*, *36*(1), 3–11. https://doi.org/10.1002/imhj.21481

Fung, B., & Duffy, C. (2024, January 29). *Kids aren't safe on social media, lawmakers say. Tech CEOs are back in DC to pledge (again) that they'll handle it.* CNN Business. https://www.cnn.com/2024/01/29/tech/big-tech-ceos-youth-safety-senate-testimony/index.html

Furrer, C., & Skinner, E. (2003). Sense of relatedness as a factor in children's academic engagement and performance. *Journal of Educational Psychology, 95*(1), 148–162. https://doi.org/10.1037/0022-0663.95.1.148

Garcia, G. M., Price, L., & Tabatabai, N. (2014). *Anchorage Youth Risk Behavior Survey results: 2003–2013 trends and correlation analysis of selected risk behaviors, bullying, mental health conditions, and protective factors.* Department of Health Sciences, University of Alaska. https://safealaskans.org/wp-content/uploads/2018/05/Anchorage-YRBS-Report-2003-2013_final.pdf

Gedo, P. M. (2011). An island in a sea of madness: The uses of theory for in-patient adolescent treatment. *Clinical Social Work Journal, 39*(2), 132–138. https://doi.org/10.1007/s10615-011-0341-6

Ghaye, T., Allen, L., & Clark, N. (2021). The holistic wellbeing of elite youth performers: U MATTER. In N. Campbell, A. Brady, & A. Tincknell-Smith (Eds.), *Developing and supporting athlete wellbeing: Person first, athlete second* (pp. 18–32). Routledge.

Ghaye, T., & Horner, T. (2023). Leadership—Time to re-purpose the pegs: Youth leadership development through sport for a post-pandemic world. In N. Schulenkorf, J. W. Peachey, R. Spaaij, & H. Collison-Randall (Eds.), *Handbook of sport and international development* (pp. 267–280). Elgar. https://doi.org/10.4337/9781800378926.00033

Gijzen, M. W. M., Rasing, S. P. A., Creemers, D. H. M., Engels, R. C. M. E., & Smit, F. (2022). Effectiveness of school-based preventive programs in suicidal thoughts and behaviors: A meta-analysis. *Journal of Affective Disorders, 298*(Pt. A), 408–420. https://doi.org/10.1016/j.jad.2021.10.062

Gilchrist, J. D., Gohari, M. R., Benson, L., Patte, K. A., & Leatherdale, S. T. (2023). Reciprocal associations between positive emotions and resilience predict flourishing among adolescents. *Health Promotion and Chronic Disease Prevention in Canada, 43*(7), 313–320. https://doi.org/10.24095/hpcdp.43.7.01

Gilman, R., Carter-Sowell, A., Dewall, C. N., Adams, R. E., & Carboni, I. (2013). Validation of the ostracism experience scale for adolescents. *Psychological Assessment, 25*(2), 319–330. https://doi.org/10.1037/a0030913

Goldberg, J. O., McKeag, S. A., Rose, A. L., Lumsden-Ruegg, H., & Flett, G. L. (2023). Too close for comfort: Stigma by association in family members who live with relatives with mental illness. *International Journal of Environmental Research and Public Health, 20*(6), Article 5209. https://doi.org/10.3390/ijerph20065209

Goldsmith, H. H., Buss, A. H., Plomin, R., Rothbart, M. K., Thomas, A., Chess, S., Hinde, R. A., & McCall, R. B. (1987). Roundtable: What is temperament?

Four approaches. *Child Development*, *58*(2), 505–529. https://doi.org/10.2307/1130527

Gullone, E., Moore, S., Moss, S., & Boyd, C. (2000). The Adolescent Risk-Taking Questionnaire: Development and psychometric evaluation. *Journal of Adolescent Research*, *15*(2), 231–250. https://doi.org/10.1177/0743558400152003

Gunlicks-Stoessel, M., Westervelt, A., Reigstad, K., Mufson, L., & Lee, S. (2019). The role of attachment style in interpersonal psychotherapy for depressed adolescents. *Psychotherapy Research*, *29*(1), 78–85. https://doi.org/10.1080/10503307.2017.1315465

Gutierrez, P. M., Osman, A., Kopper, B. A., & Barrios, F. X. (2000). Why young people do not kill themselves: The Reasons for Living Inventory for Adolescents. *Journal of Clinical Child Psychology*, *29*(2), 177–187. https://doi.org/10.1207/S15374424jccp2902_4

Haddock, S. A., Weiler, L. M., Lee, H., Henry, K. L., Lucas-Thompson, R., Zimmerman, T. S., Krafchick, J. L., Fredrickson, G. F., Yetz, N., & Youngblade, L. M. (2020). Does organizing mentor-mentee matches into small groups enhance treatment effects in a site-based mentoring program for adolescents? Results of a randomized controlled trial. *Journal of Youth and Adolescence*, *49*(9), 1864–1882. https://doi.org/10.1007/s10964-020-01267-1

Haidt, J. (2024). *The anxious generation: How the great rewiring of childhood is causing an epidemic of mental illness*. Penguin Press.

Hailu, J. (2023, November 3). When I feel like I don't matter is when I am just sad or when I feel like I am not doing anything for the world [Comment on the article "When have you felt you mattered?"]. *The New York Times*. https://www.nytimes.com/2023/11/03/learning/when-have-you-felt-that-you-mattered.html#commentsContainer

Hall, G. S. (1904). Adolescence in literature, biography, and history. In G. S. Hall (Ed.), *Adolescence: Its psychology and its relations to physiology, anthropology, sociology, sex, crime, religion and education* (Vol. 1, pp. 513–589). D Appleton & Company. https://doi.org/10.1037/10616-008

Hamby, S., Taylor, E., Mitchell, K., Jones, L., & Newlin, C. (2020). Poly-victimization, trauma, and resilience: Exploring strengths that promote thriving after adversity. *Journal of Trauma & Dissociation*, *21*(3), 376–395. https://doi.org/10.1080/15299732.2020.1719261

Hamby, S., Taylor, E., Smith, A., Mitchell, K., Jones, L., & Newlin, C. (2019). New measures to assess the social ecology of youth: A mixed-methods study. *Journal of Community Psychology*, *47*(7), 1666–1681. https://doi.org/10.1002/jcop.22220

Harder, V. S., Lor, J., Omland, L., & Rettew, D. C. (2023). Protective associations between supportive environment and suicidality among minority and majority adolescents. *Archives of Suicide Research*, *28*(2), 629–643. https://doi.org/10.1080/13811118.2023.2199808

Harris, B., Vincent, K., Thomson, P., & Toalster, R. (2006). Does every child know they matter? Pupils' views of one alternative to exclusion. *Pastoral*

Care in Education, 24(2), 28–38. https://doi.org/10.1111/j.1468-0122.2006.00362.x

Harter, S. (1990). Developmental differences in the nature of self-representations: Implications for the understanding, assessment, and treatment of maladaptive behavior. *Cognitive Therapy and Research, 14*(2), 113–142. https://doi.org/10.1007/BF01176205

Harter, S., Low, S. M., & Whitesell, N. R. (2003). What have we learned from Columbine: The impact of self-system on suicidal and violent ideation among adolescents. *Journal of School Violence, 2*(3), 3–26. https://doi.org/10.1300/J202v02n03_02

Hatchel, T., Ingram, K. M., Mintz, S., Hartley, C., Valido, A., Espelage, D. L., & Wyman, P. (2019). Predictors of suicidal ideation and attempts among LGBTQ adolescents: The roles of help-seeking beliefs, peer victimization, depressive symptoms, and drug use. *Journal of Child and Family Studies, 28*(9), 2443–2455. https://doi.org/10.1007/s10826-019-01339-2

Hawk, S. T., van den Eijnden, R. J., van Lissa, C. J., & ter Bogt, T. F. (2019). Narcissistic adolescents' attention-seeking following social rejection: Links with social media disclosure, problematic social media use, and smartphone stress. *Computers in Human Behavior, 92*, 65–75. https://doi.org/10.1016/j.chb.2018.10.032

Heath, K., Garcia, G., Hanson, B., Rivera, M., Hedwig, T., Moras, R., Reed, D., Smith, C., & Craig, S. (2015). *Growing up in Anchorage: Anchorage youth and young adult behavioral health and wellness assessment*. University of Alaska Anchorage Center for Human Development.

Heumann, J., & Joiner, K. (2020). *Being Heumann: An unrepentant memoir of a disability rights activist*. Beacon Press.

Hewitt, P. L., Flett, G. L., & Mikail, S. F. (2017). *Perfectionism: A relational approach to assessment, treatment, and conceptualization*. Guilford Press.

Hewitt, P. L., Ge, S., Smith, M. M., Flett, G. L., Cheli, S., Molnar, D. S., Ko, A., Mikail, S. F., & Lang, T. (2024). Automatic self recriminations: Development and validation of a measure of self-condemnatory internal dialogue. *Journal of Personality Assessment, 106*(5), 638–650. https://doi.org/10.1080/00223891.2024.2303429

Hill, A. P., & Madigan, D. J. (2022). Perfectionism, mattering, stress, and self-regulation of home learning of UK gifted and talented students during the COVID-19 pandemic. *Gifted and Talented International, 37*(1), 56–63. https://doi.org/10.1080/15332276.2022.2033649

Holt-Lunstad, J., Smith, T. B., Baker, M., Harris, T., & Stephenson, D. (2015). Loneliness and social isolation as risk factors for mortality: A meta-analytic review. *Perspectives on Psychological Science, 10*(2), 227–237. https://doi.org/10.1177/1745691614568352

Horney, K. (1950). *Neurosis and human growth: The struggle toward self-realization*. Norton.

Hovey, J. D., & King, C. A. (1996). Acculturative stress, depression, and suicidal ideation among immigrant and second-generation Latino adolescents. *Journal of the American Academy of Child & Adolescent Psychiatry, 35*(9), 1183–1192. https://doi.org/10.1097/00004583-199609000-00016

Hughes, J. (Director). (1985). *The breakfast club* [Film]. Universal Pictures.

Irani, F., Lamoin, A., & Lee-Jones, K. (2018). *The Children's Report: Australia's NGO coalition report to the United Nations Committee on the Rights of the Child.* https://assets-us-01.kc-usercontent.com/99f113b4-e5f7-00d2-23c0-c83ca2e4cfa2/f7db275d-5434-4949-a0dd-b5bb721b9482/Child-Rights-Taskforce-NGO-Coalition-Report-For-UNCRC-LR.pdf

Izard, C. E. (1993). Four systems for emotion activation: Cognitive and non-cognitive processes. *Psychological Review, 100*(1), 68–90. https://doi.org/10.1037/0033-295X.100.1.68

James, W. (1890). *The principles of psychology*. Holt.

James, W. (2001). *Talks to teachers on psychology; and to students on some of life's ideals*. Dover. https://www.gutenberg.org/files/16287/16287-h/16287-h.htm (Original work published 1899)

Joeng, J. R., & Turner, S. L. (2015). Mediators between self-criticism and depression: Fear of compassion, self-compassion, and importance to others. *Journal of Counseling Psychology, 62*(3), 453–463. https://doi.org/10.1037/cou0000071

Johnston, L. D., O'Malley, P. M., Bachman, J. G., & Schulenberg, J. E. (2011). *Monitoring the future national survey results on drug use, 1975–2010. Volume I: Secondary school students*. Institute for Social Research, The University of Michigan.

Kagan, J., & Snidman, N. (1991). Infant predictors of inhibited and uninhibited profiles. *Psychological Science, 2*(1), 40–44. https://doi.org/10.1111/j.1467-9280.1991.tb00094.x

Kakihara, F., & Tilton-Weaver, L. (2009). Adolescents' interpretations of parental control: Differentiated by domain and types of control. *Child Development, 80*(6), 1722–1738. https://doi.org/10.1111/j.1467-8624.2009.01364.x

Kelley, M. S., & Lee, M. J. (2018). When natural mentors matter: Unraveling the relationship with delinquency. *Children and Youth Services Review, 91*, 319–328. https://doi.org/10.1016/j.childyouth.2018.06.002

Kent de Grey, R. G., Uchino, B. N., Baucom, B. R., Smith, T. W., Holton, A. E., & Diener, E. F. (2019). Enemies and friends in high-tech places: The development and validation of the Online Social Experiences Measure. *Digital Health, 5*. https://doi.org/10.1177/2055207619878351

Keyes, C. L. M. (2006). Mental health in adolescence: Is America's youth flourishing? *American Journal of Orthopsychiatry, 76*(3), 395–402. https://doi.org/10.1037/0002-9432.76.3.395

Kidd, S. A. (2004). "The walls were closing in, and we were trapped": A qualitative analysis of street youth suicide. *Youth & Society, 36*(1), 30–55. https://doi.org/10.1177/0044118X03261435

Kidd, S. A., & Kral, M. J. (2002). Suicide and prostitution among street youth: A qualitative analysis. *Adolescence, 37*(146), 411–430.

Kihia, P. M., Iren, A. M., Mwangi, C. N., & Njoroge, J. N. (2024). Mattering and satisfaction with life: Gender and age differences among Kenyan secondary school students. *COUNS-EDU: The International Journal of Counseling and Education, 8*(3). https://doi.org/10.32388/NPHEQD

Kim, J., & Cicchetti, D. (2003). Social self-efficacy and behavior problems in maltreated and nonmaltreated children. *Journal of Clinical Child and Adolescent Psychology, 32*(1), 106–117. https://doi.org/10.1207/S15374424JCCP3201_10

King, D. L., Delfabbro, P. H., Griffiths, M. D., & Gradisar, M. (2012). Cognitive-behavioral approaches to outpatient treatment of internet addiction in children and adolescents. *Journal of Clinical Psychology, 68*(11), 1185–1195. https://doi.org/10.1002/jclp.21918

King, R. B. (2015). Sense of relatedness boosts engagement, achievement, and well-being: A latent growth model study. *Contemporary Educational Psychology, 42*, 26–38. https://doi.org/10.1016/j.cedpsych.2015.04.002

Kohn, P. M., & Milrose, J. A. (1993). The Inventory of High-School Students' Recent Life Experiences: A decontaminated measure of adolescents' hassles. *Journal of Youth and Adolescence, 22*(1), 43–55. https://doi.org/10.1007/BF01537903

Kovaleski, S. F. (2003, December 4). "All I ask is to be loved for me, Lee." *The Washington Post*. https://www.washingtonpost.com/archive/local/2003/12/04/all-i-ask-is-to-be-loved-for-me-lee/7e208485-f949-4bc8-8a29-1fb97ad7d636/

Kowalski, R. M. (2022, January 25). School shootings: What we know about them and what we can do. *Brookings*. https://www.brookings.edu/blog/brown-center-chalkboard/2022/01/26/school-shootings-what-we-know-about-them-and-what-we-can-do-to-prevent-them/

Kowalski, R. M., Leary, M., Hendley, T., Rubley, K., Chapman, C., Chitty, H., Carroll, H., Cook, A., Richardson, E., Robbins, C., Wells, S., Bourque, L., Oakley, R., Bednar, H., Jones, R., Tolleson, K., Fisher, K., Graham, R., Scarborough, M., . . . Longacre, M. (2021). K-12, college/university, and mass shootings: Similarities and differences. *The Journal of Social Psychology, 161*(6), 753–778. https://doi.org/10.1080/00224545.2021.1900047

Kowalski, R. M., & Wingate, V. S. (2024). Cyberbullying in children and adolescents. In A. N. M. Leung, K. K. S. Chan, C. S. M. Ng, & J. C.-K. Lee (Eds.), *Cyberbullying and values education* (pp. 13–29). Routledge. https://doi.org/10.4324/9781003314509

Kramer, C. S., Wilcox, K. C., & Lawson, H. A. (2020). Positive youth development as an improvement resource in odds-beating secondary schools. *Preventing School Failure, 64*(4), 301–315. https://doi.org/10.1080/1045988X.2020.1769011

Krauss, S. E., Collura, J., Zeldin, S., Ortega, A., Abdullah, H., & Sulaiman, A. H. (2014). Youth–adult partnership: Exploring contributions to empowerment, agency and community connections in Malaysian youth programs. *Journal of*

Youth and Adolescence, 43(9), 1550–1562. https://doi.org/10.1007/s10964-013-0027-1

Kruglanski, A. W., Bélanger, J. J., Gelfand, M., Gunaratna, R., Hettiarachchi, M., Reinares, F., Orehek, E., Sasota, J., & Sharvit, K. (2013). Terrorism—A (self) love story: Redirecting the significance quest can end violence. *American Psychologist, 68*(7), 559–575. https://doi.org/10.1037/a0032615

Kruglanski, A. W., Molinario, E., Jasko, K., Webber, D., Leander, N. P., & Pierro, A. (2022). Significance-quest theory. *Perspectives on Psychological Science, 17*(4), 1050–1071. https://doi.org/10.1177/17456916211034825

Krygsman, A., Farrell, A. H., Brittain, H., & Vaillancourt, T. (2022). Depression symptoms, mattering, and anti-mattering: Longitudinal associations in young adulthood. *Journal of Psychoeducational Assessment, 40*(1), 77–94. https://doi.org/10.1177/07342829211050519

Kuczynski, L., Parkin, C. M., & Pitman, R. (2015). Socialization as dynamic process: A dialectical, transactional perspective. In J. E. Grusec & P. D. Hastings (Eds.), *Handbook of socialization: Theory and research* (2nd ed., pp. 135–157). Guilford Press.

Kunyu, D. K., Schachner, M. K., Juang, L. P., Schwarzenthal, M., & Aral, T. (2021). Acculturation hassles and adjustment of adolescents of immigrant descent: Testing mediation with a self-determination theory approach. *New Directions for Child and Adolescent Development, 2021*(177), 101–121. https://doi.org/10.1002/cad.20408

Lakey, B., Tardiff, T. A., & Drew, J. B. (1994). Negative social interactions: Assessment and relations to social support, cognition, and psychological distress. *Journal of Social and Clinical Psychology, 13*(1), 42–62. https://doi.org/10.1521/jscp.1994.13.1.42

Lamonda, K. H. (2001). *The 2001 Vermont Youth Risk Behavior Survey*. Vermont Department of Health, Division of Alcohol and Drug Abuse Programs.

Larson, R. W., Raffaelli, M., Guzman, S., Salusky, I., Orson, C. N., & Kenzer, A. (2019). The important (but neglected) developmental value of roles: Findings from youth programs. *Developmental Psychology, 55*(5), 1019–1033. https://doi.org/10.1037/dev0000674

Laursen, B., & Collins, W. A. (2009). Parent–child relationships during adolescence. In R. M. Lerner & L. Steinberg (Eds.), *Handbook of adolescent psychology: Vol. 2. Contextual influences on adolescent development* (3rd ed., pp. 3–42). Wiley. https://doi.org/10.1002/9780470479193.adlpsy002002

Laycock, S. R. (1962). Fostering mental health in schools. *Canadian Journal of Public Health, 53*, 413–419.

Lee, A. Y., & Hancock, J. (2024). Social media mindsets: A new approach to understanding social media use and psychological well-being. *Journal of Computer-Mediated Communication, 29*(1), Article zmad048. https://doi.org/10.1093/jcmc/zmad048

Lee, L. K., Stewart, A., & Mannix, R. (2021). And so they wait: The other epidemic among United States youth during COVID-19. *Academic Emergency Medicine, 29*(11), 1347–1348. https://doi.org/10.1111/acem.14380

Lee, L. O., Aldwin, C. M., Kubzansky, L. D., Chen, E., Mroczek, D. K., Wang, J. M., & Spiro, A. (2015). Do cherished children age successfully? Longitudinal findings from the Veterans Affairs Normative Aging Study. *Psychology and Aging, 30*(4), 894–910. https://doi.org/10.1037/pag0000050

Legerstee, M., & Barillas, Y. (2003). Sharing attention and pointing to objects at 12 months: Is the intentional stance implied? *Cognitive Development, 18*(1), 91–110. https://doi.org/10.1016/S0885-2014(02)00165-X

Legerstee, M., & Varghese, J. (2001). The role of maternal affect mirroring on social expectancies in three-month-old infants. *Child Development, 72*(5), 1301–1313. https://doi.org/10.1111/1467-8624.00349

Leitner, J. B., Hehman, E., Deegan, M. P., & Jones, J. M. (2014). Adaptive disengagement buffers self-esteem from negative social feedback. *Personality and Social Psychology Bulletin, 40*(11), 1435–1450. https://doi.org/10.1177/0146167214549319

Lemmens, J. S., Bushman, B. J., & Konijn, E. A. (2006). The appeal of violent video games to lower educated aggressive adolescent boys from two countries. *CyberPsychology & Behavior, 9*(5), 638–641. https://doi.org/10.1089/cpb.2006.9.638

Lemon, J. C., & Watson, J. C. (2011). Early identification of potential high school dropouts: An investigation of the relationship among at-risk status, wellness, perceived stress, and mattering. *Journal of At-Risk Issues, 16*(2), 17–23. https://dropoutprevention.org/wp-content/uploads/2015/05/JARI1602.pdf

Lewinsohn, P. M. (1974). A behavioral approach to depression. In R. J. Friedman & M. M. Katz (Eds.), *The psychology of depression: Contemporary theory and research* (pp. 157–178). Wiley.

Lewis, D.-M. (2017). A matter for concern: Young offenders and the importance of mattering. *Deviant Behavior, 38*(11), 1318–1331. https://doi.org/10.1080/01639625.2016.1197659

Lewis, H. B. (1971). *Guilt and shame in neurosis*. International Universities Press.

Lindsey, E. W., Kurtz, D., Jarvis, S., Williams, N. R., & Nackerud, L. (2000). How runaways and homeless youth navigate troubled waters: Personal strengths and resources. *Child & Adolescent Social Work Journal, 17*(2), 115–140. https://doi.org/10.1023/A:1007558323191

Linehan, M. M., Goodstein, J. L., Nielsen, S. L., & Chiles, J. A. (1983). *Reasons for Living Inventory (RFL)* [Database record]. APA PsycTests. https://doi.org/10.1037/t02526-000

Liu, W., Gamble, J. H., Cao, C. H., Liao, X. L., Chen, I. H., & Flett, G. L. (2023). The General Mattering Scale, the Anti-Mattering Scale, and the Fear of Not Mattering Inventory: Psychometric properties and links with distress and hope among Chinese university students. *Psychology Research and Behavior Management, 16*, 4445–4459. https://doi.org/10.2147/PRBM.S430455

Lovibond, P. F., & Lovibond, S. H. (1995). The structure of negative emotional states: Comparison of the Depression Anxiety Stress Scales (DASS) with the Beck Depression and Anxiety Inventories. *Behaviour Research and Therapy, 33*(3), 335–343. https://doi.org/10.1016/0005-7967(94)00075-U

Lum, J. J., & Phares, V. (2005). Assessing the emotional availability of parents. *Journal of Psychopathology and Behavioral Assessment, 27*(3), 211–226. https://doi.org/10.1007/s10862-005-0637-3

Luthar, S. S., & Barkin, S. H. (2012). Are affluent youth truly "at risk"? Vulnerability and resilience across three diverse samples. *Development and Psychopathology, 24*(2), 429–449. https://doi.org/10.1017/S0954579412000089

Luthar, S. S., & Becker, B. E. (2002). Privileged but pressured? A study of affluent youth. *Child Development, 73*(5), 1593–1610. https://doi.org/10.1111/1467-8624.00492

Luthar, S. S., Cicchetti, D., & Becker, B. (2000). The construct of resilience: A critical evaluation and guidelines for future work. *Child Development, 71*(3), 543–562. https://doi.org/10.1111/1467-8624.00164

Luthar, S. S., & Goldstein, A. S. (2008). Substance use and related behaviors among suburban late adolescents: The importance of perceived parent containment. *Development and Psychopathology, 20*(2), 591–614. https://doi.org/10.1017/S0954579408000291

Luthar, S. S., & Kumar, N. L. (2018). Youth in high achieving schools: Challenges to mental health and directions for evidence-based interventions. In A. W. Leschied, D. H. Saklofske, & G. L. Flett (Eds.), *Handbook of school-based mental health promotion: An evidence-informed framework* (pp. 441–458). Springer.

Luthar, S. S., Kumar, N. L., & Zillmer, N. (2020). High-achieving schools connote risks for adolescents: Problems documented, processes implicated, and directions for interventions. *American Psychologist, 75*(7), 983–995. https://doi.org/10.1037/amp0000556

Maftei, A., & Diaconu-Gherasim, L. R. (2023). The road to addiction (might be) paved with good intentions: Motives for social media use and psychological distress among early adolescents. *Journal of Children and Media, 17*(4), 538–558. https://doi.org/10.1080/17482798.2023.2255304

Maine Department of Health and Human Services. (2022). *The importance of mattering among youth: Data from the 2019 Maine Integrated Youth Health Summary*. https://www.maine.gov/miyhs/sites/default/files/2022-06/Mattering%20Infographic%20-%20FINAL.pdf

Malti, T., & Noam, G. G. (2008). The hidden crisis in mental health and education: The gap between student needs and existing supports. *New Directions for Youth Development, 2008*(120), 13–29. https://doi.org/10.1002/yd.283

Malvo, L. B., & Meoli, A. (2014). *Diary of the D.C. sniper*. CreateSpace Independent Publishing Platform.

Marcus, F. M., & Rosenberg, M. (1987, March). *Mattering: Its measurement and significance in everyday life* [Paper presentation]. Eastern Sociological Society 57th Annual Meeting, Boston, Massachusetts, United States.

Maris, R. (1985). The adolescent suicide problem. *Suicide & Life-Threatening Behavior, 15*(2), 91–109. https://doi.org/10.1111/j.1943-278X.1985.tb00644.x

Markus, H., & Nurius, P. (1986). Possible selves. *American Psychologist, 41*(9), 954–969. https://doi.org/10.1037/0003-066X.41.9.954

Marshall, S. K. (2001). Do I matter? Construct validation of adolescents' perceived mattering to parents and friends. *Journal of Adolescence, 24*(4), 473–490. https://doi.org/10.1006/jado.2001.0384

Marshall, S. K. (2004). Relative contributions of perceived mattering to parents and friends in predicting adolescents' psychological well-being. *Perceptual and Motor Skills, 99*(2), 591–601. https://doi.org/10.2466/pms.99.2.591-601

Marshall, S. K., & Lambert, J. D. (2006). Parental mattering: A qualitative inquiry into the tendency to evaluate the self as significant to one's children. *Journal of Family Issues, 27*(11), 1561–1582. https://doi.org/10.1177/0192513X06290039

Marshall, S. K., Liu, Y., Wu, A., Berzonsky, M., & Adams, G. R. (2010). Perceived mattering to parents and friends for university students: A longitudinal study. *Journal of Adolescence, 33*(3), 367–375. https://doi.org/10.1016/j.adolescence.2009.09.003

Marshall, S. K., & Tilton-Weaver, L. (2019). Adolescents' perceived mattering to parents and friends: Testing cross-lagged associations with psychosocial well-being. *International Journal of Behavioral Development, 43*(6), 541–552. https://doi.org/10.1177/0165025419844019

Martin, A. J., & Marsh, H. W. (2008). Academic buoyancy: Towards an understanding of students' everyday academic resilience. *Journal of School Psychology, 46*(1), 53–83. https://doi.org/10.1016/j.jsp.2007.01.002

Martin, A. J., Nejad, H., Colmar, S., & Liem, G. A. D. (2012). Adaptability: Conceptual and empirical perspectives on responses to change, novelty and uncertainty. *Australian Journal of Guidance and Counselling, 22*(1), 58–81. https://doi.org/10.1017/jgc.2012.8

Maslow, A. H. (1942). The dynamics of psychological security-insecurity. *Journal of Personality, 10*(4), 331–344. https://doi.org/10.1111/j.1467-6494.1942.tb01911.x

Maslow, A. H. (1943). Preface to motivation theory. *Psychosomatic Medicine, 5*(1), 85–92. https://doi.org/10.1097/00006842-194301000-00012

Masten, A. S. (2014). *Ordinary magic: Resilience in development*. Guilford Press.

Mayes, L. (2023, November 3). I felt needed when I was riding motorcycles with my cousin and he had wrecked down the road and broke [Comment on the article "When have you felt you mattered?"]. *The New York Times*. https://www.nytimes.com/2023/11/03/learning/when-have-you-felt-that-you-mattered.html#commentsContainer

McComb, S. E., Goldberg, J. O., Flett, G. L., & Rose, A. L. (2020, December 16). The double jeopardy of feeling lonely and unimportant: State and trait loneliness and feelings and fears of not mattering. *Frontiers in Psychology, 11*, Article 563420. https://doi.org/10.3389/fpsyg.2020.563420

McDonald, B., Lester, K. J., & Michelson, D. (2023). "She didn't know how to go back": School attendance problems in the context of the COVID-19 pandemic—A multiple stakeholder qualitative study with parents and professionals. *British Journal of Educational Psychology, 93*(1), 386–401. https://doi.org/10.1111/bjep.12562

McManama O'Brien, K. H. M., Almeida, J., View, L., Schofield, M., Hall, W., Aguinaldo, L., Ryan, C. A., & Maneta, E. (2021). A safety and coping planning intervention for suicidal adolescents in acute psychiatric care. *Cognitive and Behavioral Practice, 28*(1), 22–39. https://doi.org/10.1016/j.cbpra.2019.08.003

Meza, J. I., Patel, K., & Bath, E. (2022). Black youth suicide crisis: Prevalence rates, review of risk and protective factors, and current evidence-based practices. *Focus, 20*(2), 197–203. https://doi.org/10.1176/appi.focus.20210034

Milestone, S. F. (1993). Implications of affect theory for the practice of cognitive therapy. *Psychiatric Annals, 23*(10), 577–583. https://doi.org/10.3928/0048-5713-19931001-10

Missildine, W. (1963). *Your inner child of the past*. Pocket Books.

Mohammed, S. K., Maranzan, K. A., & Mushquash, A. R. (2023). Mattering matters for students high in socially prescribed perfectionism as they transition to university: Support for a moderation model. *Personality and Individual Differences, 214*, Article 112356. https://doi.org/10.1016/j.paid.2023.112356

Moore, C. D. (Ed.). (1981). *Adolescence and stress: Report of an NIMH conference on research directions for understanding stress reactions in adolescence*. National Institute of Mental Health.

Mougharbel, F., Chaput, J.-P., Sampasa-Kanyinga, H., Hamilton, H. A., Colman, I., Leatherdale, S. T., & Goldfield, G. S. (2023, June 14). Heavy social media use and psychological distress among adolescents: The moderating role of sex, age, and parental support. *Frontiers in Public Health, 11*, Article 1190390. https://doi.org/10.3389/fpubh.2023.1190390

Mueller, C. E. (2009). Protective factors as barriers to depression in gifted and nongifted adolescents. *Gifted Child Quarterly, 53*(1), 3–14. https://doi.org/10.1177/0016986208326552

Mulderrig, E. (2023, November 3). When they tell me it almost feels like reassurance that they care and love me. But with other people, it feels like enlightenment [Comment on the article "When have you felt you mattered?"]. *The New York Times*. https://www.nytimes.com/2023/11/03/learning/when-have-you-felt-that-you-mattered.html#commentsContainer

Muris, P., & Meesters, C. (2014). Small or big in the eyes of the other: On the developmental psychopathology of self-conscious emotions as shame, guilt, and pride. *Clinical Child and Family Psychology Review, 17*(1), 19–40. https://doi.org/10.1007/s10567-013-0137-z

Muris, P., Meesters, C., & Timmermans, A. (2013). Some youths have a gloomy side: Correlates of the dark triad personality traits in non-clinical adolescents. *Child Psychiatry and Human Development, 44*(5), 658–665. https://doi.org/10.1007/s10578-013-0359-9

Murphey, D. A., Lamonda, K. H., Carney, J. K., & Duncan, P. (2004). Relationships of a brief measure of youth assets to health-promoting and risk behaviors. *Journal of Adolescent Health, 34*(3), 184–191. https://doi.org/10.1016/S1054-139X(03)00280-5

Murphy, L. B. (1987). Further reflections on resilience. In E. J. Anthony & B. J. Cohler (Eds.), *The invulnerable child* (pp. 84–105). Guilford Press.

Myers, J. E., & Sweeney, T. J. (2005). *The Five Factor Wellness Inventory manual.* Mindgarden.

National Research Council and Institute of Medicine. (2002). *Community programs to promote youth development.* National Academies Press.

Neel, R., & Lassetter, B. (2019). The stigma of perceived irrelevance: An affordance-management theory of interpersonal invisibility. *Psychological Review, 126*(5), 634–659. https://doi.org/10.1037/rev0000143

Neff, K. D., & McGehee, P. (2010). Self-compassion and psychological resilience among adolescents and young adults. *Self and Identity, 9*(3), 225–240. https://doi.org/10.1080/15298860902979307

Nolen-Hoeksema, S. (1991). Responses to depression and their effects on the duration of depressive episodes. *Journal of Abnormal Psychology, 100*(4), 569–582. https://doi.org/10.1037/0021-843X.100.4.569

Nordyke, G. (2023, November 3). A time I feel like I've mattered most was when my parents needed someone to look after my brother and [Comment on the article "When have you felt you mattered?"]. *The New York Times.* https://www.nytimes.com/2023/11/03/learning/when-have-you-felt-that-you-mattered.html#commentsContainer

Northwest Territories Standing Committee on Social Development. (2023). *Strengthening community supports, lifting youth voices: Recommendations on suicide prevention.* https://www.ntlegislativeassembly.ca/sites/default/files/legacy/cr_50-192_scosd_recommendations_on_suicide_prevention.pdf

Office of the Surgeon General. (2023). *Social media and youth mental health: The U.S. surgeon general's advisory.* https://www.hhs.gov/sites/default/files/sg-youth-mental-health-social-media-advisory.pdf

Olcoń, K., Kim, Y., & Gulbas, L. E. (2017). Sense of belonging and youth suicidal behaviors: What do communities and schools have to do with it? *Social Work in Public Health, 32*(7), 432–442. https://doi.org/10.1080/19371918.2017.1344602

141 Cong. Rec. S5543 (1995). https://www.congress.gov/104/crec/1995/04/07/141/65/CREC-1995-04-07.pdf

Osman, A., Downs, W. R., Kopper, B. A., Barrios, F. X., Baker, M. T., Osman, J. R., Besett, T. M., & Linehan, M. M. (1998). The Reasons for Living Inventory for Adolescents (RFL-A): Development and psychometric properties. *Journal of Clinical Psychology, 54*(8), 1063–1078. https://doi.org/10.1002/(SICI)1097-4679(199812)54:8<1063:AID-JCLP6>3.0.CO;2-Z

Oswald, D. L., & Clark, E. M. (2003). Best friends forever? High school best friendships and the transition to college. *Personal Relationships, 10*(2), 187–196. https://doi.org/10.1111/1475-6811.00045

Oyserman, D., Brickman, D., & Rhodes, M. (2007). School success, possible selves, and parent school involvement. *Family Relations, 56*(5), 479–489. https://doi.org/10.1111/j.1741-3729.2007.00475.x

Oyserman, D., Bybee, D., & Terry, K. (2006). Possible selves and academic outcomes: How and when possible selves impel action. *Journal of Personality and Social Psychology, 91*(1), 188–204. https://doi.org/10.1037/0022-3514.91.1.188

Oyserman, D., & Markus, H. R. (1990). Possible selves and delinquency. *Journal of Personality and Social Psychology, 59*(1), 112–125. https://doi.org/10.1037/0022-3514.59.1.112

Page, R. M., Yanagishita, J., Suwanteerangkul, J., Zarco, E. P., Mei-Lee, C., & Miao, N.-F. (2006). Hopelessness and loneliness among suicide attempters in school-based samples of Taiwanese, Philippine and Thai adolescents. *School Psychology International, 27*(5), 583–598. https://doi.org/10.1177/0143034306073415

Pancani, L., Gerosa, T., Gui, M., & Riva, P. (2021). “Mom, dad, look at me”: The development of the Parental Phubbing Scale. *Journal of Social and Personal Relationships, 38*(2), 435–458. https://doi.org/10.1177/0265407520964866

Parent, N. (2023). Basic need satisfaction through social media engagement: A developmental framework for understanding adolescent social media use. *Human Development, 67*(1), 1–17. https://doi.org/10.1159/000529449

Parke, R. (2000). Foreword. In G. H. Elder, Jr., & R. D. Conger (Eds.), *Children of the land: Adversity and success in rural America* (pp. xiii–xvi). The University of Chicago Press. https://doi.org/10.7208/chicago/9780226224978.001.0001

Pea, R., Nass, C., Meheula, L., Rance, M., Kumar, A., Bamford, H., Nass, M., Simha, A., Stillerman, B., Yang, S., & Zhou, M. (2012). Media use, face-to-face communication, media multitasking, and social well-being among 8- to 12-year-old girls. *Developmental Psychology, 48*(2), 327–336. https://doi.org/10.1037/a0027030

Perkins, D. F., & Noam, G. (2007). Characteristics of sports-based youth development program. *New Directions for Youth Development, 2007*(115), 75–84. https://doi.org/10.1002/yd.224

Perry, M. (2022). *Friends, lovers, and the big terrible thing*. Flatiron Books.

Peterson, J. (1998). Six exceptional young women at risk. *Reclaiming Children and Youth, 6*(4), 233–238.

Pinto, A., Whisman, M. A., & Conwell, Y. (1998). Reasons for living in a clinical sample of adolescents. *Journal of Adolescence, 21*(4), 397–405. https://doi.org/10.1006/jado.1998.0173

Prilleltensky, I. (2020). Mattering at the intersection of psychology, philosophy, and politics. *American Journal of Community Psychology, 65*(1–2), 16–34. https://doi.org/10.1002/ajcp.12368

Prilleltensky, I., & Prilleltensky, O. (2021). *How people matter: Why it affects health, happiness, love, work, and society*. Cambridge University Press. https://doi.org/10.1017/9781108979405

Prime, H., Walsh, F., & Masten, A. S. (2023). Building family resilience in the wake of a global pandemic: Looking back to prepare for the future. *Canadian Psychology/Psychologie canadienne*, *64*(3), 200–211. https://doi.org/10.1037/cap0000366

Proulx, N. (2023, November 3). When have you felt you mattered? *The New York Times*. https://www.nytimes.com/2023/11/03/learning/when-have-you-felt-that-you-mattered.html

Racine, N., McArthur, B. A., Cooke, J. E., Eirich, R., Zhu, J., & Madigan, S. (2021). Global prevalence of depressive and anxiety symptoms in children and adolescents during COVID-19: A meta-analysis. *JAMA Pediatrics*, *175*(11), 1142–1150. https://doi.org/10.1001/jamapediatrics.2021.2482

Radloff, L. S. (1977). The CES-D Scale: A self-report depression scale for research in the general population. *Applied Psychological Measurement*, *1*(3), 385–401. https://doi.org/10.1177/014662167700100306

Rayle, A. D. (2005). Adolescent gender differences in mattering and wellness. *Journal of Adolescence*, *28*(6), 753–763. https://doi.org/10.1016/j.adolescence.2004.10.009

Rayle, A. D., & Myers, J. E. (2004). Counseling adolescents towards wellness: The roles of ethnic identity, acculturation, and mattering. *Professional School Counseling*, *8*, 81–90.

Renick, J., & Reich, S. M. (2023). Elevating student voices and addressing their needs: Using youth participatory action research to improve school climate during the COVID-19 pandemic. *Journal of Adolescent Research*. Advance online publication. https://doi.org/10.1177/07435584231215448

Richey, M. H., & Richey, H. W. (1980). The significance of best-friend relationships in adolescence. *Psychology in the Schools*, *17*(4), 536–540. https://doi.org/10.1002/1520-6807(198010)17:4<536::AID-PITS2310170420>3.0.CO;2-I

Riehm, K. E., Feder, K. A., Tormohlen, K. N., Crum, R. M., Young, A. S., Green, K. M., Pacek, L. R., La Flair, L. N., & Mojtabai, R. (2019). Associations between time spent using social media and internalizing and externalizing problems among US youth. *JAMA Psychiatry*, *76*(12), 1266–1273. https://doi.org/10.1001/jamapsychiatry.2019.2325

Robins, R. W., Hendin, H. M., & Trzesniewski, K. H. (2001). Measuring global self-esteem: Construct validation of a single-item measure and the Rosenberg Self-Esteem Scale. *Personality and Social Psychology Bulletin*, *27*(2), 151–161. https://doi.org/10.1177/0146167201272002

Rochester Regional Health. (2018, April 19). *From ACEs to assets: Fostering resilience to improve outcomes* [PowerPoint slides].

Rogers, A. (2023, November 3). This feeling of importance and being missed makes me feel loved and fills my heart with joy [Comment on the article

"When have you felt you mattered?"]. *The New York Times*. https://www.nytimes.com/2023/11/03/learning/when-have-you-felt-that-you-mattered.html#commentsContainer

Rogers, C. R. (1951). *Client-centered therapy: Its current practice, implications, and theory*. Houghton Mifflin.

Rogers, C. R. (1961). *On becoming a person: A therapist's view of psychotherapy*. Houghton Mifflin.

Rogers, C. R. (1980). *A way of being*. Houghton Mifflin.

Rose, A. L., & Kocovski, N. L. (2021). The Social Self-Compassion Scale (SSCS): Development, validity, and associations with indices of well-being, distress, and social anxiety. *International Journal of Mental Health and Addiction*, *19*(6), 2091–2109. https://doi.org/10.1007/s11469-020-00302-3

Rosenberg, M. (1965). *Society and the adolescent self-image*. Princeton University Press. https://doi.org/10.1515/9781400876136

Rosenberg, M. (1979). *Conceiving the self*. Basic Books.

Rosenberg, M. (1985). Self-concept and psychological well-being in adolescence. In R. L. Leahy (Ed.), *The development of the self* (pp. 205–246). Academic Press.

Rosenberg, M. (1986). Self-esteem research: A phenomenological corrective. In J. Prager, M. Seeman, & D. Longshores (Eds.), *School desegregation research: New directions in situational analysis* (pp. 175–203). Springer.

Rosenberg, M., & McCullough, B. C. (1981). Mattering: Inferred significance and mental health among adolescents. *Research in Community & Mental Health*, *2*, 163–182.

Rosenberg, M., & Simmons, R. G. (1972). *Black and white self-esteem*. American Sociological Association.

Rothbart, M. K., Ahadi, S. A., Hershey, K. L., & Fisher, P. (2001). Investigations of temperament at three to seven years: The Children's Behavior Questionnaire. *Child Development*, *72*(5), 1394–1408. https://doi.org/10.1111/1467-8624.00355

Rothbart, M. K., & Putnam, S. P. (2002). Temperament and socialization. In L. Pulkkinen & A. Caspi (Eds.), *Paths to successful development: Personality in the life course* (pp. 19–45). Cambridge University Press. https://doi.org/10.1017/CBO9780511489761.002

Ruini, C., Belaise, C., Brombin, C., Caffo, E., & Fava, G. A. (2006). Well-being therapy in school settings: A pilot study. *Psychotherapy and Psychosomatics*, *75*(6), 331–336. https://doi.org/10.1159/000095438

Ruini, C., Ottolini, F., Tomba, E., Belaise, C., Albieri, E., Visani, D., Offidani, E., Caffo, E., & Fava, G. A. (2009). School intervention for promoting psychological well-being in adolescence. *Journal of Behavior Therapy and Experimental Psychiatry*, *40*(4), 522–532. https://doi.org/10.1016/j.jbtep.2009.07.002

Ryan, R. M., & Deci, E. L. (2017). *Self-determination theory: Basic psychological needs in motivation, development, and wellness*. Guilford Press. https://doi.org/10.1521/978.14625/28806

Ryan, R. M., Deci, E. L., Grolnick, W. S., & La Guardia, J. G. (2006). The significance of autonomy and autonomy support in psychological development and psychopathology. In D. Cicchetti & D. J. Cohen (Eds.), *Developmental psychopathology: Theory and method* (2nd ed., pp. 795–849). John Wiley & Sons.

Ryan, R. M., Deci, E. L., Grolnick, W. S., & La Guardia, J. G. (2015). The significance of autonomy and autonomy support in psychological development and psychopathology. In D. Cicchetti & D. J. Cohen (Eds.), *Developmental psychopathology: Vol. 1. Theory and method* (2nd ed., pp. 795–849). Wiley. https://doi.org/10.1002/9780470939383.ch20

Ryff, C. D. (1989). Happiness is everything, or is it? Explorations on the meaning of psychological well-being. *Journal of Personality and Social Psychology, 57*(6), 1069–1081. https://doi.org/10.1037/0022-3514.57.6.1069

Ryff, C. D. (2018). Eudaimonic well-being: Highlights from 25 years of inquiry. In K. Shigemasu, S. Kuwano, T. Sato, & T. Matsuzawa (Eds.), *Diversity in harmony: Insights from psychology* (pp. 375–395). Wiley. https://doi.org/10.1002/9781119362081.ch20

Ryff, C. D., & Keyes, C. L. (1995). The structure of psychological well-being revisited. *Journal of Personality and Social Psychology, 69*(4), 719–727. https://doi.org/10.1037/0022-3514.69.4.719

Sabik, N. J., Falat, J., & Magagnos, J. (2020). When self-worth depends on social media feedback: Associations with psychological well-being. *Sex Roles, 82*(7–8), 411–421. https://doi.org/10.1007/s11199-019-01062-8

Samari, E., Chang, S., Seow, E., Chua, Y. C., Subramaniam, M., van Dam, R. M., Luo, N., Verma, S., & Vaingankar, J. A. (2022). A qualitative study on negative experiences of social media use and harm reduction strategies among youths in a multi-ethnic Asian society. *PLOS ONE, 17*(11), Article e0277928. https://doi.org/10.1371/journal.pone.0277928

Sameroff, A. (1975). Transactional models in early social relations. *Human Development, 18*(1–2), 65–79. https://doi.org/10.1159/000271476

Sampasa-Kanyinga, H., Chaput, J.-P., & Hamilton, H. A. (2019). Social media use, school connectedness, and academic performance among adolescents. *The Journal of Primary Prevention, 40*(2), 189–211. https://doi.org/10.1007/s10935-019-00543-6

Sandler, I. N., Wheeler, L. A., & Braver, S. L. (2013). Relations of parenting quality, interparental conflict, and overnights with mental health problems of children in divorcing families with high legal conflict. *Journal of Family Psychology, 27*(6), 915–924. https://doi.org/10.1037/a0034449

Saritepeci, M., Yildiz Durak, H., & Atman Uslu, N. (2022). A latent profile analysis for the study of multiple screen addiction, mobile social gaming addiction, general mattering, and family sense of belonging in university students. *International Journal of Mental Health and Addiction, 21*(6), 3699–3720. https://doi.org/10.1007/s11469-022-00816-y

Scharf, M. A. (2018, November 27). *Recovering from ACEs* [Paper presentation]. MCCF Fall Breakfast, Rochester Academy of Medicine, Rochester, NY, United States. http://grmccf.org/wp-content/uploads/2018/10/ACEs-Scharf-10-27-18.pdf

Schenck, C. E., Braver, S. L., Wolchik, S. A., Saenz, D., Cookston, J. T., & Fabricius, W. V. (2009). Relations between mattering to step- and non-residential fathers and adolescent mental health. *Fathering*, *7*(1), 70–90. https://doi.org/10.3149/fth.0701.70

Schlossberg, N. K. (1981). A model for analyzing human adaptation to transition. *The Counseling Psychologist*, *9*(2), 2–18. https://doi.org/10.1177/001100008100900202

Schlossberg, N. K. (1989). Marginality and mattering: Key issues in building community. *New Directions for Student Services*, *1989*(48), 5–15. https://doi.org/10.1002/ss.37119894803

Schmidt, C. (2018). *Examining the role of interpersonal and societal mattering in the health and wellbeing of rural adolescents* [Doctoral dissertation]. University of Michigan Library Deep Blue Documents. https://hdl.handle.net/2027.42/145851

Schmidt, C. J., Stoddard, S. A., Heinze, J. E., Caldwell, C. H., & Zimmerman, M. A. (2020). Examining contextual and relational factors influencing perceptions of societal and interpersonal mattering among rural youth. *Journal of Community Psychology*, *48*(6), 2013–2032. https://doi.org/10.1002/jcop.22401

Schreurs, L., Meier, A., & Vandenbosch, L. (2023). Exposure to the positivity bias and adolescents' differential longitudinal links with social comparison, Inspiration and envy depending on social media literacy. *Current Psychology*, *42*(32), 28221–28241. https://doi.org/10.1007/s12144-022-03893-3

Semprevivo, L. K. (2023). Protection and connection: Negating depression and suicidality among bullied, LGBTQ youth. *International Journal of Environmental Research and Public Health*, *20*(14), 6388. https://doi.org/10.3390/ijerph20146388

Sendak, M. D., Schilstra, C., Tye, E., Brotkin, S., & Maslow, G. (2018). Positive youth development at camps for youth with chronic illness: A systematic review of the literature. *Journal of Youth Development*, *13*(1–2), 201–215. https://doi.org/10.5195/jyd.2018.551

Seo, H., Houston, J. B., Knight, L. A. T., Kennedy, E. J., & Inglish, A. B. (2014). Teens' social media use and collective action. *New Media & Society*, *16*(6), 883–902. https://doi.org/10.1177/1461444813495162

Sheftall, A. H., Vakil, F., Ruch, D. A., Boyd, R. C., Lindsey, M. A., & Bridge, J. A. (2022). Black youth suicide: Investigation of current trends and precipitating circumstances. *Journal of the American Academy of Child & Adolescent Psychiatry*, *61*(5), 662–675. https://doi.org/10.1016/j.jaac.2021.08.021

Shneidman, E. S. (1984). Aphorisms of suicide and some implications for psychotherapy. *American Journal of Psychotherapy*, *38*(3), 319–328. https://doi.org/10.1176/appi.psychotherapy.1984.38.3.319

Shneidman, E. (2005). Prediction of suicide revisited: A brief methodological note. *Suicide and Life-Threatening Behavior, 35*(1), 1–2. https://doi.org/10.1521/suli.35.1.1.59265

Sidmore, P. (2015, April). *Adverse childhood experiences: Overcoming ACEs in Alaska* [Paper presentation]. Northstar Behavioral Health Holistic Health Conference, Anchorage, AK, United States.

Siller, L., Edwards, K. M., & Banyard, V. (2022). Violence typologies among youth: A latent class analysis of middle and high school youth. *Journal of Interpersonal Violence, 37*(3–4), 1023–1048. https://doi.org/10.1177/0886260520922362

Smith, D., Leonis, T., & Anandavalli, S. (2021). Belonging and loneliness in cyberspace: Impacts of social media on adolescents' well-being. *Australian Journal of Psychology, 73*(1), 12–23. https://doi.org/10.1080/00049530.2021.1898914

Smith, M., Mann, M. J., Bryan, J., Mujak, I., & Campbell, K. (2022, November 7). *The model of girls' resilience: Applications to suicide prevention for young women* [Paper presentation]. American Public Health Association Annual Meeting and Expo, Boston, MA, United States.

Somers, C. L., Gill-Scalcucci, S., Flett, G. L., & Nepon, T. (2022). The utility of brief mattering subscales for adolescents: Associations with learning motivations, achievement, executive function, hope, loneliness, and risk behavior. *Journal of Psychoeducational Assessment, 40*(1), 108–124. https://doi.org/10.1177/07342829211055342

Sotindjo, T., Marshall, S., & Saewyc, E. M. (2019). Psychosocial effects of homonegative verbal interaction among high school students in Canada. *Journal of Adolescent Health, 64*(2), S5–S6. https://doi.org/10.1016/j.jadohealth.2018.10.024

Sparks, C., Dimmock, J., Lonsdale, C., & Jackson, B. (2016). Modeling indicators and outcomes of students' perceived teacher relatedness support in high school physical education. *Psychology of Sport and Exercise, 26*, 71–82. https://doi.org/10.1016/j.psychsport.2016.06.004

Sparks, C., Dimmock, J., Whipp, P., Lonsdale, C., & Jackson, B. (2015). "Getting connected": High school physical education teacher behaviors that facilitate students' relatedness support perceptions. *Sport, Exercise, and Performance Psychology, 4*(3), 219–236. https://doi.org/10.1037/spy0000039

Stebleton, M. J., Kaler, L. S., & Potts, C. (2022). "Am I even going to be well-liked in person?": First-year students' social media use, sense of belonging, and mental health. *Journal of College and Character, 23*(3), 210–226. https://doi.org/10.1080/2194587X.2022.2087683

Stephens, B. J. (1987). Cheap thrills and humble pie: The adolescence of female suicide attempters. *Suicide and Life-Threatening Behavior, 17*(2), 107–118. https://doi.org/10.1111/j.1943-278X.1987.tb01024.x

Stevenson, M. M., Fabricius, W. V., Cookston, J. T., Parke, R. D., Coltrane, S., Braver, S. L., & Saenz, D. S. (2014). Marital problems, maternal gatekeeping attitudes, and father–child relationships in adolescence. *Developmental Psychology, 50*(4), 1208–1218. https://doi.org/10.1037/a0035327

Sturman, E. D. (2011). Involuntary subordination and its relation to personality, mood, and submissive behavior. *Psychological Assessment, 23*(1), 262–276. https://doi.org/10.1037/a0021499

Su, S. C., & Flett, G. L. (2023). Psychological well-being on international students in Canada amidst COVID-19: The role of mattering and belongingness. *Research Connection, 2*(2). https://www.brandonu.ca/research-connection/article/psychological-well-being-on-international-students-in-canada-amidst-covid-19-the-role-of-mattering-and-belongingness/

Sun, J., Dunne, M. P., Hou, X.-y., & Xu, A.-q. (2011). Educational stress scale for adolescents: Development, validity, and reliability with Chinese students. *Journal of Psychoeducational Assessment, 29*(6), 534–546. https://doi.org/10.1177/0734282910394976

Tackett, J. L., & Krueger, R. F. (2011). Dispositional influences on human aggression. In P. R. Shaver & M. Mikulincer (Eds.), *Human aggression and violence: Causes, manifestations, and consequences* (pp. 89–104). American Psychological Association. https://doi.org/10.1037/12346-005

Tangney, J. P. (2002). Perfectionism and the self-conscious emotions: Shame, guilt, embarrassment, and pride. In G. L. Flett & P. L. Hewitt (Eds.), *Perfectionism: Theory, research, and treatment* (pp. 199–215). American Psychological Association. https://doi.org/10.1037/10458-008

Tangney, J. P., Miller, R. S., Flicker, L., & Barlow, D. H. (1996). Are shame, guilt, and embarrassment distinct emotions? *Journal of Personality and Social Psychology, 70*(6), 1256–1269. https://doi.org/10.1037/0022-3514.70.6.1256

Taylor, J., & Turner, R. J. (2001). A longitudinal study of the role and significance of mattering to others for depressive symptoms. *Journal of Health and Social Behavior, 42*(3), 310–325. https://doi.org/10.2307/3090217

Theriault, D., & Witt, P. A. (2014). Features of positive developmental leisure settings for LGBTQ youth. *Journal of Park and Recreation Administration, 32*(2), 83–97.

Thomas, A., & Chess, S. (1981). The role of temperament in the contributions of individuals to their development. In R. M. Lerner & N. A. Busch-Rossnagel (Eds.), *Individuals as producers of their development: A life-span perspective* (pp. 231–255). Academic Press. https://doi.org/10.1016/B978-0-12-444550-5.50016-X

Thomas, A., & Chess, S. (1989). Temperament and personality. In G. A. Kohnstamm, J. E. Bates, & M. K. Rothbart (Eds.), *Temperament in childhood* (pp. 249–261). Wiley.

Tilden, B., Charman, D., Sharples, J., & Fosbury, J. (2005). Identity and adherence in a diabetes patient: Transformations in psychotherapy. *Qualitative Health Research, 15*(3), 312–324. https://doi.org/10.1177/1049732304272965

Toolis, E. E., & Hammack, P. L. (2015). The lived experience of homeless youth: A narrative approach. *Qualitative Psychology, 2*(1), 50–68. https://doi.org/10.1037/qup0000019

Tucker, C., Dixon, A., & Griddine, K. S. (2010). Academically successful African American male urban high school students' experiences of mattering to others at school. *Professional School Counseling, 14*(2), 135–145. https://doi.org/10.1177/2156759X1001400202

Twenge, J. M., Joiner, T. E., Rogers, M. L., & Martin, G. N. (2018). Increases in depressive symptoms, suicide-related outcomes, and suicide rates among U.S. adolescents after 2010 and links to increased new media screen time. *Clinical Psychological Science, 6*(1), 3–17. https://doi.org/10.1177/2167702617723376

United Nations Convention on the Rights of the Child. (1989, November 20). https://www.ohchr.org/en/instruments-mechanisms/instruments/convention-rights-child

U.S. Senate Committee on the Judiciary. (2024, February 1). *Recap: Senate Judiciary Committee presses Big Tech CEOs on failures to protect kids online during landmark hearing.* https://www.judiciary.senate.gov/press/releases/recap-senate-judiciary-committee-presses-big-tech-ceos-on-failures-to-protect-kids-online-during-landmark-hearing

Vaillancourt, T., Brittain, H., Krygsman, A., Farrell, A. H., Pepler, D., Landon, S., Saint-Georges, Z., & Vitoroulis, I. (2022). In-person versus online learning in relation to students' perceptions of mattering during COVID-19: A brief report. *Journal of Psychoeducational Assessment, 40*(1), 159–169. https://doi.org/10.1177/07342829211053668

Van Orden, K. A., Cukrowicz, K. C., Witte, T. K., & Joiner, T. E., Jr. (2012). Thwarted belongingness and perceived burdensomeness: Construct validity and psychometric properties of the Interpersonal Needs Questionnaire. *Psychological Assessment, 24*(1), 197–215. https://doi.org/10.1037/a0025358

Van Ryzin, M. J., & Roseth, C. J. (2019). Cooperative learning effects on peer relations and alcohol use in middle school. *Journal of Applied Developmental Psychology, 64*, Article 101059. https://doi.org/10.1016/j.appdev.2019.101059

Van Sant, G. (Director). (1997). *Good Will Hunting* [Film]. Miramax.

Vélez, C. E., Braver, S. L., Cookston, J. T., Fabricius, W. V., & Parke, R. D. (2020). Does mattering to parents matter to adolescent mental health? A psychometric analysis. *Family Relations, 69*(1), 180–194. https://doi.org/10.1111/fare.12396

Vente, T., Daley, M., Killmeyer, E., & Grubb, L. K. (2020). Association of social media use and high-risk behaviors in adolescents: Cross-sectional study. *JMIR Pediatrics and Parenting, 3*(1), Article e18043. https://doi.org/10.2196/18043

Virat, M., Flett, G., Massez, L., & Przygodzki-Lionet, N. (2024). Low sense of mattering in society and delinquency among young people: An initial investigation. *Criminal Behaviour & Mental Health*, 1–16. https://doi.org/10.1002/cbm.2356

Wagner, G., Zeiler, M., Waldherr, K., Philipp, J., Truttmann, S., Dür, W., Treasure, J. L., & Karwautz, A. F. K. (2017). Mental health problems in Austrian adolescents: A nationwide, two-stage epidemiological study applying *DSM-5* criteria. *European Child and Adolescent Psychiatry, 26*(12), 1483–1499. https://doi.org/10.1007/s00787-017-0999-6

Wallace, J. B. (2023). *Never enough: When the achievement culture becomes toxic and what we can do about it*. Portfolio.

Walsh, F. (2016). *Strengthening family resilience* (3rd ed.). Guilford Press.

Wang, X., Gao, L., Yang, J., Zhao, F., & Wang, P. (2020). Parental phubbing and adolescents' depressive symptoms: Self-esteem and perceived social support as moderators. *Journal of Youth and Adolescence, 49*(2), 427–437. https://doi.org/10.1007/s10964-019-01185-x

Waterman, E. A., Mitchell, K. J., Edwards, K. M., & Banyard, V. L. (2024). Impact of peer victimization on adolescent suicidality and depressed mood: Moderating role of protective factors. *Journal of School Violence*, 1–14. Advance online publication. https://doi.org/10.1080/15388220.2024.2309569

Waterman, E. A., Siller, L., Dworkin, E. R., & Edwards, K. M. (2021). The association of stalking victimization with adolescents' depressed mood and school mattering. *Journal of Interpersonal Violence, 36*(23–24), 11768–11780. https://doi.org/10.1177/0886260519900945

Watson, D., Clark, L. A., & Tellegen, A. (1988). Development and validation of brief measures of positive and negative affect: The PANAS scales. *Journal of Personality and Social Psychology, 54*(6), 1063–1070. https://doi.org/10.1037/0022-3514.54.6.1063

Watson, J. C. (2017). Examining the relationship between self-esteem, mattering, school connectedness, and wellness among middle school students. *Professional School Counseling, 21*(1). https://doi.org/10.5330/1096-2409-21.1.108

Watson, J. C., Prosek, E. A., & Giordano, A. L. (2022). Distress among adolescents: An exploration of mattering, social media addiction, and school connectedness. *Journal of Psychoeducational Assessment, 40*(1), 95–107. https://doi.org/10.1177/07342829211050536

Weinstein, E. (2017). Adolescents' differential responses to social media browsing: Exploring causes and consequences for intervention. *Computers in Human Behavior, 76*, 396–405. https://doi.org/10.1016/j.chb.2017.07.038

Wellcome. (2021). *What science has shown can help young people with anxiety and depression: Identifying and reviewing the "active ingredients" of effective interventions*. https://wellcome.org/reports/what-science-has-shown-can-help-young-people-anxiety-and-depression

Werbart Törnblom, A., Werbart, A., & Rydelius, P.-A. (2015). Shame and gender differences in paths to youth suicide: Parents' perspective. *Qualitative Health Research, 25*(8), 1099–1116. https://doi.org/10.1177/1049732315578402

Werner, E. E. (2000). Protective factors and individual resilience. In J. P. Shonkoff & S. J. Meisels (Eds.), *Handbook of early childhood intervention* (2nd ed., pp. 115–132). Cambridge University Press. https://doi.org/10.1017/CBO9780511529320.008

Werner, E. E., & Johnson, J. L. (2004). The role of caring adults in the lives of children of alcoholics. *Substance Use & Misuse, 39*(5), 699–720. https://doi.org/10.1081/JA-120034012

Werner, E. E., & Smith, R. S. (1982). *Vulnerable but invincible: A longitudinal study of resilient children and youth*. McGraw-Hill.

Werner, E. E., & Smith, R. S. (1992). *Overcoming the odds: High risk children from birth to adulthood.* Cornell University Press.

Werner, E. E., & Smith, R. S. (2001). *Journeys from childhood to midlife: Risk, resilience, and recovery.* Cornell University Press.

Whitaker, R. C., Dearth-Wesley, T., Herman, A. N., van Wingerden, A. N., & Winn, D. W. (2022). Family connection and flourishing among adolescents in 26 countries. *Pediatrics, 149*(6), Article e2021055263. https://doi.org/10.1542/peds.2021-055263

Wicker, F. W., Payne, G. C., & Morgan, R. D. (1983). Participant descriptions of guilt and shame. *Motivation and Emotion, 7*(1), 25–39. https://doi.org/10.1007/BF00992963

Wilkinson, R. B. (2010). Best friend attachment versus peer attachment in the prediction of adolescent psychological adjustment. *Journal of Adolescence, 33*(5), 709–717. https://doi.org/10.1016/j.adolescence.2009.10.013

Williams, K. D., & Nida, S. A. (2009). Is ostracism worse than bullying? In M. J. Harris (Ed.), *Bullying, rejection, and peer victimization: A social cognitive neuroscience perspective* (pp. 279–296). Springer.

Wu, N. H., & Kim, S. Y. (2009). Chinese American adolescents' perceptions of the language brokering experience as a sense of burden and sense of efficacy. *Journal of Youth and Adolescence, 38*(5), 703–718. https://doi.org/10.1007/s10964-008-9379-3

York Region District School Board. (2017). *School Climate Survey—Mental health and well-being*. https://www.yrdsb.ca/boarddocs/pages/school-climate-survey-mental-health.aspx

York Region District School Board. (2021). *School Climate Surveys 2020–2021: Full report*. https://www2.yrdsb.ca/sites/default/files/2022-11/2020-21-Student-and-Family-Surveys-Report.pdf

Zeigler-Hill, V., & Marcus, D. K. (Eds.). (2016). *The dark side of personality: Science and practice in social, personality, and clinical psychology*. American Psychological Association. https://doi.org/10.1037/14854-000

Zhang, M. X., Kam, C. C. S., & Wu, A. M. (2024). The reciprocity between psychological need frustration and adolescent problematic smartphone use. *Journal of Applied Developmental Psychology, 91*, Article 101634. https://doi.org/10.1016/j.appdev.2024.101634

Index

A

O

P

R

About the Author

Gordon L. Flett, PhD, is a professor in the Department of Psychology at York University in Toronto, Ontario, Canada, where he has held a Canada Research Chair in Personality and Health. He is also the former associate dean of research and former director of the LaMarsh Centre for Child and Youth Research in the Faculty of Health at York University. Currently, Dr. Flett is an associate editor of the American Psychological Association (APA) journal *Canadian Psychology*.

Dr. Flett is recognized globally for his seminal contributions to research and theory on the role of perfectionism in mental and physical health. This work includes the 2022 APA book, *Perfectionism in Childhood and Adolescence: A Developmental Approach*, coauthored with Paul L. Hewitt. Dr. Flett is also known for his leading role in and many journal articles and knowledge mobilization activities on the nature and correlates of mattering. His 2018 book, *The Psychology of Mattering*, is the first complete book on the mattering construct. Recently, in 2022, Dr. Flett was the guest editor of a special issue on mattering published in the *Journal of Psychoeducational Assessment*.

Dr. Flett is also a member of the APA and a fellow of the Association for Psychological Science, which has cited him as one of the top 25 most productive authors in psychology.